Kovno
Ghetto

Wadi Rum @
Memories
Camp

Crossing the River

Crossing the River

SHALOM EILATI
Translated from Hebrew by Vern Lenz

The University of Alabama Press • Tuscaloosa

Published in cooperation with Yad Vashem, Jerusalem

Yad Vashem

Originally published in Hebrew as *Lahazot et Hanahar* by Carmel/Yad
Vashem, 1999.

The translation from Hebrew to English was made possible in part
by generous donations from Emma Lazaroff-Schaver, Southfield,
Michigan; the Aaron Friedman Memorial Fund, Mobile, Alabama;
Family Master, Easton, Pennsylvania; Memorial Foundation for Jewish
Culture, New York, New York; Association "Vehiggadta Lebinkha,"
Cambridge, Massachusetts; and Assistance to Lithuanian Jews Inc.,
New York, New York.

Library of Congress Cataloging-in-Publication Data

Eilati, Shalom, 1933–
    [La-hatsot et ha-nahar. English]
    Crossing the river / Shalom Eilati ; translated from Hebrew by
Vern Lenz.
        p.   cm.
    "Published in cooperation with Yad Vashem, Jerusalem."
    ISBN 978-0-8173-1631-0 (cloth : alk. paper) — ISBN
978-0-8173-8107-3 (electronic) 1. Jews—Lithuania—Kaunas—
Biography. 2. Holocaust, Jewish (1939–1945)—Lithuania—Kaunas—
Personal narratives. 3. Jewish children in the Holocaust—Lithuania—
Kaunas—Biography. 4. Kaunas (Lithuania)—Biography. I. Yad va-shem,
rashut ha-zikaron la-Sho'ah vela-gevurah II. Title.
    DS135.L53E3513 2008
    940.53'18092—dc22
    [B]
                                            2008018605

To the memory of my perished mother Lea Greenstein-Kaplan

and my sister Yehudith

Kovno, July 1944

I am buried under mounds upon mounds of

my life history. There I breathe

a measured and pure breath. There I offer gifts

to all that come. There I sing

in a voice strong and warm. There

I am plain as bread.

—Meir Wieseltier, *The Concise Sixties* (1984), translated by Gabriel Levin

Contents

Preface

I DIDN'T REALLY WANT TO LEAVE THAT MORNING, TO EMERGE FROM the dim warmth of our only room and my mother, to prepare to depart. But I had to. All the arrangements had been made, and now everything depended on getting past the sentries successfully.

It was a clear, crisp dawn in early spring and we may have had something to eat before setting out. Near the house I was befriended by a puppy that ran after us, and I was torn—here at last was a dog that could be mine. I pleaded with Mother to let me go back just long enough to shut the pup in our room so that if my escape failed this morning, as it had before, then at least I would have my very own dog for the first time in years.

But this time my exit was fast and smooth. The German officer was absent, and the roll call was supervised only by our people, with no interference from the guards. A few more steps and we had already reached the riverbank. Oars cut through the calm water, and I looked around me, wonderstruck. After years in the ghetto, suddenly a river, so much space, and me to sail upon it, like long ago at summer camp.

As we neared the other bank, my mother quietly removed the two yellow patches, the threads of which she had previously cut and were now fastened only with a safety pin. Her instructions were clear: once we reached the other bank I was to march without stopping through the Lithuanians standing there, cross the road, and go up the path that led into the hills. All alone, I was to walk without raising suspicion and without looking back. Further up the path, a woman would meet me and tell me what to do.

Everything went as planned, except that there was no woman waiting for me on the path. I proceeded according to my mother's instructions, going deeper into the hills, farther and farther from the riverbank and my mother. Only then did a figure with a sealed face approach me, and as she passed me she whispered that I should continue slowly; she would soon return and join me. A short while later I was following her up a steep path, and I soon found myself in the house of an elderly Lithuanian woman named Julija.

All this occurred so quickly and so easily that I scarcely grasped what had happened to me in such a short period of time. I am not sure even today, after so many years, that I have fully digested what happened to me that morning. But the next day I received the first letter from my mother, written on a rolled-up scrap of paper, to be read and then burned: "I watched you move away, my child," she wrote, and I will never forget this, "climbing all by yourself onto the bank of the river, walking past guards and people on your way to freedom. A day will come when a film will be made about your miraculous escape from the ghetto."

Like Moses in the bulrushes I was cast by Mother onto the shore of life. I therefore dedicate this story to my mother, who gave me life twice, but was unable to save her own even once.

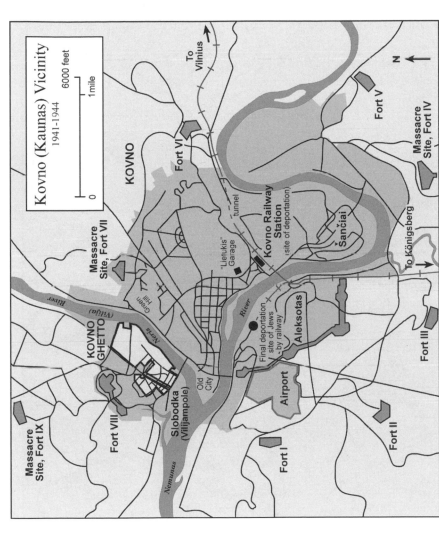

Map 1. Kovno (Kaunas) Vicinity 1941–44

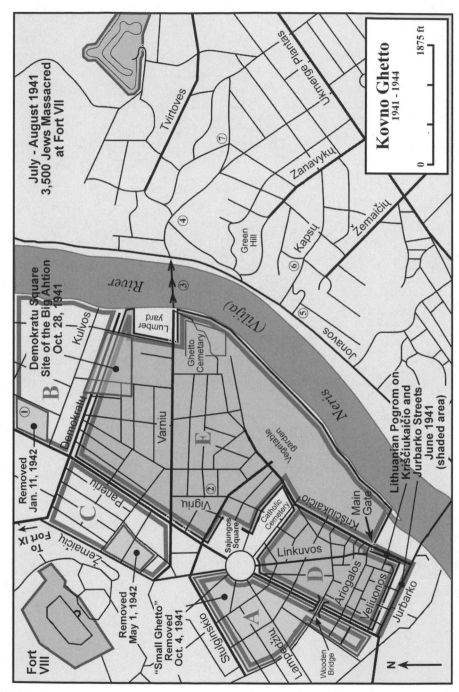

Map 2. Kovno Ghetto 1941–44

The ghetto was reduced in four phases. (The full ghetto, as of August 15, 1941, is represented on this map by the combinations of sections A–E.)

Phase A: The removal of the small ghetto plus the wooden bridge, October 4, 1941

Phase B: The northwest suburb removal. January 11, 1942

Phase C: Another north removal, May 1, 1942

Phase D: The removal of Slobodka, plus the "bottleneck," December 23, 1943

Phase E: The rest—the final shrunken ghetto until its destruction on July 13, 1944

Shalom's Route:

① Our first living location in the ghetto
② Our next living location in the ghetto
③ Crossing the river (April 12, 1944)
④ Hiding place on Green Hill
⑤ Pilz-Fabrik—my mother's workplace
⑥ My mother's possible route to visit her children
⑦ My sister's hiding place

1

How It Began

WE ABANDONED OUR FLAT AND SET OUT.

The closer we got to our allotted area the more people we met dragging things along with them. Some carried huge bundles on their heads or on their backs. Others pushed wheelbarrows or children's carriages; some even dragged overloaded tin bathtubs on the street. A fortunate few had a wagon hitched to a horse. I began to spot more and more people I knew among the marchers, young and old; they were all on the move from different directions to the same place, and this gave me something like a sense of relief.

The flow of people, which grew denser on the bridge, thinned out again on the other side of the river. I managed to notice that we had passed through a high wooden gate with two doors that leaned on a tall barbed-wire fence that stretched out and disappeared into narrow alleys. We were now in the ghetto. It seemed huge to me, broad and endless. The fence at its edges didn't bother me at all.

The new arrivals poured into the houses to find places for themselves. Quarreling broke out over an extra room, over a private corner, over the right to put a stool in the common kitchen or to stretch a clothesline. They argued and bargained and raged, unwilling to resign themselves to the conditions imposed upon them. We dove into that turmoil, and there was no turning back.

For years I have tried to recall what I had been dreaming the moment before I woke that Sunday, trying to persuade myself that I was still dreaming, what my feelings were during the last seconds before the thunder came. One day I will wake and it will be a regular Sunday morning in my hometown, Kovno, on June 22, 1941, one of the longest days of the year.

At first I attached little importance to the sounds that woke me. Together with the explosions, I heard gunfire, which was somehow already familiar to me. I had first heard similar noises on the riverbank during summer break the previous year. On that fine morning I was attentively watching a tennis match between relaxed, white-clad vacationers, when airplanes suddenly began performing odd maneuvers high above us. One after another they would dive with a loud roar toward a large tube-shaped sack that another, slower plane was pulling. While we children on the ground were engaged in a furtive struggle over the privilege of retrieving tennis balls for the players on the court, the planes in the air abruptly opened fire at each other in several short, sharp bursts. We were startled, but those among us who knew assured us that these were only maneuvers, and thus we learned a new word. The tennis players went on with their game, and this was a sufficient hint for me that it is better to pretend that all was well. Suddenly, at no great distance from us and with no warning sound, a sooty brass shell fell to the ground. We rushed to look at the oddity that had dropped from the sky. Perhaps it was dangerous? Every bystander had a suggestion about what to do with it and whom to deliver it to—the police or the soldiers patrolling in pairs—anything as long as it was taken away from the sharp-eyed boy, the lucky devil, who had first discovered the strange thing. So the peaceful tennis lawns of a summer resort were the scene of my first contact with the sounds and weapons of war.

Several weeks before that Sunday morning I had gone with my parents to see a famous movie about Lenin. In one scene, a pretty young woman with dark eyes and black hair, Fanya Kaplan, was preparing to kill the great leader. Smoking a cigarette, deep in concentration, she lined up a number of small bullets on a tabletop. One was given to understand—perhaps my mother explained this to me—the connection between these seemingly innocent details and the barrel of the gun that the young woman aimed later at the much-loved man, just after he had finished a rousing speech to a group of factory workers. There was a dry cracking sound, and Comrade Vladimir Ilyich dropped to the floor in a pool of blood. My parents broke into a fierce argument on our way home from the movie theater. He was a loyal Zionist and she a confirmed communist. Father wanted her to be the kind of housewife who would fix meals for him on time, while she—her friends called her Umru (Yiddish for "unrest")—wanted to save the world. Mother condemned the assassination attempt wholeheartedly, while Father said, "You saw how she pondered, how thoughtful and serious she was, how hard it was for her to decide." This film was my first meeting with the tools of destruction and death.

Thus the sound of guns going off, which I heard in my sleep and was hidden in the depths of my memory, should not have disturbed me. The house was quiet. Apparently no one but I had awakened.

I was trying to fall back to sleep, but then—a knock on the door. At this hour? In came the Schirms, the photographer and his wife, who had no children and lived half a flight above us. They were already dressed, apologizing for disturbing us so early, at half past five in the morning. "Can you hear it? Do you know what's going on? Is it war?" Father, still half asleep, had opened the door. He shrugged. He thought he had heard some thunder in the distance—but war? With my eyes closed, I followed the animated conversation and called out confidently and authoritatively: "Those are airplanes on maneuvers like the ones we saw last year at summer camp." The adults gathered around my bed, eagerly drinking in my words, which gave me a great deal of pleasure. They continued to question me, listening to my decisive explanations, clearly hoping to persuade themselves that I was right. The Schirms seemed to calm down somewhat. They had been on their way to see relatives in town, but now they decided to wait a while, at least until the seven o'clock news: surely someone will explain things then.

The rumbling sounds from beyond the horizon did not cease. Heavy and earthshaking, they rolled toward us in waves like a rainstorm. Even though the skies were clear, something seemed to thicken in the distance like a little cloud that swelled to engulf us, and the frightening word, spoken first by the Schirms, rolled inside, filling the entire flat until we couldn't ignore it anymore. War? Returning to bed was impossible, and Mother was not at home. Summer vacation had just begun, and she, a nurse, had been hired to go with a group of children the day before to the summer resort. We planned to join her in a day or two, to our great joy, according to a detailed itinerary that I had memorized. That same day, Uncle David was due to arrive by bicycle with a friend from a distant shtetl. Both teachers, they were delegates to the national teachers' conference that was to begin the next day in Kovno. They had a full agenda for their stay in the city, the details of which they had carefully planned long ago and coordinated with us by telephone. War was simply out of the question.

Only a week before, the previous Sunday afternoon, my parents had been talking with their guests, who were teachers: "So there is going to be a war," one of them summed up, and I remember rushing to Mother in a way I had never done before, entreating her, pleading, "Mother, don't let there be war! Don't let it happen!" as if my mother had the power to erase the latent dread that had suddenly revealed itself in my outcry.

I used to sit on the wide window ledge in our flat, high on the fourth story, looking out like a captain from the bridge of his ship. The lower walls of our building were very thick; it had apparently been a monastery in previous centuries. Only our floor, the top one, was a flimsy addition. Although the outside walls were covered with tin sheeting, it was very damp, which gave Mother severe rheumatic pains for the rest of her life.

Seated safely on the window ledge, I loved to look out into the distance. From here everything seemed firm and secure, spread out below as from a high mountaintop. At my feet lay roofs of houses, churches, and monasteries. Far to the south I could see the contours of the great river that traversed our city, and beyond it rose the steep green hills.

South of this slope spread the large airport, lying in wait for the days to come.

We lived in the lower city, at the meeting of two rivers. From this ancient corner the town had grown and climbed the surrounding hills, spreading beyond the banks of both rivers. The city was surrounded by ten huge fortresses from World War I, each surrounded by a deep moat or mound. Each had underground halls of red brick and contained iron gates. In the years to come, some of them served as execution sites for thousands of Jews, especially the forts numbered 4, 7, and 9.

Every spring the old quarter was prone to flooding. The thick cover of winter ice, which turned the whole river into a glorious skating rink, would crack and buckle and break off in huge chunks, piling one on top of the other at the juncture of the rivers, preventing the water from bursting through to the sea. The pent-up streams would invade the land, seeping into the basements and lower stories. Although the water never reached us, on spring nights I would imagine the lapping sounds of water about to emerge from the deep cellar beneath our home. Silently, the water would rise higher and higher, and by the time it burst through, the bells of the firemen would already mingle with the anguished screams of the drowning people crying for help. Was it not too late? Could we not have been better prepared?

At the tip of the peninsula created by the juncture of the two rivers, the cathedrals, monasteries, and Catholic churches were huddled. The streets there were narrow, paved, and clean. Mustachioed janitors thoroughly scrubbed the droppings of carriage horses from between the pavement stones. Novitiates in pairs and nuns with starched collars pattered through the street. Through large shop windows ornate, glossy, and lacquered coffins peered out at me. From here luxurious funeral processions with big candles, a priest bedecked in white vestments, and children's choirs would set out with ceremonial splendor into the main street beneath our window. One day near this area, my mother rescued a small Lithuanian child from the wheels of a bus, one of the modern snub-nosed kind that had been introduced that year to our city. Mother returned the boy to his parents who were busy selecting a coffin, but added a word or two about parents' responsibility for the lives of their children—making it all the more difficult for them to return a word of thanks to a Jewess.

The walls of the Jesuits' buildings in our quarter were thick and still. Their lowest windows were high, almost invisible to the children playing beneath them. From within the walls of that mysterious building on Mapu Street we sometimes heard the tremulous sob of a violin. Perhaps there was a conservatory within, or maybe some tortured monk was airing his laments. But the children said the house was bewitched and that anyone who dared to touch or lean against the wall was doomed to die. With dread we would dare one another to come close to the wall, touch it for an instant, and flee with a burst of nervous laughter. It was indeed a cursed house: before many years had passed, almost none of the Jewish children who had touched its walls were still alive.

It seems that nothing I remember from the prewar years remains as vivid and in such sharp focus as our summer vacations at the resort. Each holiday was always an adventure from which I returned filled to the brim with impressions, the raw material for daydreams and fancies for the rest of the year. The intense preparation before embarking on the voyage; then boarding the *Parakhod,* the steamboat whose engines were already roaring, proclaiming their power; the anchor raised; long poles pushing between the posts of the pier as it receded from us; and there we were in the heart of the river—would our boat not sink at once?

Once on land, we found ourselves in a small village—one or two main streets, summer houses for rent, several sweet shops, a grocery store, and a bakery. Swans floated in a fenced lake surrounded by a promenade with a bandstand. Children and adults knocked wooden balls through tiny wickets, playing croquet. Jews from the whole country, from the big city and from shtetls, gathered together for the summer. They played cards and checkers, read Jewish newspapers, and chatted endlessly. Even the famous Jewish magazine was available here, featuring photographs of the violinist Yascha Heifetz, the British minister Hore-Belisha, and the famous actor Maurice Schwartz, and you could feel proud of so many well-known Jews, talented and distinguished among the people of all nations.

To the north of the village and surrounding it stood a forest. Forest air, as everyone knows, is very healthy, especially for city dwellers. The trees in the forest were tall and close together; between any pair of them we could tie a *gamak,* a hammock of thick woven canvas, and swing till we were dizzy.

And beyond the forest—when we dared to venture beyond it—lay another land of wonders both tempting and frightening. Endless plains, fields of golden grain heaped with sheaves, and paths twisting and disappearing. At crossroads we would often encounter a kneeling figure bowed in prayer at the feet of the crucified Christ or his mother, the Madonna. The Savior would be huddled under a little roof with an abundance of withered flowers and burned-out candles at his feet. This was a country of devout Catholics who had not forgotten the Crucifixion. When they passed us we always hastened to greet them, but they never returned our salutations; we were strangers here.

At night at the resort there was the sigh of the wind in the trees, fear-sowing chirps and cackles, violent storms accompanied by tremendous peals of thunder, lightning stripping away all cover of darkness, and no escape. I was all alone, like the delirious child facing the stern Erl King in the poem Mother loved to recite. Only closing your eyes tightly, desperately burrowing deep into the blanket, or even far under the bed, might help.

Sometimes a house would burst into flames. Amazing is the speed with which a family's home can burn up before your very eyes. Was it lightning that set it aflame? Fire engines would hasten to the scene amid sounds of bells and sirens, surrounding the burning house, and panicked Jews would crowd around the fire chief, almost touching the hem of his mantle. They pressed close to hear his every word. Strong and tall, his feet rooted firmly in his land, he would answer their questions patiently. Will the fire spread? Or do they have everything under control this time? Are their own houses, God forbid, likely to burn? Worried and helpless, they would hang on his every word. What to do, what to do!

It had been going on all year, come to think of it, not just during that week— the word "war" was on everyone's lips. The frightening word had become a permanent part of everyday life ever since the Russians, "at the request of the masses," had invaded and taken over the three tiny Baltic states. Our diminutive president, whose face I knew from postage stamps, took his car and escaped immediately, first to Germany and later to South America.

When the Russians arrived, we were visiting Mossik's family on Green Hill, and from then on our families were close. I considered Mossik my best friend, with whom my eyes were opened gradually from the fog of infancy. Like us, Mossik's family had a girl and a boy who were about the same as my sister and I. We were still at Mossik's when we heard unfamiliar sounds in the street outside their home. They were the tanks of the Red Army entering our city; here I saw them for the first time. The surprise was great, and the changes that ensued were far-reaching. Nothing was ever the same again.

The tanks rolled into town, one after another, in an endless column, for several long hours. They continued westward, apparently toward the Prussian border not far away. Young soldiers stood atop the tanks, smiling and cheerful, dressed in their best uniforms covered with medals, holding bouquets of flowers. They looked as if they could not be happier to be on this mission to save us from oppression and slavery. Now we had no cause for alarm—a mighty power, under the command of the most progressive government in the world, had spread its canopy of protection over us. Enthusiastic supporters, principally Jews, could not contain their joy. They stood in groups on street corners, waving flowers and banners, and singing songs of the Red freedom, blessing and adoring all that day and all that night. And there are those who say that on that night the fate was sealed for years to come of not only this tiny country but also the Jews within it. The Lithuanians ground their teeth and never forgave those who exulted during the time of their distress.

Mother was enchanted by the coming of the Red Army. Growing up I had heard the first notes of the anthem, the "Internationale"—the opening theme of the Comintern station on Radio Moscow ("H" on the panel of our old-fashioned radio).

The hope of salvation had now come in flesh and blood with the help of the steel monsters. What joy—seldom is a person fortunate enough to see the beginning of his dreams come true. Mother happily took me to see Gliare's *Red Poppy* ballet, and in the meantime people began to sing, "If war breaks out tomorrow, / If battle breaks out," to conduct aerial maneuvers, to dig public shelters, and to demonstrate the use of gas masks.

In Rotushe Square, next to our house, the authorities dug a model bomb shelter and invited everyone to see it. I trailed behind my father, who was, as usual, deep in conversation with a friend during the tour through the twisting and dimly lit underground leviathan, full of hallways, ventilation slots, and sharp corners, as well as buckets of sand, shovels, and pickaxes. We went through it in single file, each creeping close on the heels of the person ahead. With great relief I discerned at last the light at the other exit, from which we emerged into the square.

Mother believed with all her heart that a new life had begun. Still, that same year she had written to her friend Nathan, a writer who had moved to Palestine, quoting Gorky, her favorite author: "Some trees rot away slowly, others end their lives in fire. How I wish to end in flames, not in decay." She did not know how prophetic she was.

In Mother's vision I was to have a brilliant future in the new era. At age seventeen I would finish the lyceum and go on to higher studies. All the universities of the immense new country, from the Baltic Sea to Vladivostok, would be open to me, and all professions and disciplines would await my selection. The horizon was broad and bright; nothing could stop me from plucking the fruits of the intoxicating future. So what had I to do with war? The newspapers were full of accounts of battles in faraway places with names that ran all together for me, like Dunkirk and the Cyrenaica Peninsula. About the war in our backyard, the one in neighboring Poland, I heard nearly nothing, except for the great cruelty of the Germans, who dropped coins and candy that were coated with poison from planes to kill the children of Warsaw. What did I know of war?

A week before war with Germany broke out came the night of deportations. At first we didn't know what was happening—all night large canvas-covered trucks drove through town. Lights came on in various flats; confused voices were heard, as well as children crying. Something mysterious and alarming was going on around us. Brief telephone calls in the morning and rumors that flew throughout the day clarified the gloomy picture somewhat: many Jewish families had been imprisoned on Saturday night and were taken who knew where. They were given an hour's notice to prepare themselves, among them old people and children, with only the fewest of possessions. Their pleas, their protests, their tears were all in vain. Now I tried to imagine what it was like to be taken, helpless and under guard, to an unknown and threatening destination, while your friends watched you from the slits of windows.

That weekend of deportations marked the beginning of the gradual disappearance of my friends. They faded away one by one, taken and swallowed up, while I remained behind almost alone, a great and unsolved riddle within me to this very day.

Thus there were signs all along that war was coming. So why was nothing done, why did people stand by, indifferent, like the vacationers around the fire chief? Why?

Years later I asked my father about this, one of the few questions I ever managed to ask him. He said that by that time there was nowhere to escape to and no way of escaping. Who could get away at the time, and where would they go? Well-connected businessmen and community leaders had fled the country many years before. My parents not only lacked the means to travel and to obtain a visa—a visa required a substantial sum of money—but they were also bound by commitments and surety for loans taken both on their own behalf and for relatives. They were both the only members of their shtetl-dwelling families to have permanent jobs in the big city, so they were naturally approached for help, either in emergencies or to help someone emigrate to Palestine. And it was unthinkable to go leaving unpaid debts behind. And once the war began, how were they to escape with two small children? And again, where would they go, especially since they were convinced that this was but a short episode until the sleeping Russian giant awakened.

The first morning of the war went hazily by, refusing to clear. Explosions grew more frequent; columns of smoke rose and came near. Maneuvers? The radio continued to spout inanities, but the street woke up early and convulsed; trucks roared by frequently; and motorcycles went by in relays, things the like of which had never happened on a Sunday morning.

Across the street, in flats confiscated from priests, lived the families of Russian officers. We watched a flurry of activity—curtains being removed, chandeliers being detached from the ceiling. Through the naked windows we witnessed feverish packing into large crates. Then we saw a truck parked nearby, into which the Russians carried their belongings. The situation must have really been serious then. The brother of Sioma, the student who lived in our flat, was visiting for the weekend, and they began to fear their plans were about to be ruined. And Mother wasn't home.

The hours crept by, the radio did not provide any information, and anti-aircraft guns started firing, causing great alarm. The short bursts seemed aimed directly at our windows. Sirens sounded from distant suburbs. Through the window, in the distance above the airport somewhat toward the south, I saw a bizarre dance of airplanes. Like the up-and-down movement of the needle of my mother's new Singer sewing machine, they started diving and climbing. Tiny bulbs sprayed around them, and black smoke mushroomed in their wake, exploding upward. Whose planes were these, and who was chasing after them? Were they actually enemy planes that had come this far? And if so, shouldn't we be staying away from the windows and heading for the cellars, heeding the national guard, who of late had been filling our ears with alarm drills?

Father didn't know what to do. He lay on the sofa reading a book, while my little sister maneuvered between Sioma's room and Father's lap. Two fingers of her left hand stuck in her mouth, her right hand forever twisting her curly hair.

Her teeth had left sharp lines on the upper joint of her fingers; I warned her again and again that they would fall off if she kept on sucking them, just as my parents had warned me that my pee-pee would fall off if I kept playing with it. My father, a teacher, a historian whose thesis was on the Spanish Inquisition, was now reading Dubnov's *Chronicles of the Jewish People.* Eight months later Father was exiled to Riga, Dubnov's home town, and he would later describe his experience there, which included writing a chronicle of the great historian's last days.

If Father had taken us both in his arms at that moment, like an animal saving its offspring and, like Lot, had escaped eastward without looking left or right, we might all have remained alive. Somehow we might have made it into the heart of the USSR, and ever-vigorous Mother would certainly have managed to follow us.

At one or two o'clock in the afternoon Foreign Minister Molotov gave a statement at the beginning of the news, informing the nation of the low and despicable act that had taken place that morning. With no forewarning or stated cause, the Germans, only yesterday allies, had begun to attack along the broad expanse of our western border. But the brave Red Army, backed by the entire Soviet people, would retaliate and repel with all their strength the forces of evil that had so treacherously invaded our homeland. All were called upon to raise the banner, to report, each to his post, and be vigilant until final victory was achieved.

Immediately we began applying strips of cloth to the windowpanes using a white flour paste, as instructed by the national guard. Someone bravely climbed up to the attic above us to make sure that a barrel of water and sandbags had been stored there, again obeying instructions.

In the last issue of *Ogonyok,* the colorful official weekly, my eyes had been drawn to a new device for locating airplanes, an apparatus of interlocked horizontal and vertical pipes that could hear and see a great distance. Thanks to this important invention, the article said, our forces could now detect the approach of enemy airplanes from far away. I hoped that since morning they had already managed to equip every unit of the Red Army in our area with these miraculous devices.

In the meantime I was shooed away from the window for fear of "shrapnels." I imagined these shrapnels as something like flying snakes, scurrying and looping through the air until they found their victim. Sioma's brother gave me sounder advice—whenever I heard a siren I should get under a doorframe, a relatively safe place to be in case a bomb fell—*bomba* in our language, a word with a heavy and frightening sound. No bombs fell in our neighborhood, but from that time onward I spent hours skipping from doorway to doorway, trying to guard myself against a direct hit and staying out of the path of flying shrapnel. In retrospect I think it was then I began my personal escape journey, which in time would lead me beyond rivers and seas.

The explosions came nearer and multiplied. Fighter planes dared to venture into the skies of the city itself, and the anti-aircraft guns seemed to choke with rage and anger. The walls and frames of the house seemed brittle, and my wide window ledge held dangers. Clearly, in a matter of minutes the bombs would be falling on us. Even so, Father hesitated to take us down to the Meltzer family one story below. He didn't like to bother people and ask favors of them, he said. But go we did, thus entering their affluent flat for the first time. Their grandson, Mishka Kapulsky, was my classmate. Their thick-walled flat exuded comfort and security.

Father brought us news from time to time as he climbed up and down between our flats, his anxiety growing. What was happening with Mother? We had heard nothing from her, nor did the phone ring. In the meantime, Uncle David had arrived with his bicycle. David was upset and confused. What would happen to the teachers' conference scheduled for tomorrow? Perhaps he should call and find out. When we were allowed back up to our flat for a short time in the evening, before we were hurried back downstairs, I caught a quick glimpse of the intriguing belongings our uncle had brought with him, now arranged on the shelf we had cleared for him in our closet—shirts and towels neatly folded, razor and scented soaps, cologne, cufflinks, combs, ties and tie clips, apparently bought specifically for David's trip to Kovno. Everything was tidily packed in a way I had never before seen in my house.

Finally we got good news. Mother had returned at last and would soon come down. She entered in a flurry, excited by all that had happened to her, still incredulous. The day before she had set out on a riverboat with the children to the OZE (International Jewish Communal Health Association) camp. They arrived, settled in, and prepared the summer camp routine. But early in the morning they woke to the roar of airplanes and the sounds of guns and bombs, and didn't know what to do. They tried calling the city and the camp management, but there was no answer. The staff was left alone with the responsibility for several dozen children. They decided to try to return immediately to the city. But how would they accomplish this? Then like a fairy godmother the riverboat appeared, still sticking to its schedule. The captain was hesitant about taking so many children onboard on such a day. They begged, pleaded, and promised him extra payment, and at last he agreed. They sailed before the confused children could learn the meaning of their sudden return. The adults did their best to calm them, pretending all was well, although the banks of the river teemed with sights of war—a burned vehicle spewing smoke, shots and explosions on all sides. While they were still sailing, just outside the city, German planes burst over them. They took a daring gamble by herding all of the children onto the deck, urging them to wave at the planes with their white hats. The first plane dived down and approached the boat; they held their breath. The children waved to the fighter plane, which, at the very last minute, when it was very close to the boat, turned aside and climbed back skyward. Are German pilots heartless? Upon discovering that children were on deck, they spared the boat. Only a few days later I found it hard to believe our innocence in accepting Mother's version of events. During the rest of their journey home, they saw the bombers dive down bridges and attack roads and structures, with only occasional fire being directed back at them.

The Russians seemed to be in full retreat from all directions. The city's entrances were blocked with cars and carriages, and panic and tumult reigned. Mother and the children were lucky to have been on a boat; otherwise they might never have made it into the city. As soon as they docked they had to contact parents and find cars to bring every last child home, and it had not been easy. That was why, even though she had been in the city for several hours, she had not been able to come home until now, her sense of responsibility for the children in her care having taken precedence. Did any of them survive the coming years? A painful and pointless question.

Mother's arrival cleared things up somewhat. Now we could attempt to decide what to do—should we stay or flee? The question was based on an illogical assumption—but what was logical in the events of that day?—namely, that the Russians might retreat beyond our city. If so, we should flee as fast as possible. Like the contraction of a muscle grown taut in time of danger, Mother began bundling together a number of things that seemed at that moment most necessary. She took several items of food from the pantry, which was almost empty in anticipation of our upcoming summer holiday; and she dressed us in our best and warmest clothes, even though it was high summer.

After fifteen minutes, the activity ceased, the hands slackened—perhaps because it was so hard to decide what to take and what to leave, and especially where to go and how to get there with two small children. On the roads there was danger of attacks from both the German planes and the Lithuanians. The German border was so close—they had only to force a crack in the Soviet wall and in an instant our tiny country would be overrun, with us stuck somewhere behind, on the roads or in the forest. What was the point of running? So it was decided: we would stay. Mother put things back in their places and announced that we would move to the cellar. Thus it sometimes happens that fate is decided in an instant; we can never know whether the decision is the right one for the given moment.

There was no point in escaping, or indeed any place to go, after six in the evening of the second day of war. That is the general conclusion people reached later, after analyzing and reanalyzing the sequence of events, trying to grasp and digest for the thousandth time exactly what took place.

Sioma and his brother, young and apparently independent, began talking of escape from about noon of the first day. They wavered throughout the first day and were still not gone on the morning of the second.

Scene: Monday afternoon. Sioma is sprawled on his back on the sofa in his room in a kind of paralyzed torpor. It is clear he has no desire to move from here, but apparently he must go. My four-year-old sister stretches herself upon his stomach and, as if reading his thoughts, is whispering with soft, kittenish charm, "Don't go, Sioma, don't leave." *End of scene.*

Within a matter of hours, Sioma and his brother suddenly shook themselves out of their lassitude and got up and left. Sioma's room was left neat and tidy, and on his clean drawing table lay a row of sharpened pencils. Sioma also played the violin—where was the violin? Later we were glad to hear that at 6:00 P.M. on Monday the last train had still managed to leave our city for the east. There was a chance that Sioma and his brother may have gotten away at the last minute and were now far away from here. But—it seems to me it was Wednesday—suddenly the telephone rang. This alarmed us—a telephone call, these days? It was Sioma, calling from the house of relatives here in the city. Yes, they had set out, were delayed, and here they were again. He was just able to ask how we were when the telephone call was cut off. We never heard from him again. In the ghetto we didn't see him or his brother.

Uncle David and his friend, who had come for the teachers' conference, hurried home that Monday morning. They cycled along the country's main road toward their shtetl in the northeast. They left most of their handsome new possessions, now of no use to them, packed in our closet. Survivors from their village remembered two teachers who left on their bicycles for the big city on the first day of the war but never came back.

More and more troops were retreating through our streets. Early in the morning the first wagons had appeared, a little sheepishly at first, but in the next few hours their numbers grew. As at Catholic funerals, here, too, the soldiers plodded slowly along, surrounding the wagons, which were also bedecked in fresh branches like green shrouds. At first I did not understand why they covered themselves with cut branches, as if they were playing a big Scout game.

As the hours passed, the stream of wagons grew. The wagons were gloomy and their horses were very tired, most of them dragging a cannon or mortar behind them like a piece of useless junk. It was a huge army, retreating in a kind of anti-march. Where were the triumphal tanks of the year before? As the hours passed, the soldiers' heads hung lower and they held onto the sides of the wagons like drowning men. In groups and alone they moved like shadows, oblivious to the explosions and sirens. More and more of the plodding soldiers were bandaged, and through the tarps of the wagons, which were pulled by tired horses and which now had red crosses drawn on the sides in an untrained hand, stretchers could be seen, dangling legs in every direction.

And when we finally understood that this was war indeed, and that we were in the middle of it, did I see much of it? On the morning of the first day I mustered the courage to look out a little. As the day wore on, it became too frightening. From that point I only heard the war from the depths of the cellar, curled up, wrapped, and tense, with eyes shut and ears wide, wide open.

It was damp and stifling in the cellar. That is where I once thought the flood waters would rise to drown us. A long obstructed passageway, a dim lightbulb, a row of compartments. Toward evening, we tried going back up to our flat, but the strong volleys of shots, the incessant explosions, and the flames that started to crown the broad horizon in glowing scarlet sent us scurrying back down. There at least we didn't see anything. Mother brought blankets down and we made room for ourselves among pots and old baby carriages. I didn't know at that time that it was only the first time I would hide among pots and carriages. A day will come that I'll owe the rest of my life to such junk. Even through the thick walls of the cellar we could feel the din of wagons which, like those festive tanks, never stopped moving all night long. These were the much-reduced remnants of a defeated army.

That Monday night, as we were preparing for another night in the cellar, an immense explosion occurred, dwarfing all others preceding it; immediately another explosion followed. The very molecules of air seemed to break into bits as though our house were crumbling above our heads or the earth were shaking and opening up. We later discovered that it was the two main bridges over the two rivers of the city, on both sides of our house, being blown up by the Russians, one after the other. It was six in the evening, the second day of the war. They had not spared even their own people, so we heard. When the explosions went off, the bridges were full of vehicles and people. They now had no chance of joining their own forces and returning to their homeland.

Now, on urgent reserve duty, gliding like an albatross, gazing like a hawk from an immense height. I look into their houses and peer into their yards, snoop in their fields, and sniff their mountains. Prepared and alert, I observe their constantly increasing strength. With professional detachment I count the factory chimneys that have been added, new roads that have been paved, electric lines and water pipes that have doubled in number. Will war come again? Will it suddenly break out yet again?

I estimate the volume of underground fuel reservoirs, wondering about piles of concealed ammunition. Who are they for? How long will they last? I try to peep under sheds and camouflage nets—are new cannons hidden there, are tanks ready to emerge? For years I have been deciphering military aerial photographs. Like ancient diviners examining the liver of a young calf, I bend over the stereoscope, examining the minute clues sketched in the emulsion of the film before me. Like those haruspices, I, too, look for signs and portents, trying to prognosticate events before they materialize, know in advance things that may happen before too long. As I have said, I no longer like surprises. Those bronze shell casings that fell onto the grass of the tennis courts in the resort the summer before the world war broke out were early omens that continue to affect my life to this day, like a long-sustained underlying bass note.

For so many years I had ignored my burden, and my hand—the hand of a professional editor who makes a living from scribbling—would grow heavy as lead, unable at times to scratch so much as a letter on the blank page beneath it.

(A child's memory: what do I really know about what happened? Have I investigated, collected documents, taken testimonies? What then can I tell, other than what has infiltrated and reached me, absorbed and adapted by a child whose senses were very sharp, it is true, but who would still be only eleven years old at the end of the war. No scientific journal would accept my testimony for publication—but this is my story.

In fact, my real story is the one happening as I write, the story of my attempts to gradually open my bundles of memory and continue functioning at the same time, to be "all right," alert and ready to go, so that I should never be taken by surprise. Never to stop, never to hesitate, like the morning when I crossed the river, only to march straight ahead, as Mother told me. Only thus is there any hope of survival or rescue.)

The loud explosions that evening signaled that nothing would return to the way it was before. The sounds changed over the next few days: fewer explosions and more shots; less in the air, more on the ground. Fighter planes stopped flying overhead; cannon fire was not heard. From rooftops and corners peered the heads of Lithuanians, who enthusiastically took potshots at the remnants of the Red Army.

We remained holed up in the cellar. We could do nothing but wait, and wait some more.

On Wednesday a bizarre silence reigned. We felt it even in the depths of the cellar as soon as we woke from our sleep. There were no shots; no sounds of people running or wagon wheels turning. Silence was all around us; our very breathing stopped: what silence was this?

Little by little out of the silence came distant, unfamiliar sounds, approaching ever nearer and nearer. It was not the roar of engines or the thunder of planes. The sound grew louder and more distinct. At first we didn't believe our ears—it was all so at odds with the circumstances. It was the sound of singing. Sharp and distinct, the song of troops coming from the distance into the city. Not with the gallop of horses or the rolling of tanks, however. As in the days of Assyria, of Rome, of Alexander the Great, row by row, rank upon rank, the conquerors approached in a slow march, heavy but measured, while singing their undoubtedly ancient soldiers' hymn.

Ah li la lo la la
Ah li la lo la la

Thus they had sung in the Franco-Prussian War, during World War I, and only a few months previously in Poland, Belgium, and France. To this day it still haunts me; I can write its score.

Ah li la lo la la
Ah li la lo la la

Platoon by platoon, each marching and singing the same song. Consequently, the music reached our ears in discordant, chaotic notes, like the waves of a river when boats move past one another.

Ah li la lo la la
Ah li la lo la la. . . .

They sang with might and self-assurance, pride and mastery: the victory song of the conquerors, new lords of the land.

The city lay submissive beneath their feet.

And we, down below, deep in the cellar, held our breath like helpless cubs. Ready, attentive, waiting. They have come, they are here. What does their song of celebration mean for us?

That's how it began.

2

Summer

The First Days

A new day broke and we, deep in our cellar, held our breath; the Germans had indeed arrived. We remained there for a few days more; only our parents emerged from time to time. Later, even we children dared to return to our flat, feeling somewhat ill at ease, exposed upstairs on the fourth floor; the dark cellar seemed warmer and safer.

Although the front was moving eastward, the shooting never ceased. News flowed in from all sides that was hard to believe at first—they were shooting Jews. Lithuanians were going from home to home, especially in the ancient quarter of Slobodka, across the river, slaughtering entire families with knives and hatchets, as in the days of Chmielnicki.

There were also kidnapings. People who left on simple errands would cross a street on their way home and were seemingly swallowed by the earth. Some were ordered to report for conscript labor and never returned. Hundreds, thousands even, were gathered during those first weeks of war and were never heard from or seen again. There were rumors of concentrations of prisoners on the outskirts of various cities being held in the withering July heat without water or food. It looked as if the Lithuanians had begun settling their old accounts with the Jews.

Mossik's father was among those arrested. And Abrasha, Arke and Maimke's father, also disappeared; he was arrested while they were returning from a failed attempt to flee during the war's first days.

The last photograph of those who were taken to the Seventh Fort, in the eastern part of the city, shows them crowded and jumbled together. They stand there in long rows—about six thousand of them—their ID cards in hand, ostensibly waiting to be sorted and classified. They are like those, perhaps, who quietly waited at Babi Yar, ignorant of what was happening on the other side of the rampart and in many other places as well. No explicit information ever reached their families, who continued to wait for their loved ones during the coming years, seizing on every scrap of rumor, refusing to be comforted.

What is "Germans"? And why did this name frighten us so? My mother's family came from the region of Kurland on the Baltic coast, which is saturated with German culture. During World War I, thanks to the German conquest, she had studied in German in a good elementary school, and she knew many German songs and poems. One day in the ghetto she returned in good spirits from a day's hard labor felling trees in the forest. She and the others in her group happened to be accompanied by an elderly German sentry, with whom Mother had had a good talk—she had even sung one of her childhood songs to him, only to discover it was a song he had learned as a child as well. Together the two of them, prisoner and guard, sang "O Tannenbaum, O Tannenbaum, / wie grün sind deine Blätter" (O Christmas tree, O Christmas tree, how green are your leaves). For a moment my mother almost felt human again, that all was not lost after all. Much later I was surprised to hear that melody in one of Mozart's violin concertos: he, too, was—for me—German.

Most of the Germans moved on, leaving behind military patrols wearing steel helmets whose profile freezes my blood to this day. With them, a new and terrifying entity swept in—the Gestapo. At times they went out hunting with lists made out in advance; their dungeons swallowed people all the time—no Jew returned alive from there. Alongside the Gestapo new units appeared wearing especially frightening uniforms—black lapels, brown lapels, the skull and crossbones on their caps. A regime that flaunts a death-head! And everywhere, whenever one dared to lift his eyes, was the swastika, a symbol of brutal and terrifying violence, flapping high atop poles, menacing from the insignia on armbands.

On one of the first days after the Germans entered the city, an old *Feldwebel* (field sergeant) entered our yard. In a panic, we children scattered to all sides, but he calmed us with his questions. It seemed he was a medic on the way to the front. He wanted to know how we were and what we needed. When he heard that Jews were forbidden to buy food in the customary stores, he took some of us to the nearby bakery, where he paid for several loaves of hot bread with his own money, bidding us to share it among ourselves. We were amazed and jubilant: here were Germans of the kind my mother remembered. How then to gauge the degree of danger around us, the antelopes asked each other, while predators gazed upon them from the surrounding bushes, their faces sealed.

Salvos of commands fell on everyone. It was forbidden to own weapons of any kind, military equipment, or radios. Hiding soldiers were to be handed over, to give information about collaborators with the previous regime. It was forbidden to send signals, to make broadcasts, to leave lights on at night, to possess incendiary newspapers or literature, and on and on. The orders were signed by the Kommandant of the city, who had a new, markedly Germanic name, Kauen. To these were added special orders targeting only Jews—they were forbidden to leave the city or to use radios or telephones, they were permitted to shop in only a few stores, and they were allowed to be in the streets only during certain hours. It was strictly and absolutely forbidden to enter certain areas of government offices and military installations, and more. All of the decrees and orders were worded with the same brutal ending: "Violators of this regulation will be shot"—*wird erschossen werden*—plain and simple.

Although these orders were harsh, Jews could feel a certain relief—the period of chaos and wild bloodshed sustained by the Lithuanians came to an end. From this time on there was a master, a sovereign, whose commands and decrees, although severe, and whose voice, although offensive and violent, nevertheless made a clear demarcation between what was permitted and what was forbidden. It was, after all, a regime that gloried in the slogan "law and order."

Jews continued to be shot, however, in the streets, in the doorways of houses, through lighted windows, from unexpected distances. From this point onward and for three years to come, in addition to massacres and organized killings, shootings occurred almost daily. The daring few who tried at first to protest and who sought meetings with the Kommandant to appeal in person this decree or that in general never returned. Or, at best, they returned, beaten and bruised, so that everyone around them would learn the lesson of the nature of the new procedures now in effect.

The first days of limiting the sale of food to Jews were a treat for us children, especially for those whose features were not distinctly Jewish. For want of a better alternative, my parents now had to depend on me, to treat me as a valuable partner. As soon as I saw that the butcher shop across the road had received supplies, I left the house—once, twice, even a third time, at intervals—to buy whatever was being sold in rations. From the butcher shop I would rush to other shops in the area, though without straying too far, and buy whatever I could at these places, too. Thanks to my excursions, different kinds of foods and sausages reached our table, the likes of which we had never seen even during ordinary times—as long as the Soviet currency was still accepted. For a brief period of time I was the family's provider, and I was proud beyond measure. Before long, however, these trips became too dangerous, and my few days of glory ended.

Before the war, Mother and I took a memorable, intoxicating walk in the morning into the city. We were on our way to the municipal bus station at an early hour, before the buses had begun to run. The streets were still sleepy and empty, with industrious janitors scrubbing and washing the sidewalks in front of houses. I was utterly amazed that we could walk unhindered through the main avenue of the city, and proud that Mother could rely on me to rise early and walk so far. The last time we spent a whole day together was in Zhezhmer, the shtetl where Aunt Libe and Uncle Shmuel—they were both teachers of Hebrew—lived with my cousins Rivkeleh and Zionah.

During the first days of the war this municipal bus station was the site of one of the cruelest massacres in our city. Lithuanians herded scores of Jews into the Lietukis garage and beat them with any piece of iron they could find—bars, keys, hammers, and screwdrivers. None was left alive. The streams of blood were washed and scrubbed from the cement floor with the hoses used to wash the buses. And my aunt and her daughters, it is said, were pushed into a mass grave and buried alive.

A few days after the new military regime was established, Jews were prohibited from walking on the sidewalks. Jews were ordered to march in single file and, when meeting any German soldier or other uniformed person, to lower their heads and remove their hats, which they were obliged to wear. I remember being unable to sleep the evening the order was issued. Would people really obey such a humiliating command? Morning came, and through the drawn curtains of the wide window, I watched what went on outside. For the first few hours no Jews were on the streets; it was as if they were putting off their errands for as long as possible. But later, one by one, figures with bowed heads began to appear, passing rapidly as ordered on the sides of the road, as if pursued by demons. In the days that followed, we became accustomed to it as a matter of course. Sometimes, as a prank, I would try to go around the rule. I would move diagonally from our house along the pavement until it met the street, as if I were going to go down the road, and then I would move diagonally again to the adjacent gate.

It was not always possible to circumvent the rule—Lithuanians were on guard, eager to be hard on the Jews. Mother returned home one day and said, with a wry smile, "I got what I had coming to me." A year or so earlier—she had come home excited on that day, too—a gypsy woman had been brought to give birth at the hospital where Mother worked. "No longer to crouch on the ground among clods of earth and filth / under black canvas tents or the starlit skies," wrote my mother elatedly, several weeks after the event, in the last of her poems published by the newspaper. "In a soft bed will you bear your child / between white sheets," she continued, in praise of the new, enlightened regime. On that day, a gypsy woman had caught my errant mother taking a few steps on the sidewalk and had upbraided her with sharp words and insults.

A flood of rumors and news overwhelmed us. Rumors about what was to become of us here, news about what was happening to Jews elsewhere. In the meantime we were told that without exception every Jew must wear the yellow Star of David, one on the left side of the breast, the other on the right side of the back. The order included precise measurements and even a sketch, with instructions as to how the patch should look and the materials from which it must be made. In a few days, another order came, repeating emphatically that the patch must be sewn on, in permanent stitching, and must be on every article of clothing, outer and inner layers alike. Nothing was left out.

First the order to use the edge of the road, then the order to wear the yellow star; later came the order to move to a special ghetto—the actions seemed to be taken straight out of Father's history books. Mother sat down at her Singer and stitched yellow patches for us all.

The first days wearing the Stars of David passed uncomfortably enough, as if we had been branded with the mark of Cain. But in time we grew so accustomed to them that when I looked out through the ghetto fence at passersby on the other side, I would take the absence of a yellow patch on their clothes as a defect of some sort, like a bland dish of food without seasoning.

The summer dragged on, in spite of the war. There was no more talk of summer camp, rivers, or sailing. Everyone withdrew into his corner and waited fearfully for the next blow. Everyone looked cautiously around to see who was left and who was missing.

Prominent people among the Jewish population were rushed to the city's central command and under direct threats were told to assemble a committee to represent the Jews to the authorities, "for their own good." Their insistence that they were not sanctioned to represent anybody and had no authority to undertake the office was to no avail. Objections because of ill health and fresh bereavement were rejected as well. For lack of other options a number of brave men, Dr. Elkes especially, shouldered the burden of representing the rest. These representatives were called the Ältestenrat, the council of elders. They had to summon all their strength to appear before the Germans and do their bidding, making cautious attempts at negotiations. They never knew, when attending these meetings, whether they would return; they said the prayer of *vidui* (deathbed confession) before they went.

And what of the shtetls? We were greatly concerned about the fate of our families there, but we knew nothing. As we learned later, members of the death squads, the Einsatz-Gruppen (operational detachments), reached hundreds of villages and shtetls during the first months of the occupation, systematically executing Jews in towns and villages, one after the other. There were four Einsatz-Gruppen in all of eastern Europe, whose members were recruited and trained in the months before war. A few hundred Germans only, they reaped the first great harvest of death. In our region, it was the Death Squad Sonder-Kommando 3 of Einsatz-Gruppe A, a few dozen Germans in all, who conducted the execution of tens of thousands of Jews in the shtetls. Their work was made easy thanks to the willing and eager help they received from Lithuanians, who in effect carried out the German objectives.

They rounded up the Jews in my grandfather's village and locked them in the synagogue, the mighty stronghold of normal times. Through the windows they saw the jeering, hate-filled faces of their former neighbors. Such were the Lithuanians, whose ancestors were still worshiping Perkunas, the god of lightning, when Maimonides published his monumental works. For generations Jews and Lithuanians had lived together side by side, making deals and asking after each other's health. Now the concealed enmity burst forth and knew no bounds. At Grandfather's synagogue, from time to time one or another of the besiegers would squeeze up to the window and announce to the petrified prisoners that soon they would be killed, one by one. Several days later they took all the men to pits prepared for them in a distant grove, the one by the railroad station.

The last moments of my grandfather's life were accounted for by a witness. When the Jews of Vidukle were led to the killing pit during the hot days of August of that year, the rabbi, my grandfather, straggled unwillingly at the end of the column, stubbornly refusing to quicken his pace. From his hiding place, the sole survivor from the village heard the Lithuanians tell the story as they returned, content with the deed their hands had performed.

My grandmother and all the women and children were imprisoned in the synagogue for three more weeks. The sole survivor reported how the women prayed ceaselessly in front of the ark and scrolls of the Torah, but to no avail.

On the Ninth of Av—of all days—they were taken, this time in wagons, to a long, open pit at the margins of the old Jewish cemetery, and there they were dispatched in the same manner as the men had been.

On the eve of the war my extended family included seven families—twenty-nine souls in five shtetls and one city, not counting the large branch of the family in nearby Belorussia. By the end of the war, only two had survived.

Thus even Jews saw the order to move to a special ghetto as a plausible or at least possible necessity.

The Germans allotted a month to complete the move to the ghetto. They asserted that this was the only way they could guarantee the safety and possessions of our people from additional pogroms on the part of the Lithuanians.

At first everything happened slowly, as no one was in a hurry to go. The area set aside for the ghetto was the old Jewish suburb Slobodka, which had grown up across the river in the preceding centuries as a typical Jewish shtetl at the entrance to the city. To it they annexed an adjacent quarter on the east where Lithuanians lived in wooden houses surrounded by gardens. These two neighborhoods were set aside for all the Jews of the city. The Lithuanians were ordered to vacate their houses and lots and to exchange them for the flats of Jews in the city. This was certainly a harsh measure for some of them, but the rewards were great—they could choose among the finest and most centrally located dwellings in our city, completely furnished and fully stocked. When we finally moved, Mother insisted on dragging a sack of coal and kindling along with her from our cellar. "There's winter to think of," she said.

The days went by; we had no place to go, and our anxiety grew. Once or twice my parents went to scout the area of the planned ghetto, but wherever they went, the Lithuanians there said they had already exchanged their dwellings, and the Jews who had already moved claimed that all the places around them were taken. Only once did my parents manage to bring candidates for an exchange to our flat. With their noses in the air and contemptuous faces, the Lithuanians looked around—fourth floor, damp in the walls—they had better prospects elsewhere.

The stream of wagons and wheelbarrows rolled toward the bridge, their numbers growing day by day. Peasants from all over the surrounding district hastened to the city with their wagons to profit from the transfer of the Jews.

The time allotted by the Germans to find an apartment was up, and we had nowhere to go and no one to turn to. An unequivocal announcement made it clear that the date for moving would not be postponed, and any Jew found in the city limits beyond the set date would face dire consequences. Already there were almost no Jews to be found, and the ring of hostility grew tighter. My parents decided to wait no longer. They gathered a few belongings, suffering not a few qualms with regard to some books, and we set out. The plan was to live temporarily in the flat of a teacher friend who had agreed to put us up until we found a place to live.

Five days before the deadline, we left our apartment and set out.

LOCKED GATES

August 15, 1941, came, a mere eight weeks since the disturbances began, and the gates of the ghetto were locked. Everyone was now inside. For a few weeks, people continued to move from place to place in search of a corner for themselves. Occasionally new families were brought in, having survived by some miracle. From a population of about thirty thousand in the first days, only a few thousand remained at the end of three years.

Aggressive people took up the largest apartments and most spacious settings—after all, they had given up fine dwellings and many possessions in the city. However, even those who had nothing at all to offer were sent to the ghetto. Stealing and insolence abounded, the strong prevailing over the weak. In the end, did any advantage accrue to the vulgar and pushy people over the more refined? Reality shook them up and jumbled them, pressed them together and ground them up, and in the long run the strong had no advantage over the weak, nor the aggressive over the meek. In the end it was hard to tell one kind of person from another. To quote the movie *Shoah*, "From the gas cells, when the doors were opened, they fell out in one solid block."

In the meantime my parents had to continue making the rounds in search of a place for us. Friends and acquaintances who occupied more space than was allotted to them now became unapproachable strangers. To me, everyone was a stranger. But I was told once by Dr. Gurvitch, Ettele's mother, "This was not a concentration camp or work camp where total strangers were forced together, free to turn tooth and claw against their neighbors. These were members of your own community, with whom you had lived for years; you knew them in different, more respectable circumstances, now suddenly showing a different side of themselves, often an ugly and repulsive one. This was one of the most hurtful things about the ghetto."

By chance, my father met Mottel Podliash's relatives. Mottel was a very simple, ordinary man. Years ago, while a student, Father had lived like a member of the family in Mottel's flat on Green Hill, which was barren and crammed with children. Now it was Mottel's daughter Beila who, upon hearing of our family's hardship, decreed laconically, come to us. By this time Mottel and Beila's husband were already gone—they had been among those taken to the Seventh Fort. The diminished family now included Hinda, Mottel's second wife; Beila; a younger brother; and a pair of young twins. They now lived in the easternmost part of the ghetto. After several trips back and forth with our belongings, we moved into their flat, which consisted of two rooms and a kitchen. They hung a sheet across the middle of the larger room and said, "Here's where you'll live." Afterward, Father never stopped praising them and telling how our salvation came not from institutions and not from friends, but from Mottel's family—simple, warm-hearted, and unpretentious people.

We had scarcely put down our things before I began exploring. Everything was new to me, unfamiliar and intriguing. Most of the buildings in the ghetto were made of wood, similar to those we lived in at the resort. There were also three or four apartment blocks—cheap four-story quarters for laborers that were built of concrete and left unfinished by the Soviets. The blocks' silhouettes dominated the view, serving as a landmark and a signpost. In our part of the ghetto, the garden suburb, the houses were small, with one or two floors, and were surrounded by fields of green. Some of the previous residents had improved their property with ornamented wooden fences and flowerbeds, leaving them against their will to the Jews. Trees? I do not recall any trees in the ghetto. There were empty lots between the houses. The roads in some areas of the ghetto were unpaved, but wide and straight, laid out in both parallel and perpendicular lines.

North of the ghetto the land was higher. A road cut diagonally across the slope, rising gradually from left to right. To the south, the border of the ghetto hugged the riverbank, its dunes blocking our view of the water and the city on the opposite shore. Along the river, inside the ghetto, stretched a long, unpaved road; at its eastern length were rundown factories built of red bricks. An abandoned sawmill by the river marked the farthest southeast corner of our new pale of settlement.

To me the ghetto seemed a huge expanse, and the trip across it from end to end, a long and adventurous journey. Through the center of the area allotted to the ghetto passed a main road leading to the northeastern part of the country, a route that was important to the Germans. They fenced both sides of this road, excluding it from the ghetto and cutting it into two parts—the only connection between them was a high, arched bridge for pedestrians. The bulk of the ghetto, the "big ghetto," lay to the south, spreading to the riverbank. North of the big ghetto, bordering the foothills, was the "little ghetto." At its center was one of the open areas that had doubtless been built to beautify the growing city.

The wooden bridge became the umbilical cord of the ghetto. It astonished me to see how such a high bridge was built out of nothing but boards and planks. As soon as it opened, it teemed with people; there was never a moment when it was empty. Some had business crossing it; others, like me, went out of curiosity. From its dizzying height I gazed around me, as from a high tower. I was a little fearful about looking down on the road below, both because of the great height and because of the German vehicles that constantly passed below. Before long the bridge was dismantled, there was no more little ghetto, and once again it was impossible to look down from on high at the Germans.

To the west was the Jewish shtetl. For generations our people had crowded here at the side of the main road leading into the big town, where, at the time, Jews were forbidden to reside. At the edge of this quarter, facing the city, stood the main gate of the ghetto. The shtetl had muddy alleys that were narrow and twisted, and old houses with mossy roofs that leaned against each other, clustered beside the synagogues and schools, as in Chagall's paintings. Among them, like a precious stone, was the famous Slobodka Yeshiva, a house of Torah known in all corners of the world. My father had taught for years in one of the newer institutions of that quarter, the Tharbuth ("Culture") School.

At first my parents forbade me to leave the house. But gradually they relented, preoccupied by their own worries. These outings were a great relief for me after the two months of tension. I had never before appreciated the warmth and security that came from living with one's own kind, Jews only.

Among those brought together in the ghetto I found acquaintances from different times and places—friends from kindergarten, from school, from summer camp, and from the waiting room of Dr. Kamber, the pediatrician—a kind of grand reunion. We began to find out who remained and who was missing. Ever since my good friends, the brothers Arke and Maimke, had returned from Helsinki the summer before with stories of stoplights that changed colors from moment to moment, I imagined that the entire outside world was adorned with marvelous signposts of this kind. Now, both the brothers and I were shut in the ghetto where we could only dream about the world outside and imagine what was happening to our missing friends.

I was a boy from a "good home," and during the first period in the ghetto I suffered not a little for it. I couldn't bear the vulgarity, the violence, and the profanity all around. I learned a new word, employed by my discomfited parents to deal with their new surroundings—*Unterwelt* (underworld). In other words, we will never sink so low, we will not be counted among them. Once, in our first days in the ghetto, I joined Mother when she went to the butcher's, where they doled out small rations of meat. The line was backed up and we waited a long time, anxious lest the supply run out before our turn came. Just as we reached the counter, a poker-faced woman jumped up from behind us and claimed it was her turn, and she got the last rations of meat. What could my mother say to this brazen woman? How should she respond? Frustrated and defeated, she hissed loudly through clenched teeth, "May a black spot stain your conscience forever!" Thus spoke my mother, the poet, to the woman with strong elbows who made her way out of the butcher shop without batting an eyelash, her booty under her arm. I learned an important lesson that day about the way of the world.

In time the ghetto fence took on a clear and rigid identity of its own, and I came to know its course and every detail of its contours and configurations. It divided the world into two. As the days passed, my world became constricted into what was inside the barbed wire. Everything outside became a cipher that I gazed at through the fence, as if through a clear but impenetrable curtain.

In the first weeks in the ghetto, procedures were declared, routines were fixed. The self-governing body for the ghetto—the Komität—appointed officials and aides; established offices, departments, and storehouses; and issued food tickets and work permits, all in accordance with the Germans' instructions.

But the Germans never stopped their duplicity. By dusk on the day the gates of the ghetto closed, scores of people who had been caught at random in the streets were executed. And though the Germans repeatedly insisted that such things would not happen in the ghetto, three days after the gates were closed another disaster occurred. Five hundred and thirty-four people with higher education, who answered a summons to volunteer for a special assignment "requiring broad knowledge," failed to return from their first day of work. All the appeals and attempts to investigate were fruitless. Family members of the missing persons worked ceaselessly to gather information, but the Germans asserted firmly that their relatives had been sent on a special secret mission and that before long they would be sending letters. A few weeks later, in fact, postcards began arriving, signed by some of the missing persons. We know now that this was part of a campaign of deception—all those who were taken were murdered at the Ninth Fort on the first day.

Work was required of everyone, and it fell to the ghetto authorities to enforce the rule. The Komität had a Jewish police force whose members sported blue and white bands on their sleeves and who wore special caps. They affected military manners and gave orders in Lithuanian. Side by side with the Germans, they watched over all those coming and going at the gate.

If the fence was like a diaphragm, such that anything happening along it affected the breath of the ghetto, the gate was its very heart, the place through which the life of the ghetto came and went. Through the gate came search and confiscation patrols, squads for selection and arrest. Here supplies were brought in; food was smuggled (some say arms as well); and a lucky few were able to escape.

Passage through the gate occupied everyone. At dawn and at dusk the work brigades exited and reentered. When they left, the people were carefully counted; when they returned, they were not only counted but thoroughly searched as well for smuggled food or valuables they might have obtained by barter with Lithuanians. A dangerous game of cops and robbers developed, each side improving its stratagems to defeat the other. Smugglers might get off with confiscation of their goods, overnight arrest in the local jail, and a turn in the hard labor brigade the next day, but they could also be taken to the dungeons of the Gestapo in the city to wait miserably with the other hostages who were regularly gathered there until their fateful dispatch to the Ninth Fort, the main execution site of Jews in the coming year.

The hardest of the work brigades was the airport brigade, the one destined for the Aerodrome. No one wanted to be enlisted in it, and everyone did their best to avoid it. After a five-kilometer march south across both rivers, workers had to perform various manual tasks under harsh supervision and in any weather, on day or night shifts, digging and quarrying, loading and carrying. The Germans were expanding the airport, the one whose bombing had ushered in the war that first morning. Every morning and evening a crisis broke out at the gate over filling the quota of workers for the brigade. The Germans announced that the ghetto existed solely by virtue of this brigade. Accordingly, every able-bodied man in the ghetto was assigned to join it in turn. The police force was enlisted to execute the order. They failed at times to meet the quota, especially for the night shift, which left for work at sunset. Then, for want of an alternative, the police would snatch workers from any day shift brigade returning from work, sending them out for another shift of hard labor.

MY UNIVERSITIES

My universities, the first period in the ghetto, countless impressions.

Neighbors: Across from us lived a Parisian family, a mother and her daughter, thrown by chance into the ghetto. A foreign language, fragrances, manners, and dress from another world. The little girl was somewhat younger than I. She had long blond ringlets tied with colored ribbons. Her dress was always spotless; she wore colorful stockings and shiny shoes. She seemed to have come straight out of a children's tale, perhaps "Sleeping Beauty." The two spoke only French between themselves; the sound of their conversation was like pleasant music, distant and appealing.

The fairy-tale girl always held a doll or two; they, too, were combed and neatly dressed. The climactic moment for us, however, was the appearance of her biggest doll, a life-sized toy that could make human noises and sing songs. Occasionally my sister would be allowed to hold this doll, or push one of the smaller dolls in a tiny but matching carriage, while all of us looked on admiringly. Like creatures from another world the French family spun around us, and I was intoxicated.

The gardens beside the houses: I first saw dwarf nasturtiums there, their angular flowers, their polygonal fruit, their sharp aroma. There were vegetable patches among the houses, left behind by the Lithuanians. One day, as if by a prearranged signal, people suddenly appeared from all sides of the plot, tearing up and trampling the plants. At first I did not understand what all the commotion was about, all the feverish digging in the dirt around me, until I saw their baskets filling with potatoes. I ran straight home to tell of my discovery and find a basket so I could get a share of the spoils. To my surprise, when I came back, all was quiet—no one was there, and all that remained was the shorn and trampled field.

So I learned that day both how potatoes grew and about lightning raids that became the custom in the ghetto. The vegetable gardens were still perceived as belonging to the Lithuanians, and touching them was prohibited. But there are restrictions that people cannot abide. People watched each other, and as soon as one person crossed the barrier, in the blink of an eye the entire field was plundered and stripped. With the aid of family members, receptacles prepared in advance, and an efficient division of labor, the harvest was gathered and brought speedily to hiding places, all before the police could be summoned. They were even able, these aggressive plunderers, to rid themselves of children like myself, keeping them at a distance and preventing them from enjoying even the smallest scraps from the feast.

In our house, my efforts to join the plunder were not accorded much glory. I was given to understand that our family did not indulge in certain kinds of lawlessness and looting, even if "everyone else was doing it." Order must be maintained, rules must be obeyed.

My hill: Behind our house, as in several other places within the ghetto, was a large pit, evidently the result of an excavation. In it grew wild plants and reeds. Here I found ants, beetles, and grasshoppers to play with. I pulled their limbs off one by one and built ghettos for them. I spent hours alone here in my private corner on a mound of dirt that was my ship and my airplane, and I its captain and pilot. Here no one fenced me in or set limits on my imagination.

The dog Belka: As her name suggests, she was all white, and beautiful. Perhaps her previous owners had abandoned her in the ghetto, though she could have come from anywhere. She was short-haired, small, agile, and friendly. For the first time in my life I had a dog, and I was beside myself with joy. She had two yellow spots on her left side, one on her torso and another on her snout, which amused everyone who saw her—a truly Jewish dog she was, wearing our mark of disgrace as required. I spent entire days playing with her and even dug a den for her in the mound at the bottom of the pit, pretending that I was burrowing out a long tunnel that would take both of us far away.

But other times came, and Belka disappeared, as if sensing the changes about to take place. Perhaps she simply slipped through the barbed-wire fence and found a quieter corner. At least we were not forced to deliver her to the authorities when the order came, some time later, to hand over all pets. For many years afterward I longed for a dog of my own.

Trading through the fence: The alley where we lived on the edge of the ghetto was convenient, relatively speaking. The fence blocked its end, leaving us a somewhat concealed corner. Consequently, it was possible to exchange goods through the fence with Lithuanians in the neighborhood. At the time, the sentries were not overly zealous, interpreting the injunction not to approach within two meters of the barbed wire with a certain laxity. Between the rounds of the sentries from one end of their beat to the other, it was possible to get things done.

I used to watch in bewilderment the hasty commerce being conducted over the fence. Across from us, just around the corner of a building, stood a Lithuanian woman, apparently aimlessly. My mother would wave her hand or flap a woolen skirt or a colorful towel up and down to arouse her interest. After a few vain efforts, the Gentile woman would stir and begin waving her own items of trade—eggs, butter, meat. Then the vocal part of the transaction would begin; they haggled over the terms of exchange. When they agreed, both would look hastily left and right, spring simultaneously to the fence, trade the goods in their hands in an instant, and retreat to their starting corners. Sometimes the lengthy bargaining would end without result.

Over time Mother came to know some of the traders, and they recognized her. By peeping through the window, Mother could judge in advance whether it was worth her while to venture out that day. Occasionally she would decide not to trade that day, only to discover that other women were getting a good deal, and immediately she would rush to join them. Other times, Mother would return to the house disappointed, like a fisherman who waits hours only to gather an empty net—no one had appeared on the other side.

And thus, while our bundles grew smaller and our belongings became fewer, our table sometimes had better food than usual, depending on the day's trade. Mother, who had once dragged firewood from the city to the ghetto, now changed her mind—there was nothing to save and no point in hoarding. What could be traded should be traded now, without delay.

School: In the midst of all this, there was an effort to establish a school for the children of the ghetto. My parents were pleased and so was I—it was time I returned to my studies. Under normal circumstances, I would have been entering the fourth grade. In the two-story building beside Democrats' Square near our house, they assembled children of varying ages and tried to divide them into classes according to similar levels of knowledge. We were brought together in groups for discussions; we may even have been taught some Torah. Sometimes we were all brought together in a larger hall on the ground floor, where a man wearing a skullcap would preach a long sermon. In my case, however, it was the public singing at the close of these sermons that took hold. Together with these a number of similar songs from my mother are stored in my memory, such as the vigorous protest of Rabbi Yitzhak ben Levi of Berdichev, who contends with the Holy One, Blessed be He, over the hardships He inflicts on His own people, the children of Israel, for no sin of theirs. There would be days when these songs would become my priceless possessions, my only solace in times of distress.

Decrees and confiscation orders followed close upon one another: electrical appliances and radios, cameras and record players, jewelry, gold and silver utensils, brass and copper tools, samovars, candlesticks, cooking utensils—all were required for the war effort. We received replacements for our brass handles for doors and windows made of a gray alloy. I was impressed by the coordination involved in the exchange. Later, in winter, we had to give up furs, then books—the latter an unbearable decree.

On the heels of confiscation orders came the search parties. They moved from house to house through the entire ghetto, inspecting to ensure that the inhabitants had delivered up everything as commanded. Panic broke out when the search parties came near—the Germans were coming! For many, and certainly for us children, this would be our first direct encounter with them. Because we lived at the far end of the ghetto, we had to wait several days before the Germans reached us. The inspections were very thorough, and we heard stories of insults and beatings, angry outbursts and humiliations. But in general the inspections passed peaceably enough. Some managed to move endangered items at night from an area that had not yet been combed to one where the searches had already ended.

One day, unexpectedly, a curfew was announced in our quarter. All were ordered to enter their flats, prepare identification papers, leave the doors to rooms and closets open, and put valuables on the table for inspection. Our turn had come.

Mottel's family consulted Mother about a few valuable items that they still had and had not given up before—would it get them into trouble? Mother suggested, "Put the items in an out-of-the-way place, without actually hiding them. If the searchers see them, they can take them, and will have no complaint against you." We ourselves had nothing to fear except for a package of good leather for boot soles that Mother had received by trade through the fence; now she wondered what to do with it.

They came suddenly and stormed in—a few German officers accompanied by Jewish policemen who ran before them like Puss in Boots, shouting "Achtung!"

AchtungAchtungAchtungAchtungAchtungAchtungAchtungAchtung

A pair of syllables—one word, ostensibly ordinary, and yet even today it can freeze the blood in my veins.

Shining boots, dark uniforms, diagonal leather chest straps; belts on which heavy, well-oiled pistols were hung, ready to open fire in an instant. Black or brown lapels, gleaming visors, decorations and buttons, swastikas on their shoulders, solid leather riding whips or flexible canes in leather-gloved hands, batons held with elegant carelessness beneath their arms—for the first time the Germans stood in my house.

Loud voices commanded us to show our papers and identify ourselves one by one; I tried not to be seen and didn't dare raise my eyes. They turned this way and that, combing the surroundings with hungry hawk eyes. While one of them began rummaging through cupboards, another one fixed his eyes on Beila and announced that he wanted to do a body search on her. With a sort of knightly gesture he motioned her behind the curtain. Our attentive ears heard muffled voices and embarrassed giggles. Later, she said that when he ordered her to undress, she explained to him why she had a bulge in her middle, which had first aroused his suspicion. Never mind, he told her, I'm a doctor. So I found out that Beila was well along in her pregnancy. While one officer searched Beila, the other was casting about for some place else to search. On the spur of the moment, Mother made a quick decision—she went to the shelf near the ceiling and took down the partly hidden package of leather, extending it with a few words in good German. Satisfaction spread across the face of the officer, and, together with the other, who had finished with Beila, they turned and left the apartment without disturbing us further.

After this incident I asked my mother if she had planned her actions. She said she didn't know how she would behave in advance—she had gambled intuitively. In the coming years I learned a lot about Mother's daring in taking risks and gambling: had she not taken certain risks, I would not be here to write these words.

The officers left and we were relieved. If these were the Germans, perhaps things weren't so terrible. Perhaps they had grown tired of the searches, or perhaps their trained eye told them that there was no point in searching our house further. And perhaps the package Mother had surrendered did the trick. That evening my mother and father had an argument—might the Germans not have left on their own, without the sacrifice of a valuable possession?

I went out to see what had happened in other houses. Around us I discovered buildings torn apart like feather pillows—doors unhinged, tiles uprooted, belongings thrown about. Not everyone was as lucky as we were. Never before had I encountered such a vivid illustration of manmade chaos. In the days to come there would be nothing novel about it.

3

Autumn

STRANGE DAYS

In my private world, the first few months in the ghetto were a kind of immense game of make-believe in which everyone participated—Jews, Lithuanians, and Germans. Soon, I imagined, every one of us would return home and life would resume its normal course. But the facts were different. True, the inspections and confiscations had ceased, work brigades left in an orderly fashion, we continued to go to school, and the Komität offices kept working at full steam. But from time to time, for one reason or another, people would be taken to the Ninth Fort. The most trivial transgressions, such as failing to wear the yellow star, attempting to send mail, or not lowering the head as required, led to imprisonment or execution.

The Germans began issuing, in limited quantities, special family permits certifying that the possessor was employed in work that was vital to the German war effort. Those who were left out worried—what would become of them? People began striving to obtain these "good" permits. Ironically, the permits required the stamp of a ghetto commander, a man named Jordan, and they consequently came to be known as "Jordan Passes"—our Jordan River, the one in the atlas that Arke, Maimke, and I so often used to study.

Once they stopped Father on the wooden bridge and nearly took him away. He managed to get out of that one, but as a result he took the trouble to obtain a "Jordan Schein" too. For a minute I was allowed to hold the two white, narrow certificates, one in his name, the other for members of his family—seemingly innocent strips of paper, but what power they held, almost magical properties.

One morning the little ghetto was closed, a curfew was announced, and all the residents were assembled in the square. The sorting began—those with certain work permits were released and sent to the big ghetto, while others—hundreds of them—were loaded into trucks and taken in the direction of the Ninth Fort. All the rest, including the sick and the elderly, were left standing for several hours in the central square, surrounded by guards. Germans lay behind machine guns, their fingers on the trigger. A machine gun was even stationed on the wooden bridge. At the same time there was a house-to-house search to find anyone hiding. New orders were issued, and additional Germans took up firing positions all around. All the rifle barrels were now trained on the people in the square. Something decidedly inexplicable was about to happen here at any moment.

Then suddenly—so we were told—just as in a play, a motorcycle came roaring in, its rider waving a sheaf of paper from a distance and shouting: "Halt! Stop!" The commander of the operation took the document from the messenger's hand, scanned it briefly, and ordered, "Everyone disperse!"

Those who were taken to the fort returned before long, unharmed.

Some viewed this as a miracle from heaven, divine intervention at the last moment. Skeptics claimed defiantly that the entire event was intentionally staged to frighten the Jews into reporting more diligently for work. After all, was it reasonable to suppose the Germans would fire machine guns into a defenseless crowd of men, women, and children who had never done them any harm? And so openly, too, in a public square of the city, right beside the country's principal road? Henceforth, the events of that strange day were known as the Fake Aktion.

A mere three weeks later the little ghetto was surrounded once more. Once again all the ghetto dwellers were ousted from their homes, and once again the meticulous sorting began. While everyone was standing there, a column of smoke began rising from the nearby hospital. The Germans had set fire to it with its patients, doctors, and nurses still inside—none was allowed to escape. Those who were seen jumping through the flames were shot. The cries and screams of people burning alive fell on those standing in the adjoining square.

Afterward, the Germans tried to claim that the hospital had been a hotbed of contagious diseases that endangered the entire city and their army. The possibility that the ghetto was the source of plagues, especially typhus, was used for years by the Germans as a kind of bogeyman to express their loathing of and revulsion for the ghetto and its inhabitants. More than once it prevented them from entering the ghetto, as if the overcrowded ghetto were not of their own making.

Holders of the "Jordan Schein" were sent to the big ghetto this time too, but about two thousand people without permits were taken to the Ninth Fort, never to return. Among them were all the residents of the home for the elderly and the ghetto orphanage—institutions located, as it happened, in the little ghetto. At this time, a decree was published ordering the complete evacuation of the little ghetto. The survivors were forced to find new quarters immediately, without their belongings. This time fortune went against those who had occupied the nicer villas on the hillside.

The little ghetto, its evacuation now complete, remained empty and fenced off, rather than being returned to the Lithuanians. Some nights voices could be heard there, and flashlights pierced the darkness, but by the next morning all would be quiet within.

We soon discovered that the Germans used the little ghetto as an overnight way station for transports of Jews from central Europe. They would let them off with only a few possessions from the train that had brought them from Vienna on their way to points east for resettlement: their heavier baggage would catch up with them later, they were promised. The next morning the travelers would be taken straight to the Ninth Fort. Workers from our ghetto were sent to the train station and to the little ghetto to collect the belongings they had left behind. Were it not for the tags attached to the elegant leather suitcases indicating the names of their owners, our people would never have known who the overnight guests in the little ghetto were.

During the next few days the sentries grew more diligent, and the shots at night along the fence, at any spark of light, grew more frequent.

End of October

Tuesday

One Monday about two weeks after the holidays, announcements appeared on the walls ordering all the ghetto inhabitants to report the next morning not to work, as usual, but to the nearby Democrats' Square for a general head count. The order allowed no exceptions, even for the elderly and infirm. Homes were to be left open. The notice ended in the familiar brutal manner: anyone found at home after 6:00 A.M. would be shot—*wird erschossen werden.*

The bustle began in the predawn darkness. Lights came on, doors slammed, voices scolded at children. Some made hot drinks or swallowed a hasty bite, as families began streaming in a quiet, orderly manner toward the square. Not a soul knew how long the count would last; the more practical brought along sandwiches and bottles of hot water.

In the early half light it was impossible to estimate the number of people gathered. In the grayness of the autumnal dawn I gradually began to perceive the square and its surroundings, packed with people, as I had never seen it before.

Among them were respectable and prominent people, some of them world famous. All stood here together—a crowd numbering nearly thirty thousand. We soon met friends and stood together with them. The day drew on and everyone waited.

Little by little we could feel a certain movement in the mass of people, shifting toward the southern edge of the square, the side closest to the river. It was understood that an inspection of some sort was taking place way off at the edge of the crowd, though with extreme sluggishness or over-thoroughness, and we could do nothing but wait. In the meantime, we had noticed that many German guards were surrounding the square, so there was no point in thinking about slipping away early back to our homes.

So we stood where we stood. Because the day was cold, without sunshine, people moved about a bit, shaking arms and legs, running in place, and talking with one another. Father, as was his custom, made the rounds in search of friends and acquaintances. Such an opportunity: all the Jews of this great city were together in a single place. He often exchanged witticisms with friends laced with his usual dark humor. However, for all his circulation in the vast sea of people, he was none the wiser as to precisely what was going on.

The day dragged on and slowly two or three broad lines of people formed, moving southward at slightly different speeds. The question arose—which line to join? Should we try to hasten the inspection, or should we hang back? On the one hand, it might be best to get it over with; on the other, perhaps in the course of the day the Germans would grow weary of the entire effort and dismiss the last of us without checking us at all. Which was the better option, no one could say.

At any rate, it was now noon. Movement in the lines was now more apparent; we were clearly headed toward a certain spot. We could distinguish both more Jewish policemen and more German guards. There the lines of those waiting were defined and delimited. Where those who had passed the search had gone wasn't clear. At any rate, the dwellings and streets close to the square still seemed, from my vantage point, deserted and empty.

According to the rumors filtering back to us from the front of the lines, the Germans were examining each family separately. Immediately people began rehearsing, to themselves and to their families, what to say and how to answer when questioned. It was generally agreed that we should make the best impression possible—that we should appear healthy, youthful, skilled, and motivated to work, for the Germans had always insisted that the purpose of the ghetto was to aid their war effort. Large families split into two or more units, and older family members managed to pair themselves up with younger ones.

We got closer and closer to the front of the arena until we were standing in lines of about eight people each. The rest of the square beyond the barrier of sentries was empty, hemmed in mainly by Jewish policemen who were helping to keep order. A little way from them, standing apart, was a group of German guards. These were shabby Wehrmacht soldiers from the local garrison, rifle and belt dragging, crumpled caps on their heads, and sagging gaiters on their boots. Normally they guarded the ghetto fences and served as escorts for the work brigades. A wretched bunch, most of whom were getting on in years or in poor health, they were tasked with guarding the Jews instead of fighting on the Eastern Front. Now they were straggling back to accompany groups from the inspection grounds in some unspecified direction.

In the center of the square, at a distance from all the others, the dreaded SS men were stationed. They were the focal point of the activity. Spit-polished, in black uniforms with heavy pistols in their holsters, they were dictating which direction to send everyone who passed them. Even though we could see groups being sent from here to there, we could not deduce any particular pattern, either from the direction they were marched in or from the composition of the groups.

At some distance beyond us, toward the river, was a large open lot, a kind of shallow bowl like the one we had in our yard. To the left, on some sand mounds overlooking the river, stood a few shacks that belonged to the abandoned sawmill at the edge of the ghetto. Looking closely, I could see a large number of people there, apparently ours. None of us knew why they were being held there.

Scene: A Jewish policeman holding two children approaches one of the German officers. He halts several paces from them, stands at attention like a well-drilled soldier, and with lowered head makes a request. The patent gestures of subservience apparently have their desired effect; with a slight nod, the German officer assents. The policeman turns aside and, still holding the children and breaking into a slow but stylized trot, begins crossing the open square, across the shallow pit by the river, straight to the people among the shacks on the mounds. After a few minutes, the policeman returns by the same route, still trotting, but this time alone. A whisper races through the crowd. Unclear as the patterns of sorting have been, it is now obvious that the sawmill is the preferred destination. "They get everything, the German slaves," say the people, grinding their teeth. *End of scene.*

The patience of the Germans was apparently wearing thin, for they began moving ever-larger clusters of people past them. The suspense grew. We found ourselves suddenly being headed off by policemen. They cut us off from the mass behind, surrounded us, and began moving us forward as a separate group, apparently in preparation for sorting. Father, having fallen a bit behind at that moment—probably wrapped up in conversation with someone—was suddenly on the other side of the chain of policemen now cutting between us and those behind, unable to rejoin us. Mother did not lose her wits for even a moment and cried out. The policemen tried to calm her: "He will join you later; don't worry; he will be right behind you." But Mother would have none of it—he was the head of the family; without him we would not budge. While this was happening, the mass of people around us was shoving and pressing slowly forward. "I don't know where I found the strength all of a sudden," she said later. With my sister on her arm and me holding on behind her with all my might, Mother heaved us all backward, broke through the chain of policemen, seized Father, who, confounded, had frozen in his tracks, and pulled him with all her strength to join us. So forceful was her tug that the nearest policeman made no effort to stop her.

Still agitated by our near separation from Father, we did not notice that we were now part of a group slowly passing by the Germans. Achtung! The lines stopped dead. I breathed deeply, bit my lips, and held tightly to my parents. Rows were counted, there was a momentary pause, and then came the order to keep moving. In front was a Jewish policeman, at the sides and behind us a German sentry or two, and in between was our group, consisting of fifteen or twenty rows, with six to eight people in each. We heard voices among us—"Oy, yidn, we're going left, that isn't good." But others cried out, "No, they said go right." Yet another voice, perhaps that of the Jewish policeman marching beside us, his face betraying no emotion but with a friendly look in his eyes—"Yidn," he whispered, "it's all right, all will be well."

Within a few moments we were being marched along the east side of the square. I held Mother's hand tightly; beside her, Father held my four-year-old little sister in his arms. From my place at the edge of the group, I had a good view of what was happening all around us.

The crowd remaining in the square watched us through the chains of guards, trying to guess which way we were headed. For a moment it seemed to me as if we were walking on a raised stage, as in a theater, with the audience watching our movements. I felt bashful and tried to march well, showing restraint and self-discipline. We continued marching along the edge of the square, further and further to the north. My heart sank. The lead policeman slowly began to turn the group in a deep semi-circle, like a boat in mid-river, and by degrees we found ourselves facing back to the right, in the direction of the sand mounds, the sawmill, and the shacks. A sigh of relief broke out among us—thank God, we are in the good direction.

We were just finishing the large U-turn when the next group swept past us. They, too, were first marched north, in the same direction we had gone, but with this difference—they were accompanied only by German guards, not Jewish ones. Something compelled me to watch their faces intently. For a moment, my gaze focused on a young woman marching on the edge of the row. Her face had a concentrated expression that became engraved in my memory, as if she were already in a strange and different place, far from us.

So near did they pass by us that we could hear talking among them, voices murmuring for something. Maybe their calls were directed at us. At times I still seem to hear the voices. Little did I know that I was confronting at close range a group of people being led by blind chance to a fate completely different from our own.

They receded farther and farther from us. And we, after another short march, arrived at the mounds of sand beside the river. Crowds of people were waiting on the docks, waving and cheering. Our family arrived at the shore in one piece and joined the thousands who had been waiting there since morning.

All were excited and relieved. Thank God it was all behind us. Everyone exchanged stories, telling their fears and worries, describing how it had been for them. The question weighing on all our minds at the moment was what would happen to those still waiting to be sorted, and what was the fate of those sent in the other direction. Rumor had it they were being taken to the little ghetto. We heard stories of people who refused to be separated from their family—the elderly, the lame, the infirm. In most cases, the sorters had granted their requests and sent them together—to the left. In other cases, we were told of family members who had been brutally torn from one another.

The same SS officer who had waved his hand *links-rechts, links-rechts* figured prominently in all the stories of sorting; it was he who decided the fate of everyone who came before him. Even after he grew tired, he took a seat and continued his work, not stopping the entire day. Today I know that his name was Rauke, and that he also directed the Aktion against the five hundred members of the intelligentsia.

We didn't have to wait much longer that day. The Germans were evidently tired of the whole affair and during the last hour they began channeling people in the two directions simultaneously, *links-rechts, links-rechts,* in larger and larger groups each time.

We were still excitedly exchanging stories when a German officer emerged, jumped upon a table or chair set out for him, shouted "Achtung!" and began speaking. His words were brief, to the point, and not arrogant. I did not understand all he said, but the upshot was that all the people assembled in our group were to remain in the ghetto. His last words, however, I remember clearly: "As long as people work, all will be well. If not, kaput." Achtung, halt, kaput—the entire story of the ghetto in three short words. After a day of suspense and anxiety, a rumble of assent arose from the tired but attentive crowd, almost a cheer. The German descended from his stand, and the crowd began dispersing to their homes.

We went home, too. It was twilight. The cold evening air descended upon us all. Hungry and tired, we tumbled inside to find that no one had touched the things in our open flats during the day. While Mother prepared food, the neighbors gradually began returning to their own dwellings. Mottel's family was late in coming, as were the French woman next door and her golden-haired daughter. Mottel's people were all hardworking. All night we left the doors open in case they had been delayed. Or perhaps they would be freed to return later. People trickled in from the neighboring flats, asking whether we had seen this person or that, and we began to realize how many had yet to return home. Friends and relatives began conspiring in groups how they might steal, under cover of night, into the little ghetto, smuggling blankets and food to their loved ones—all those people had left that morning with nothing, and the night was so cold.

That evening, or perhaps in the early hours of the next morning, Father, who was hidden behind the partition, suddenly asked me whether I could recall exactly the closing remarks of the German officer. "If not," I quoted, "alles wird kaput sein."

Father was pleased. I felt as though I had given him important information. I asked no more questions, but I knew that Father, the historian, was secretly writing historical notes of some kind—the chronicles of the Jews in the ghetto.

Like a drunkard I staggered to bed without even undressing. Not even the sounds of gunfire along the fences, more of them than usual, especially from the direction of the little ghetto, kept me from sleeping deeply that night.

WEDNESDAY

Mottel's family had not returned by the next morning. After I had eaten something I returned to the square. Until yesterday it had been nothing to me, only a huge lot, an empty space of no consequence beside the houses in the ghetto. I doubt I even knew, at the time, its pretentious name—Democrats' Square. To the west the buildings multiplied and that was where most of the ghetto was, while to the east the garden suburb houses merged gradually into the quiet countryside. Now the square was empty except for stray Komität workers who were picking through the piles of possessions and refuse left behind. Whatever they collected they piled along the road that cut across the square, which was also the road to our house.

While walking and looking about, my eye fell on some strangely shaped lumps among the mounds of rubbish. I passed the lumps several times from a distance until I mustered the courage to get closer. From afar, they looked like sacks stuffed full of old clothes. I was torn between an instinctive aversion and a fascinated attraction to the fearsome mystery laid before me—these were human corpses. I had never seen corpses so close up. I could have even touched them had I wished; there was no one there to prevent me from doing so. They lay there all tangled and crowded, each person sunk in on himself as if in deep thought, elderly people taking a lazy afternoon nap. Their faces were as white as that of the milkmaid who fainted at summer camp; their eyes were closed. Nothing moved. So this is how the dead look, I thought. Was this a glimpse of death's arrival, so calm, so relaxing? I felt that this was an important question for those days.

And why were they here, of all places, along the wayside? I suppose they had been sick or very old people who, with their last bit of strength or the help of their family, came out for roll call at dawn the day before, and, having reached this place, here they stayed. Their end may have been brought on by the long wait in line with no food or hot drink, or perhaps the evening chill had done them in. Perhaps no one had come to take them back home, so they had stayed in place until they froze to death. The cunning of the old! They alone had the power to elude the sorting.

It was several days until the last of them was cleared away.

While I stared at them, wondering, afraid, curious, standing still or passing uncomfortably by them, faint sounds of shots came to my ears. I looked up, seeking the source of the gunfire, which was erratic. The sounds were far away, so it took several seconds for me to discover their point of origin—somewhere along the road that started beyond the roofs of the little ghetto. Now I could make out large numbers of people, slowly climbing the hillside in small clusters, each group separated from the others, and surrounded by many guards.

Because of the great distance between this scene and me, it seemed to be taking place in silence. It surprised me to realize that this road, which was visible to all as it rose diagonally from left to right, was already mostly full of people. Had I not looked up to find the source of the gunfire, their march would have been completed unheard and undetected. Who were they, and where were they headed?

And then, only then, did the data from my sight and hearing come together in my mind, exploding into an astounding conclusion that was impossible to accept and unbearable to comprehend: here, in front of our eyes, they were leading our own people, those who had been separated from us last night, in an undeniable direction—to the Ninth Fort.

The meaning of these things, revealed to me so suddenly while I stood beside the frozen corpses of the elderly, was so terrifying, so shocking, that I could not stand it, child that I was, for another instant. I abandoned the dead old ones and ran for dear life back home, to Mother.

I suppose that my childhood ended right then—its innocence, the privilege of being unafraid. From that moment on my understanding of human existence was changed; it became more melancholy and sober.

A kind of mute cry seemed to enfold the whole ghetto. People stood still in the streets, in doorways and windows. All eyes were glued to the rising column of people in the distance. A quiet moaning broke out everywhere, growing louder and louder. It was a grieving and mourning for children, parents, friends, and relatives—a lament for themselves. Petrified, in disbelief, they saw how their kin were sent to their end, before their very eyes; they could not raise a hand to save them.

Even at a distance we could see the movement of the groups, which were slow, wavering, and unwilling to go forward. Within the lines we could make out, even from afar, eddies of uncertainty, swaying, wavelike attempts, in vain, to stray to the left or the right. Any way but forward, any way but straight ahead, although the determined guards ran back and forth, raising their rifles and shoving, beating, and firing. Like unwilling herds of cattle that are prodded to the slaughterhouse, the lines of people were unable to go any direction except forward.

What did they feel during those moments? For they too, like us, understood where they were headed and what lay at the end of the road. They had stepped out yesterday at dawn for nothing more than roll call, leaving doors open and cooking stoves lit to warm the next meal. Innocently they had left their homes for a few hours, and suddenly it had become their last hour.

The lines of people continued to climb higher and higher. Where were so many people coming from, so many groups? Sometimes another hour went by before a new group ascended the path, then yet another.

They walked solemnly and meekly as if to a funeral—their own. And we, below them, across from them, stood choking with tears and frozen with horror. Silently we followed them with our gaze. On no other occasion have I witnessed a mass funeral as large, a funeral of so many escorts and escorted alike.

There were no more questions, no more doubts. It was suddenly all very clear: the long sorting process of the day before; the little ghetto that had stood empty for several weeks; the detention of people there for a cold night without blankets or food, and now, this morning, the march to the place of their destined destruction. And all in plain view, in full daylight, with all those who remained in the ghetto, and with them tens of thousands of people from the city and the surroundings, looking on, seeing how the Jews were sent to death.

So the Germans were really killing Jews. All those pretenses, those tendentious explanations and reassurances—all of it a monumental lie.

And suddenly, with a jolt, I grasped the fateful significance of the arbitrary *links-rechts* wave of that one-man judiciary. Yesterday the same could have happened to our family. The random blink of an eye separated me, standing in the empty square that morning, gazing about in shock, from those being led up the hill. And my father may have been saved that day from a certain death thanks to Mother's quick action.

And the group of people who had passed by us going to the north whose breath we could all but feel—strangers though they were to me: I little realized then that I would have such a large part in their remembrance, if only for the few minutes of their last steps. I felt almost as though I had returned from among them.

In the afternoon the last of the groups set out, and the hillside path sank back into its former state of anonymity. The transport had ended and not a soul remained in the little ghetto.

Evening arrived. The noise of the city subsided. We were still confused, and our measure was not yet full. Muffled, unfamiliar sounds reached us from a distance. Like summer webs carried by the wind, half heard, half stifled, the intermittent sounds of gunfire drifted down to us from the hillside. Not in sporadic, isolated shots but in continual volleys of machine guns in long and angry bursts. The heart refused to credit the ears: man, at this very moment, your brothers and sisters are being executed. You hear the sounds, but there is nothing you can do, nothing. You may cry out, or go mad. Nothing will help.

The gunfire kept coming, with short intermissions, for several days. There were those who insisted that the shots were surely military exercises, merely maneuvers—maybe the Russians had returned, having parachuted behind the German lines. But several days later, the Lithuanians on the other side of the fence, with undisguised pleasure, filled in with color and detail that which we tried with all our might not to admit—everyone had been killed there.

Since then I have only to see a drawing or painting with a diagonal line rising from left to right in the background and I am transported there again as if by a magic wand. And so it is with music as well—Mahler's first symphony, for instance, the second and third movements: first a slow funeral march, accompanied by deep rhythmic drumbeats against a background of a meandering Jewish tune, and I cringe, accompanying the marchers' slow progress up the hill. Then suddenly, after a brief silence, a paralyzing scream bursts out from dozens of instruments and I choke in tears, hold my head in desperation, and cannot be consoled. I am there.

The Following Days

During the next few days some of the survivors of the mass executions began returning. By some miracle they were able to crawl wounded from the pits, from between the layers of massacred bodies, and in the darkness of night return stealthily to the ghetto. They were able to tell of the last hours of those who had been taken there, but the members of the Komität hid them well and swore them to secrecy, lest evil befall us all. However, their testimony sifted down to us all in spite of the secrecy and was not forgotten.

I also now know that the Lithuanians were active participants at the Ninth Fort, just as they helped execute the shtetl Jews. A company of Lithuanian locals acted hand-in-hand with a company of Germans. Half the soldiers from each company stood ready to fire, while the other half brought the people from the citadel's yard to one of four large excavations (fifty meters long, two meters wide, a meter deep) prepared by Russian prisoners of war a few days before. Water stood in the pits. The first to be killed (in groups of one hundred) were beaten with iron bars and rifle butts in order to force them to stretch out naked at the bottom of the trenches.

Then there was my cousin Rachel. She had wavy hair, long eyelashes modestly covering blue and dreamy eyes, a young girl's fine-featured, slightly bashful face. She was seventeen when she came to us, and I fell in love with her immediately. She was also in the square that day. A few weeks before the war broke out she had reached us from the townlet of Mazheik in the north. It had long been my mother's custom to encourage her relatives to get out of the shtetl and acquire a profession in the big city.

Mother's sister Feigeh consented to send her eldest child, Rachel, to us for studies. She brought from her shtetl not only her charm but also delicious smoked meats from the butcher shop that her parents owned. She lived with us a few weeks until she enrolled in a course for nurses, and a few weeks later she accompanied us to the ghetto.

There, however, with the problems of space that we had, we found no place for her except with Sarah, Mother's cousin, who came from the same shtetl. On the morning of the big Aktion, Sarah asked Rachel to stay with her neighbors, an elderly couple, during the sorting, so as to help them pass the inspection. Rachel stayed with them when they were sent to the left.

Mother tore her hair with sorrow; she refused to be comforted. Her anger with Sarah knew no bounds. She couldn't forgive her for bringing about the death of the little lamb. A deadly hatred grew between them, and to the last days of the ghetto, Mother did not exchange a single word with her. The gulf was so great between them, so terrible the ban, that even I, many years later, could not have anything to do with Sarah, the only surviving member of my mother's family.

Intermediate Epilogue: Years Later

I spent the summer of 1977 in Washington, D.C., to pursue my studies. One Sunday I decided to look at the White House and join the bustle at a time when visitors from all over the nation were thronging there to meet the president of their country.

In an improvised arena on the south lawn stood a noisy, celebrating crowd of people, waiting. Orchestras played, flags waved in the breeze, choirs sang. Every so often, according to raised signs, a new group from among those gathered would wend its way toward the entrance of the building. At the same time, the group just emerging from its tour would pass beside them before dispersing. As one group went in, the other came out. They moved quietly, without raising their voices. The light was soft; the grass was quiet; the square was large. Suddenly something was very familiar to me, very close. Surprised, I found I was choking anew, after so many years, at the scene of the big Aktion in Democrats' Square. Shocked and upset, I left the place immediately, in turmoil.

And again—November 1995 in Jerusalem. I set out early in the predawn darkness, and from all the alleys around more people emerged, joining a silent walk in the same direction. The sky cleared in the east, the warm clothes that I put on grew heavy. A queue of people formed long before our destination. The crowd kept order; no one pushed or shoved.

All night long people had been streaming to this place from all over the land, and even at dawn the line was not short. The light was gray and the many waiting people, eight or ten abreast, moved forward slowly, too slowly. Coming the other way were those who had already been there; they too were silent, their faces grave. Tens of thousands had come to say farewell to the prime minister, who was assassinated the night before. As for me, as soon as I began waiting in the silent crowd, a feeling of suffocation fell upon me, of deep oppression, that grew as I moved forward in line, as though fifty-four years and one week had not gone by since the big Aktion. I turned around and went home.

Later I mentioned in passing what had happened to me in Washington to Danke, my friend since kindergarten. We were in the ghetto together, and he had even survived Auschwitz. Danke, in turn, told my story to his brother Urke, who was older than we were and, accordingly, had been given in the ghetto the enviable job of Eilbote, errand boy for the Komität, and sported a special ribbon on his sleeve. Urke told him that he had had a similar experience. While in Greenland he reached a remote spot with his companions and watched a flock of penguins crowding together on an ice floe. Urke was suddenly struck by the thought, a reflection, that astounded him: "just like in the big Aktion."

For all of us, Democrats' Square is still implanted deep within. Sometimes it seems as if a part of me is still unsure that I was saved, as if it is ready for the bubble of time allotted to me to burst.

In Rehovoth in May 1967, I thought my time was indeed up. The streets on my way to the university that morning were emptier than usual, and I was pedaling my bike to the research laboratory with particular heaviness. My hands shook as I prepared the experiments planned for that day, thinking how foolish it was to occupy myself on such a day with the development processes of the color of orange peels. Earlier that morning the radio had announced that the Egyptian ruler had closed the Straits of Tiran, blocking access to Israel's southernmost port. I did my best to make sure that my lab notes would at least be clear and legible. It was apparent to me there would be war. That night, I heard the footsteps of the telegraph messenger at two in the morning on the damp lawn outside our open window even before he rang the doorbell. I leapt up, my heart skipping several beats. Within a quarter of an hour—I still remembered how to get dressed fast—I was already among those leaving their homes.

My two children were still fast asleep, two innocent, golden-headed toddlers surrounded by dolls, some large, others very large, which held and sheltered them. Miriam's warm glance accompanied me to the door. My eyes were moist and my throat very tight. I hate leaving the house before dawn; I hate partings.

People lamented, grieved, and went to work. Scarcely a household was untouched, scarcely a family not torn apart. About a third of the ghetto's population, nearly ten thousand people, were killed in that Aktion, which came to be known forever after as the big Aktion.

And people went back to eating and feeding, quarreling and hoping. They were gradually worn down, sinking into their misery and excruciating pain, but no one lost their mind. No one had the leisure to mourn. The pressure of forced labor, the shortage of food, and the fear over what was in store for those of us still alive left no room for prolonged grief. Flats remained shut, windows dark, doors sealed off by the Komität. Absence, like a separate being, was always present, oppressive and demanding. Space was filled by missing faces: the nights overflowed with them, their ghosts wandered everywhere. They dwelled with us as long as we had strength for them. Thus it is with Aktionen—this time, and the times to come.

Several days passed, and a wagon with ghetto policemen began making the rounds from house to house, like the stretcher carriers during the black plague in Father's history books. They opened the sealed flats and loaded up their contents. The neighbors had beaten them to it—the rustle of doors quietly opening and closing could be heard at night all around. My parents decided to keep their hands clean; they would not take part in such things. But when we saw the furnishings of our Parisian neighbors' beautiful flat being loaded onto the wagon, Mother couldn't help asking for one small favor of the Jewish police officer—to leave with us the large doll that my little sister had loved so much. "Impossible," he answered sternly, and when the job was finished, we saw him leave with the doll under his arm.

Mother later regretted her foolishness in sticking fast to high moral scruples under conditions in which they no longer had any place. There came a day when she needed every penny she could get, first to keep her children from starving, and then to save them. Household goods, especially cloth articles of any kind, became the common currency during those years. And why should I complain about the Jewish policeman? When the day came, he and all his colleagues were marched to the same fortress of death.

Two years later the Germans began removing, burning, and grinding the remains of corpses at the Ninth Fort, trying to cover their tracks. For these efforts they used crews of Jews who were destined to die, in particular those who were caught escaping to the forests, as well as captive Russian officers. One Christmas night some of these laborers succeeded, by daring ruses, to escape from the fort and some even returned to the ghetto. But that is another story.

4

Winter

Little time was left to lament and mourn. One wintry Sunday, the weekly day of rest, we were ordered to evacuate within four to six hours. We had to clear out of our quarter and move to the west, to the other side of Democrats' Square. This was German logic, cold and severe: since the ghetto population was diminished by at least a third, the ghetto territory could now be considerably reduced. Part of the shrinkage had already taken place by eliminating the little ghetto, and now compression began anew. The process repeated itself over the coming days—the ghetto's territory was lessened piece by piece, and the remaining population became more and more crowded. Time and again people had to take their belongings and find a dwelling in some corner, and soon there were nearly no family apartments. In time, two families found themselves sharing a single room, and there was no end to the quarrels and bitterness. How were we to find a new place to stay and move to it in a matter of hours? What were we to take? What should we leave behind? Shock and bewilderment. Father was sent to spy out some other place, and Mother began packing furiously. And what would become of our great treasure, the spare logs on the side of the pit in the yard? How could we give them up? And then a kind of miracle happened: at midday a group of men and women appeared at our doorstep, like the three angels, and said, "We've come to help you." They were teachers, father's former colleagues. We were overcome with emotion and gratitude. They did not linger, as time was short; each of them picked up an object and took it over the evacuation line. Nor did they disdain to take the large wooden beams—two or three pitched in and dragged them across the snow with a rope. I was a bit embarrassed that such well-known and respectable people should work on our behalf at a job that had something demeaning about it. But they took their work seriously, approached it with determination and without hesitation, coming back a second and third time without appearing nearly as disturbed as I was about their social standing. The power of friendship!

It happened on an especially cold day, when the temperature was below minus thirty degrees Celsius. But I do not remember it being particularly cold, perhaps because of my excitement.

Where were we to take our belongings when we had no new place yet? It was decided that we would store our things beside Ruchamah's house until we found a new home. Ruchamah was Arke and Maimke's mother; she also belonged to the family of teachers and lived in the center of the ghetto, not too far away. Although they lived on the second story of a large wooden house, they had a shed in the yard that had enough room for most of our belongings. We were invited to spend the first night with her, and in the end we spent several weeks there until we found a place of our own close by.

While we were crossing Democrats' Square for the last time, a new fence was already being stretched behind us. Once more we had changed our dwelling, the second time in the last six months.

Our new home was a wooden corner house, single-storied, that commanded the intersection of Vigriu and Grinius and had a garden in front. Once the house had been white with a bluish tint, and it had had a flower garden. Remains of the garden were still visible during the first winter, but later its traces disappeared entirely. Our room was the corner one, with a door through which, in better times, the family must have stepped out to the porch and the garden to sit and sip a cup of tea. We placed our wardrobe up against that door in the corner, and thus I was able to locate its remains when I returned years later.

Three or four families lived in the rooms of the flat. The main family, who had been there the longest, consisted of a polite and pleasant elderly Yekke couple (Jews of German origin) and their daughter, whom my memory insists on calling Rayah, although her name may have been Lisa, which seems more appropriate. The way to our room led through the communal kitchen. We did not ask who had lived there before we arrived, how they had disappeared and when. We lived there for two and a half years, and I do not remember any serious quarrels, probably thanks to Rayah's family. Our room in the corner gave us a lookout advantage, which was important in the ghetto—our two windows faced different directions. Because of the empty lots near our house, we could also see Arke and Maimke's house. It was very important to be always on the alert, to look and listen.

In the yard stood the toilet, sheds, and a small house belonging to the Gafano-vitches. Their elderly, pleasant-faced mother spent the day quietly and diligently making *papirosn*—homemade cigarettes—which her sons sold with great success. In the second wing of the house, which also had a small separate staircase of its own, lived one or two other families. Beneath the house lay a cellar with a broken-down door, full of junk and remnants of old furniture.

I do not remember how we got along with two adults and two children in a single small room. My parents had a bed and each of us children had one. A small shelf for books and various household utensils was also crowded in, as well as a table, used mostly for preparing food.

In our former dwelling at the edge of the ghetto, where the nasturtiums grew, I was still an innocent city child, enraptured by the charms of gardens and yards. Echoes of dangers reached me from a distance, storming somewhere beyond the square. By contrast, the house at 44 Vigrių was in the heart of the ghetto, and our fingers felt its pulse beat day and night. From our windows we could see the Komität building, where the Ältestenrat resided, and by it Varnių Street, a major artery cutting across the ghetto, through the northern end of which the Germans entered. In addition, not long after we moved in, in a special shed near the fence not far from our dwelling, the headquarters of an NSKK company (auxiliary forces of the German army) were established, which from that point on sent night patrols along the interior of the fence and also—in pairs—into the main streets of the ghetto.

From our new entrenchment the ghetto seemed diminished and more crowded, the surrounding houses small and transparent, and we ourselves very much exposed. But it was here that my world stabilized, as much as possible. Here routines, friendships, and acquaintances were formed for the years to come. I matured here. And I owe my very life, among other things, to the chain of circumstances that led me to that house, and thus to the good fortune that brought us to live there, thanks to Ruchamah, who took us into her house close by on the first night after the evacuation.

First winter in the ghetto. The mass raid on the potato fields took place in late autumn, and when the cold set in, similar raids started on everything made of wood. The first victims were the picturesque fences like the one surrounding our new house, followed by gates, cornices, lattices, gardening sheds, and structures in yards and on porches—even telephone and electric poles were taken. As with the potatoes, these items would be descended upon, as if by a swarm of locusts, and in an instant all would be sawn, dismantled, torn, and dragged away. Those who had the audacity and strength would even penetrate into houses and yards. I learned a lot during these days about ways of dismantling, sawing, and chopping wooden posts. I had only to hear certain sounds coming from a distance and I would rush to the place and try to join the party. Gradually the houses became more and more naked and exposed, and the ghetto came to look like an ugly plucked fowl. From then on the difference between the two sides of the ghetto fence was discernible not only in the upright posture of those outside it, but also in the enfolding of trees, fences, and fresh flowers that continued to wrap the houses over there, emphasizing the image of bleak desert on this side, like a photographic negative.

At this stage of my accelerated adolescence, I was ready to take part in any act of plunder. Ghetto life turned out to be rich with situations of semi-anarchy from which those who were alert and quick could reap considerable advantages. The terms "permitted" and "forbidden" became extremely flexible. I sensed that social success, even among us children, now sided with those who snatched rather than with those with good manners. My parents were not happy, to say the least, with the manners I picked up on the street. They repeatedly tried to forbid me to take part in various lootings and acts of plunder, although it meant renouncing—as they never tired of saying—the material advantages to be derived from my diligent efforts. But they were hard put to withstand the prevailing winds. Other parents gave up trying, or made no attempt to interfere—this was no time to raise questions about education and morals. And I wanted to be like everyone else, to shake off my image of a scholarly child from a good home. I wanted to compete with my peers and succeed. I wanted to bring things home, to feed the family as I had done during the first days of the occupation. In spite of themselves, my parents would come to recognize the importance of my contribution to the family and would shower me with praise.

February

It was deepest winter, and the tinsmith business was booming in the ghetto. Stoves, cooking ranges, lanterns—I found it hard to understand how, under ghetto conditions, they managed to produce such complex tin items, or from whence came the raw materials. In our house a heating stove was installed; its jointed chimney pipe ran horizontally across the room and protruded through the window. The pipe was a source of pleasant heat and could be used to hang laundry on, but it was also a perpetual source of worry. It had to be watched constantly to be sure that it was properly sealed, that the smoke going through it was reaching the outside lest we be asphyxiated in our sleep or, at the very least, wake with a bad headache. There was no dearth of stories about people who had grown tired of it all and who, by plugging the chimney, had cut their own journey short.

The situation seemed to stabilize. The Germans repeatedly and pointedly promised that there would be no more Aktionen. In the meantime, everyone was preoccupied with collecting things to use as heating fuel and food to supplement the thin rations. Once in a while a rare supply of meat with a unique sweetish taste would arrive. Various jokes circulated about it to make swallowing easier—that it was meat from horses killed in battle. Maybe these were the same tired horses that had passed beneath our windows during the first days of the war and had reached no further.

Work brigades went out regularly, even the one for the airport, where work was especially hard in winter because of the mud and snow. But everyone hoped that continued employment meant that there was some guarantee for our continued existence. The treasury of German curses that we children picked up from adults—a seemingly useless byproduct of work on the brigades—we passed along to one another. There were the old terms that had always been poured upon us, such as the following:

donnerwetter—thunder weather/blast, hell
verfluchte Jude—accursed Jew
schweine, schweinerei—swine, swinishness
hunde—dog
Scheissjude—shit Jew

To these were added more specific abuses directed by taskmasters to the labor gangs.

untermensch—subhuman
verwurfe—monster
dreckige bande—shitty band
schneller—faster
los, los—forward, get a move on
tempo—pace, rhythm

This, too, was one part of my "universities."

Encouraging rumors reached us from the Eastern Front about the ravages of "General Winter." While winter weighed heavily on us, too, it had also blocked the Germans at the gates of Moscow, taking its toll in casualties. Hospitals in the city filled with the wounded, and the ghetto workshops were flooded with special orders. Those who knew history and other seers of salvation hastened to draw encouraging parallels with the adventures of Napoleon on that same route, and for a while people's outlook brightened somewhat.

The Komität and the Jewish police routines became more entrenched, and with them flourished an outrageous and galling protectionism. The public gradually grew accustomed to the burden of domination imposed upon it, venting its frustration, among other ways, in bitter and biting ghetto songs about the "shishkas" (pine cones), that is, the senior members of the Komität, who behaved like lords with blatant favoritism. One day I managed to persuade my parents to agree to my suggestion that I too be allowed to take a peddler's box and set up shop by the Komität fence to sell small goods. Many boys peddled items of various kinds throughout the ghetto, and I wished to do it, too. During our migrations from one dwelling to another, we had collected a number of small items that were of no use now that we were crowded into a single small room. I claimed we could get a few pennies (Pfennigs, to be precise) for them. Among our treasures were a few pairs of shoelaces, some bars of soap, round chicory sticks, pieces of bluing for laundry, and tins of shoe polish. Some had remained in the pantry of Mottel's family, others perhaps came from the articles Uncle David had brought with him on his vacation. Hesitantly, after repeated refusals, my parents agreed that I could set out with my merchandise the following day. My joy knew no bounds. They got me a little box, we arranged the goods in it in a certain order, and they even discussed with me the techniques of setting prices for each item—whether I should put out written price tags or, like a seasoned merchant, only proclaim prices orally so that I could change them during the bargaining.

I was proud to be a partner at last in shouldering the household burden—after all, we never stopped discussing, on a daily basis, how we might obtain a few extra crumbs. And in preparation, early the previous afternoon—it was a Thursday—I went to the Komität building to find the spot I would stake out the following morning. I also had a very important decision to make about how to display my wares—should I stand, or should I sit on a brick that I could bring with me, with my box on the ground beside me?

As always, people were standing about at the Komität, checking the various announcements that were regularly hung on the wooden fence, the only one that remained at the time in the entire ghetto. A fresh notice that people were crowding around drew my attention. It was a call for five hundred healthy people who could work well for temporary work in Riga. Volunteers would receive particularly good conditions and larger food rations, and would return several months later. Suitable people, and anyone who wasn't scheduled for work the following day, were ordered to appear at 10:00 A.M. for roll call and selection. The announcement was straightforward and not particularly threatening, and the reaction of the people reading it was not agitated either. When I went home, I told my parents about it, while I continued energetically with the arrangements for the important event the next day.

That Friday was a sunny winter day, the sixth of February, the coldest month of the year. Snow gleamed in the empty lots, accentuating the narrow pedestrian paths. I was ready to go on my way that morning, but to my great disappointment, my parents prevented me from leaving—anxiety had set in over the demand for workers in Riga and the upcoming roll call. We had many good reasons to be suspicious of every roll call and conscription of volunteers. My parents had also decided that even though Father was scheduled for a day at home, he would not attend roll call for several reasons—he was already enrolled in the airport brigade, and he was on the school staff, which might still renew its activity. But the primary reason was that he had secretly been appointed ghetto historian. The Komität members would undoubtedly cover for his failure to appear.

Although no curfew had been called, the ghetto seemed rather empty—the brigades had gone to work, and those remaining were principally the elderly, children, mothers, and people from the night shift who had just returned to their houses. Dressed in warm winter clothes, disappointed and frustrated, I played in the empty lot in front of our house, trying to console myself by rolling a large snowball that I planned to make into a snowman. From winter to winter, the size of the snowballs that I could roll and pile up was a challenge and a gauge of my growth and strength. It was almost noon when Father came out and asked me to join him—he had decided to go to the selection lot. During the course of the day, all the houses would be inspected anyway, and he preferred to get it over with because he had a lot to do. He had also consulted senior officials who had promised he would not be taken, no matter what happened. It would take him half an hour, no longer. For extra security, he asked me to come along.

I willingly complied—gone were the days when I had taken walks with Father through fields or wandered with him to the libraries and newspaper offices. The selection was taking place in a lot on the other side of the three apartment blocks; when we arrived, the crowd was very small. The inspection process was proceeding slowly, conducted by Jewish policemen with a German or two in attendance, and there was no particular tension. Additional soldiers were stationed some distance away, but they did not interfere. People arrived in a thin, trickling stream, showed their documents, and intended to return home. But then something different and unexpected began happening—everyone who came was detained and not allowed to return home.

Those in charge claimed that the delay was temporary, perhaps only for re-inspection, since a general search of the ghetto would be starting soon anyway. But since some people were allowed to go home after all, we began to grasp that all was not going smoothly. Father tried to persuade the sorters to let him go home as well, and even hinted that he had special duties. The person in charge agreed with him and promised him that a senior member of the Komität would be arriving soon and he would no doubt set matters straight. Father then requested that they at least allow his little boy to return home in the meantime. They agreed to this, so on the spot I took to my heels, left Father, and hurried home to tell Mother what had happened. We had agreed that if Father did not follow me shortly, Mother should alert the authorities. But where was Mother at the time? Why had Father gone to the selection lot even though they had decided otherwise in advance? We thrashed out these questions over and over again during the coming days.

> *Scene:* On my way home, I am about to cross Varnių Street, which is paved and somewhat raised from its surroundings. Just as I am about to step down to the road leading straight home, I glance up momentarily and see from afar, in a direct line ahead of me in the middle of the road, the figure of my mother hurrying toward me. From a distance we recognize each other, and for an instant we pause, I alone, she with my sister in her arms. We understand everything. *End of scene.*

This image has haunted me for years; it feels like Munch's *The Scream*—everything frozen in anticipation of a terrible disaster just about to happen.

A few more seconds, and we were moving toward each other. Mother listened to me tell what had happened, and then she quickly trudged past me, my sister hanging on her hip and I running behind them. For some reason I felt a need to defend Father against Mother's anger. It appeared she knew nothing of Father's plans. She had stepped out to the neighbors' house for a minute, and when, upon returning, she neither met him nor found me, she knew in her heart that something was wrong.

We hurried along, retracing my steps back to the selection lot. There suddenly appeared before us a column of marching people, row after row, surrounded by guards with rifles at the ready, being led toward Varnių Street. Who were they? Where did they come from? For a moment I didn't understand—everything was conducted with such purposeful silence, with no complaint or protest. All that could be heard were the quiet murmur of marchers, the vigorous crunch of feet on snow, and a few harsh rebukes from the armed escorts, nothing more.

Then with a jolt I realized that these were the very men that I had left behind me only moments before in the selection lot; they were now being led away already. Had Father been released? Mother ran forward to search the marchers' faces up close; I ran behind her. Whether she heard his voice or recognized his face, she was shortly in the marchers' way—she in front, I in back, recoiling from the approaching columns and from the Germans surrounding them—when a sharp cry broke the air: HALT! As if she had not heard the clear order, Mother turned to the German, ready to explain to him in fluent German that there was some mistake—they had no need of her husband in Riga; his family was staying here; here was his tiny daughter in her arms; he himself was a vital worker; she could bring papers to that effect immediately. However, he seemed uninterested in her pleas from the start. Taking no heed of her, he only raised his rifle, pointing it straight at Mother, and repeated in a louder, more strident tone: "Halt! Halt!"

HALT!

HALT!

HALT!

HALT!

I closed my eyes and turned to stone.

The column stopped. The entire world stood still. Everyone looked to see what would happen. My mother stumbled slightly as she stopped in the middle of her running near the entrance to a house, froze in place, my little sister in her arms. Opposite her, four or five steps away, stood the German, the butt of his rifle locked against his shoulder, his head cocked to one side, the barrel of the rifle aimed at Mother, his finger on the trigger—ready to fire, standing position.

Mother only emitted a short, stifled "Oh!"—not loud at all. Darkness had descended, even stars could not be seen. Time seemed to crawl by.

The German gave a derisive growl—maybe he meant to laugh—and he slowly lowered his rifle. The earth renewed its movement and the column its march. A few seconds more and the column disappeared from sight.

In shock, we stayed where we were. A minute, two minutes, an hour? It was a stillness that stretched to infinity. Slowly, defeated and exhausted, we began plodding back home—my mother, my little sister, and I.

As soon as we arrived home Mother began running to senior officials and friends, urging them to do something, to cancel the decree. It appeared that the ghetto authorities had failed to round up five hundred volunteers as commanded, so they started collecting everyone who came their way without much sorting. They had even commandeered brigade men returning from work in order to meet the quota. They were all being held in the train station and hadn't yet been sent on their way. Members of the Komität were attempting to return a number of essential persons from those taken, and the Germans had promised to cooperate. Thus they tried to calm Mother—everything would be done to bring Father back.

That afternoon and evening, a painful ache spread into my legs. When I had felt similar aches before, they had been dismissed as growing pains. This time, however, the pain was worse than ever before. Were they perhaps rheumatic, of the kind that often afflicted Mother? She offered me a hot water bottle (*garelke*) and covered me with a warm blanket, but nothing helped. True, I had been running around all day in the cold and snow, but I had been doing that for days. Mother took camphor alcohol and started rubbing my calves and thighs with slow, wavelike motions (she was ever the compassionate nurse), but the pains only grew. My groans gradually turned to wailings that could be heard outside. I refused to be calmed.

What must Mother have been feeling? Instead of hurrying out to stand guard and wait for Father, she had to stay at home and care for her sobbing son, massaging his legs but achieving no relief. Only toward midnight did I finally fall asleep, probably from exhaustion. Father said that Mother had been unable to make inquiries to try to get him released because she had one of the migraine attacks from which she had suffered in the past. Perhaps that is what happened, or perhaps that is merely Father's interpretation.

When I woke up the next morning, I did not find Father in our room. The pain in my legs had disappeared as if it had never been, and only the strong odor of camphor hung in the air, a smell I would not forget for years.

As for the train, it was delayed in the station all that night, and in the morning it left. A few of those taken away came back, but Father was not among them.

Later, some parts of the picture fell in place for me. As it happened, Father was listed among those who should have returned. Komität workers later claimed they had called his name several times in vain. Father maintained that no cries reached his ears in the crowded railcar. He was tired and overwhelmed; how was he to hear voices from the platform? When I heard this, I was unable to suppress the thought, a snide one perhaps, that Father must have been wrapped up at the time, as usual, in conversation. And why did his seekers give up? It is possible that another man, quicker and sharper than Father, answered in his place, was whisked out of the car, and was sent back to the ghetto. Father has a different story, laced with cynical sarcasm. The very fact that he had been looked for came to his knowledge—adding to his pain—only several days after the event. During a stop at Keidan on the way to Riga, he was called out of the train. When he turned up, he was scolded for not answering the call in the railway station in our city. "Trying to get out of supporting your wife and children, eh?"—thus he was reprimanded by the German, a man "with a strong sense of duty."

Mother remained convinced that if she had been free that evening and not compelled to attend to my pains, she would not have given up and Father would have been returned. To her credit I must say that although she dwelt often on the subject, I never felt that she blamed me directly. Her heart was bitter and heavy about Father to the end of her days. Why had he gone out to the square, and why did he trust the promises of the officials? She was out of the house only a short while, and look what happened. Moreover, the ghetto itself was never searched to fill the quota; they had only taken the innocents and shlimazels who were at hand and left with them. And on and on.

Once and only once has my Father addressed the issue, and only in passing, for we do not discuss these topics too often, and he has not yet heard what I remember about those days, perhaps because of his unwillingness to touch painful scars. I mustered the courage to ask what had suddenly made him decide to go to the selection lot that day. Father only shrugged his shoulders with embarrassment—he didn't know then and even now he has no clear answer.

THE NEXT DAY

The following day we were a smaller, amputated family. It had happened so suddenly, almost inadvertently; it was hard to get used to the fact that from now on we, too, were among the afflicted families. Similarly, after the war I found it hard to get used to the idea that without a father and mother, I, too, was considered an orphan, like those miserable children I had seen before the war, walking in the public gardens in a long column, two by two, dressed in uniforms.

From that point on the three of us were left alone, a mother and two young children. How strange, how inconceivable—until yesterday his corner had been there, his clothing, his things, his little notes, and in an instant he was gone. A foundation stone of our world had been displaced overnight. And even though we felt from the first that he had not been executed immediately, that he had been taken somewhere and might even return soon, it was hard for each of us, perhaps for my little sister more than my mother or me, to grow accustomed to his absence.

And my mother, who had struggled so hard in the past against being chained to the kitchen among pots and pans, against an ordinary life in which she was destined to do nothing but raise children, was now in spite of herself solely responsible for our very existence.

Some time after Father was taken we received a message from him. He had indeed been taken to Riga and was living and working there. Why had the Germans transferred those five hundred men there (later we learned the number was closer to four hundred) from our city, as well as thousands of Jews from other places? And why had they found it necessary, as I now know, to kill Riga's tens of thousands of original Jewish inhabitants?

Those who were transported to Riga eventually found ways to send us letters, and we were very moved. Already this set me apart from the rest of my friends whose fathers were missing—they knew nothing of their fathers' fate. Riga was not far away; there were those who traveled back and forth between the ghetto and Riga. Sometimes letters would arrive by regular mail between the two cities, carried by communications personnel, a Latvian there, a Lithuanian here. In Father's letters—the letters of a graduate of a Lithuanian university, written in fluent Lithuanian—each of us had a fictional Lithuanian name, figments of Father's creative imagination. I became Saulutis ("son of the sun"); my sister was Yulite; Mother was Liah; and Father himself was Isidoras. The correspondence lasted for a rather long while, with sometimes long spans of time in between letters. It was madness—routine mail passing between two planets, both of them out of this world.

I recently heard from Father that a few months after being taken away, the Germans permitted a few families from our ghetto to join their loved ones in Riga. I remember Mother once making efforts to send an urgent letter to Father, asking for a quick reply. Perhaps she was asking his advice about just such an opportunity then being offered to her.

So it was for the rest of our time in the ghetto: from time to time, a Hamlet-like, fateful question would pose itself to Mother about her family and her two cubs, and alone, in utter darkness, she had to decide whether to seize the initiative, to interfere with the course of things, to deviate from the path we were on. And Mother would decide. And this time, too, as was often the case, she decided that we would stay put. From where I stand now, from a purely selfish point of view, it was the right decision. The move to Riga would probably have benefited my parents themselves, probably increasing my mother's chances of survival. But in hindsight her chances of rescuing us in strange and unfamiliar surroundings would certainly have been minimal. At some point, we survivors are destined, cruelly and at the cost of feeling guilty all our lives, to fall in with the sequence of steps that led eventually to our rescue. My friend Shlomit, a child my age who was imprisoned in a ghetto in Poland during the war, left through a gap in the camp fence against her father's wishes. She never saw her parents again, and she carries the feelings of guilt to this day.

From then on, Father left the circle of our lives. The events of his life were now inseparable from the fate of the Jews of the Riga ghetto, with all its storms and vicissitudes. I know only a little of it. He was put to work ironing in a tailor shop. Like all the others transported from our city, he was held in a separate section of the ghetto, although he was not cut off from the rest of those imprisoned there.

Even in the Riga ghetto, Father managed to follow what was happening, to engrave events in his memory, and even to send a report to our Komität—it has survived in his handwriting—about the hardships and condition of those exiled from our town. In addition, years later he reconstructed, with the eyes of a historian, several chapters of that ghetto's story, including an account of the arms stockpile for an uprising that never took place. And they are written in the chronicles of the Riga ghetto.

5

The Quiet Season/Childhood in the Ghetto

A Kind of Preface

People in the ghetto became more and more accustomed to their peculiar condition. Life before the war became wrapped in the veil of a distant fable. Vain hopes of sudden miracles and last-minute salvation were held no longer. The war front receded gradually, hovering somewhere between Moscow and Stalingrad, and what was happening there—the rumor mill was our only source of information—did not help things in the ghetto. The Germans, for their part, made it known repeatedly that only faithful and diligent work in the brigades would save us from calamity.

One tends to think of the anxieties and fears, the efforts to escape and be saved, that filled people's thoughts as happening to all ghetto residents. But I was largely unaware of what it meant to go to work every day at forced labor. Day in, day out, months on end; what a waste of years! People sought ways of joining easier brigades, seeking special "protection" (it was called "vitamin P") to get assigned to workshops in the ghetto or in the ever-growing Komität departments.

Study groups sprang up, as did a choir and an orchestra, and home-based industries flourished, run usually by women or elderly people, including embroidered goods, tailoring and sewing, carpentry and tinsmithing—any product that could be moved and smuggled through the ghetto gate for trade with the Lithuanians. Dr. Gurvitch and her daughters, for instance, developed a home-made method, which soon became widespread, of printing colorful headscarves with beautiful designs and fast dyes. They were not difficult to make, and before long most of the Lithuanian women in the city and in the villages around it were wearing kerchiefs produced by Jewish women in the ghetto.

And throughout this time, there was ceaseless movement in the streets of the ghetto. This was doubtless the sight we presented from the other side of the fence: figures in layers of clothing, all marked by the yellow star, continually gathering, moving between houses and through streets devoid of vehicles, among buildings stripped of any wooden facade or ornament, with never a dog or a cat to be seen. It was conspicuous especially on weekends—everyone visited everyone else, if they still had anyone to visit. It was a way for the ghetto body to release its accumulated tension.

Sometimes, too rarely, warning sirens would reach us from the direction of the city, followed by muffled buzzing sounds from high in the sky, like the delicate murmuring hum of gathering angels, an indistinct, otherworldly presence passing high above without sending us any clear message, without leaving any traces. Much strength of soul and patience were required in those days.

Bubble within a Bubble

"The quiet season"—thus we called the days after Father was taken, a period that lasted about a year and a half, even though the chronicles of the ghetto overflow with endless descriptions of harsh events during this time. It was as if we were trapped inside a bubble of air in a sinking ship—for the moment we breathed and hoped, but not a soul knew whether the diminishing air would last until the rescuers arrived.

Within this pocket of air, a bubble within a bubble—for the space of two winters and summers—was the life we children led. Like minnows swimming confidently through the clear waters of a tidal pool, unaware of the receding ocean, of the fast-approaching tide, so were we. Ignoring as much as possible what was happening around us, our childhood went by. We were left to our own devices during the day, with no school—it had been outlawed—and no parents since by then our mothers were compelled to work outside the home. We played and played from morning to night. Like a vine, whose roots grapple with obstructions and send down shoots even among stones and boulders, we kept on growing. In retrospect, those of us who were destined to live gathered experiences to last a lifetime; those whose fate was already sealed, even though they did not know it, grew like plants in distress that hurry to bloom, trying to accomplish all that they could. But at the time, each of us might have belonged to either group.

Each morning my sister and I would wake up to find our mother already gone to work. Food would be ready on the range; beside it would be a note explaining what the dish was and how to warm it up. I almost saved one such note from my mother, and its memory still wrenches my heart.

I have relatively more memories of this "quiet" season than of other periods. I would have been, in normal times, in grades four and five in school.

I would help my five-year-old sister get dressed, we would have something to eat, and out I would go. Our elderly neighbors were there to be called upon if necessary, but we usually spent all day in the streets or in our friends' flats—for they had no parents at home either—doing what children do and looking after ourselves.

What did my sister do with her friends all day? They dug in sand, made mud pies, and fed them to their dolls, recounting to each other their babies' superior qualities and the troubles they had with them. They had a large number of babies. It seemed they never stopped bearing and raising children. Where in fact did they see that happening? At that time bearing children was forbidden in the ghetto. And how do I have such a distinct memory of this little girl custom? Perhaps I observed it only in my own children, and not in the ghetto at all. Things are gradually mixing up; it becomes harder and harder for me to distinguish between then and now, between those who were close to me in the past and those in the present.

At noon we would meet and heat up the food Mother had prepared. Though we separated during the day, we knew we had to keep track of each other, and not at a distance either. My sister always had to inform me of her whereabouts and to return home by dark, all according to Mother's instructions. I was the big brother and, in Father's absence, together with Mother, responsible for my little sister. She rebelled more than once. Still I forgave her each time.

The Gang

We seemed to have plenty of time on our hands, time filled with much activity. I do not remember this period as being boring or wasted in idleness. I spent most of the day with my friends Arke and Maimke and their friends. When the weather was good and conditions were right, we were outdoors; this was the great time of games. On cold, rainy, or "bad" days (days in which an Aktion was expected), we stayed in someone's flat. In winter we built snowmen and had snowball fights, like children all over the world. Very few of us had real sleds made of arched wooden slats on steel blades, the kind I had dreamt for years of owning, and they were greatly envied. By this time they had probably been handed in, if only because of the steel blades. Instead, we improvised and made sleds out of a broad plank resting on two narrow, polished slats. We would slide them in every direction we could push them. The large open pits that had been dug in several lots were great attractions; one with especially steep sides became the favorite spot for dangerous sliding. We would speed down from directly opposite sides; often there was only a hair's-breadth difference between a daring descent and a head-on collision. One of the surviving ghetto photographs shows children running with their sleds in just such a pit. One of the children might be me.

Among the indoor games we played for days on end were not only chess, checkers, Monopoly, and various card games, but also other types of competitions. Victory in these helped determine one's social standing. I liked those for which we had to compile the longest list of authors, places, or objects beginning with a certain letter. I wanted very much to succeed among Arke's and Maimke's peers, and in contests of this sort I was at my best.

In summer we played various ball games, although real balls were scarce. My friends introduced me to the game of soccer. When we couldn't play soccer outdoors and we tired of chess, a new game rose to eminence—table soccer played with buttons. Button soccer was invented and developed by ten- to thirteen-year-old children in the Kovno Ghetto. On a large plank or table, we drew a detailed soccer field using colored lines. On each side of the center line we stationed eleven player buttons, different colors for the different sides, sized according to their positions on the field. The ball was a small, smooth, brass button. Using a spoon or a curved knife blade, we would press the round edges of our player button, propelling the ball-button forward toward the opposing team's goalpost. Each side took turns propelling the ball, several children manning its players.

This thrilling game occupied much of our time, and we often found ourselves so engrossed in the game that we came home late and worried our parents. It was a complex project, requiring a great deal of organization—finding a very large board, drawing the field with clean lines, setting it up in a room large enough to hold it, and policing the excited spectators to keep them from sprawling all over the table. Therefore, a set of detailed rules and regulations was created, similar to those used in the real game. A referee ruled on what was permissible and what not. My friends were good at following the rules and regulations. Maimke, with great astuteness, was forever testing the limits of the law; Arke, his senior by two years, was a rock of honesty and fairness, all responsibility and sobriety. His face would flush red with anger at his younger brother's provocations, the liberties he took, playing however he liked.

I do not remember the names of the main organizers, but their faces are ever before me. The wish somehow to reconstruct their names with someone's help rises uncontrollably, some sign by which to identify them—but there is no one to ask, no one with whom to clear the matter up.

Among my friends at the time was one extraordinary child who lived across the empty lot, opposite our house, and who stood out among us by virtue of his seriousness and his excellent manners. His German-speaking family was from Austria, apparently brought here by the vicissitudes of war. Their spotlessly clean flat was full of all kinds of books and embroidery. Johann proudly showed me his collections: sparkling mineral crystals, dried plants, insects with tiny pins piercing their backs. Best of all was the microscope through which he could examine things, and the drawings he made of his observations, executed in fine, precise lines in a special notebook. At the time, he seemed like a magician or wizard, conversant with distant worlds.

While he showed me his treasures, his parents looked on with pride, taking a polite interest in their son's guest. I felt a wordless respect toward these people who succeeded in raising a barrier between themselves and the ghetto fence. I am not entirely certain of the boy's name; perhaps it was Hans. But I am certain that he came from Innsbruck. Someday, perhaps, when I meet someone from that city I will ask whether he knows anything about this family.

Abandoned Goods

In the summer and winter we roamed about, snooping, collecting, and hoarding. By then people had begun to lose their vitality, and they tired of dragging the remnants of their old homes with them, often simply leaving things behind. Daily routines were upset, and things fell apart; one of the results of this whirlpool was abandonment. The contents of a flat whose inhabitants had been uprooted or had passed on would be simply left, as well as a pile of discarded personal items—one person's calamity was another's fortune. And, like ever-scouting ants who alert their comrades, we developed special senses to discover and descend upon abandoned possessions.

A flat abandoned by its owner seemed to have lost its soul, and its bundles of possessions were like so many dead bodies. We would go indifferently past the old clothes, bed sheets, worn shoes, and household utensils scattered all over. How did people come to have so many pins, spools of thread, and buttons? Among wrinkled curtains and broken suitcases bundle after bundle of family photographs, ripped packages of personal letters tied with ribbons, honorary certificates, genealogical records, scriptures and prayer books would spill out. Entire lifetimes would pour through our rummaging fingers without making us blink.

We were after brass buttons, stamped picture postcards, locks, alarm clocks with gears we could take apart, czarist banknotes with fabulous watermarks, and German marks bearing intoxicating values in the millions. We never found anything of any real worth, but, like fevered gold diggers, we continued to nourish our burrowing obsession, overturning, emptying, scattering in our search for that unique, rare, we-never-knew-quite-what that might be waiting for us under the next heap. Oh, that hopeless greed.

In addition, I always searched for books, and more books.

Books: An Old Love

In being taken away from us Father was spared the anguish of the book Aktion, which fell upon us several weeks after he was exiled. The decree was to give up all books—a senseless idea, impossible to accept, yet at that stage in the ghetto's existence, we were nearly beyond incredulity. With heavy hearts we set off to place our books at one of the collection points. Mother dared to leave a book or two at home, as did others. Shulamit and Izzia Rabinovitz, our loyal friends from the ghetto, did wonders, leaving many books at home. Years later, Shulamit told me how, even when they moved into the ghetto, they had deliberated among their many items of furniture and their sizable library. She had decided the books were preferable. Now they arranged a special hiding place behind an interior staircase. During the next two years, I was one of the regulars who enjoyed this hidden treasure.

Handing the books over took place at a relatively gradual pace. The books were transferred from the initial collection points to the great yeshiva building, while many remained lying about the collection points and along the road. In the yeshiva the books were sorted, and most of them were taken away. The rest stayed where they were, with a strict prohibition against taking them back. I would linger about these places, tunneling and browsing among the mounds of books, moved by an infinite want.

Scene: Varnių Street, the ghetto's main artery. I am engrossed in burrowing through a pile of books near the blocks of flats. While bending over a steep pile of heavy volumes, I glance up and see none other than Zelda, coming straight toward me from across the street. Is it she? I have not seen her for years, not since the end of second grade. I remembered a slender face; blond, boyishly short hair; chubby, dimpled cheeks; almond-shaped blue eyes that looked at you with a dreamy, confusing gaze. She was a princess among the girls of the class, the object of my secret infatuation. Now her face is sunken and ashen. She pulls her younger sister behind her, both of them dressed carelessly in tattered clothes. Could it be? Her appearance grieves me. She was one of the girls whose heart I had tried to win by promising, among other things, that I would smooth their collection of wrinkled silver foil overnight, using a miracle machine I had. And so every day I would bring them sparkling new sheets of foil in place of the old ones they had given me—all to make them like me more.

Sheltered by the heap of books, I now covertly examine Zelda, and notice, with a certain satisfaction, the wretched appearance of this former object of my fantasies. Sadness reflects from her slender face and her almond eyes. The cruelty of a child. When she advances toward me, I crouch behind the encyclopedias. She passes, and I never saw her again. ***End of scene.***

I read books—in all hours, in all circumstances; in bad weather, by day and by night; by oil wick and by carbide lantern; during the long waits for Mother to return from work; and during the anxious times we spent expecting something bad to happen. I drank in everything that came my way in Yiddish, Hebrew, or Lithuanian, not disdaining even Gothic or Cyrillic script. Some of the books I came across were offbeat and bizarre publications—I read them all, a rich and stimulating kaleidoscope that an ordinary child might never see. I swallowed it all and soaked it up.

There was some excellent fiction. Trembling with pleasure, I read *Twenty Thousand Leagues under the Sea* and other books by Jules Verne, about Vinetto by Karl May, and alongside these, with my romantic mother's warm recommendation, Romain Rolland's *Jean Christophe*, as far as I could understand it. One day my mother returned from her Sunday meetings with *History of Human Culture, Part I—China* in her hands. I opened the weighty book; we looked together at the rich and colorful illustrations printed in the frontispiece, and the rustling of celestial wings filled our tiny room; we were seized by an exaltation as if we were entering a high and spacious hall, my mother and I.

But most captivating of all were Captain Nemo and his courageous crew of sailors aboard the *Nautilus*. With keen intelligence and wisdom he overcame all obstacles. Walls of undersea rock could not stop him; he sailed around icebergs and to the poles of the earth, and even made his way through the Suez Canal.

When in distress, he holed up with his crew on a secret, isolated island that belonged to them alone, and from a fortress-like rock—I can still remember how I
imagined its appearance—they repulsed their evil attackers with rifles. Oh, how
I longed to be one of Captain Nemo's crew! In a secret tunnel my mother, my
little sister, and I might reach the riverbank, there to board the *Nautilus* and sail
away to distant shores and another life.

Until such time as the submarine arrived, I would immerse myself in plans to
revive and make a garden of the Sahara Desert by a simple and logical method: a
network of canals would divide the huge wasteland into a checkerboard pattern
of squares; through them the waters of the Mediterranean would flow, irrigating
the land and bringing happiness to mankind.

One day Arke, who knew that I was an avid reader, asked me matter-of-factly
whether Eskimos weren't a very strong people. I was so pleased that he would
turn to me as to an expert, so flattered by his interest, that I jumped on the
bed and there held forth to him, with growing enthusiasm, while my feet got
tangled in our woolen blanket, on the height and strength of the Eskimos, sons
of the vast spaces between Greenland and Iceland, giants nourished by the fat of
seals. With my arms gesturing toward the ceiling, I demonstrated to the amused
Arke how a single Eskimo, were he to find himself under the wooden bridge of
the little ghetto—while it still existed—could raise it like Samson uprooting the
Gates of Gaza and pulling down the pillars of Ashkelon. We—Arke, Maimke,
and I—urgently needed fearless heroes. Little did we imagine how much we
would need their help.

The Tale of Ileda

One day before my father was taken to Riga I found myself standing by the
Komität building fence and reading a notice hanging there, wrinkling my brow
and trying to understand what it said. The announcement forbade residents of
the ghetto, from a certain date onward, to bring children into the world. Anyone
who disobeyed the rule—the implications were always clear—would be punished with the utmost severity.

I came home and told my parents, full of wonder. They answered me non-
committally—there was nothing in their response to lessen my wonder. But the
announcement and warning seemed to have an effect: babies in the ghetto became rarer and were no longer seen outside. Parents who took chances raised
their children in secret. Dr. Gurvitch told me that she helped deliver a baby girl

whose parents named her Geulah, salvation. And I have read about another girl named Ghetta.

Many years later we met a young couple in Rehovoth, immigrants newly arrived from the United States. The pretty young woman had black, curly hair and brown eyes. She was full of energy, restless, constantly smoking. She worked for the Jewish Agency, welcoming immigrants at the airport, and her scientist husband studied at the Weizman Institute. I knew she was a relative of Lazer, one of our neighbors in the ghetto, and so I asked her about herself. While her two children played with ours in the yard, she told her story—slowly, without enthusiasm, in marked contrast to her previous lively manner. It turned out that she was one of the children born in our ghetto. Since she was born during the prohibition against bearing children, her parents, in protest, named her in Hebrew and called her Ileda, "No-birth." They had her smuggled out of the ghetto as a baby, and they themselves later perished. Had it not been for a relative who sought her out, Ileda would probably have led a peaceful and quiet life as a Lithuanian in all respects, in spite of her dark hair.

Fate ordered it otherwise. She was taken to the United States by Lazer and he adopted her; there she had lived a moderately affluent life. I felt close to her when I met her in Israel, the warmth of a partner in fate. "Does your special name not embarrass you," I asked. "No," she smiled, "the name sounds exotic, and people simply accept it without asking questions." "Are you happy now, Ileda?" In the sadness of her shining eyes and her obvious restlessness, I discerned her discomfort. Some time after we met, we were informed that Ileda and her husband had decided to return to the United States. They had sent their children on before them, while they, somewhere between Athens and Rome, plummeted like a rock into the deep waters with their plane, which had exploded in the air. The curse of Ileda's untimely birth caught up with her thirty years later through a terrorist's bomb.

THE RIVER

In all of this, like an eternal refrain, so close and so unattainable, the river never stopped flowing, silent and free, toward the great ocean somewhere far in the west.

Usually we children never saw it. I suppose it would have been possible to sneak beyond the cemetery or the workshops to slightly higher areas near the embankments and view it, or to the mound near Democrats' Square, where a German guard was now stationed beside the gate leading to the river. From other vantage points one could look far to the west and see the remains of the great bridge that led to the city, which had collapsed at the beginning of the war. Beside it stretched a military pontoon bridge over which the Germans moved heavy vehicles and the brigades marched on their way to work. Leisure boats no longer sailed there, and lumber barges were also rare.

During the second year, some work brigades began crossing the river by boat, morning and evening, straight from the ghetto to their work sites on the other side. Pilz-Fabrik brigade was one of these. Work in the felt-boot factory was exhausting and wearing. With bare hands the women had to knead the clumps of felt, softening and preparing them for washing, so they could be fashioned into boots for German soldiers at the front. For Mother with her rheumatism, working in the intense humidity was like being stabbed with a knife every day. Yet this workplace made constant contact with Lithuanians, particularly women, possible. During the day they could bargain and barter almost without supervision. It was not for nothing that many tried to join this brigade. The head of the brigade was Dr. Greenberg, a decent man, an X-ray specialist. He excelled at getting along with the Germans and meeting their demands while still safeguarding his people as much as possible. Mother joined the brigade by chance, as a substitute worker, and, having seen its advantages, clung to her place with all her might and never let go.

Control over the gates leading from the factory to the river was lax, which made smuggling a little easier. From time to time, however, for their own reasons and without advance warning, the Germans would cancel the boat transports, rerouting the brigades through the main gate, catching people by surprise and subjecting them to more rigorous inspections and confiscation, which often resulted in overnight detention in jail, if not worse.

Ghetto Songs, Choir, and Orchestra

The ghetto sang songs. As soon as people recovered from the first shock, ghetto songs spread. They were based on familiar tunes to which new words were fitted, and they were passed from one person to another. The songs were about everything, missing not a single aspect of the new reality. The descriptions were sometimes naive and sentimental, sometimes bitter laments, but they were also humorous and hopeful for better times. They were a kind of underground communication for a persecuted community trying to keep its courage up. As children do, we were among the first to memorize the words, copying them diligently onto any half-used page. These in turn became yet more items in our endless barter and exchange. Many songs can be found in various anthologies.

And there was a choir, with four voices. Choir members were both children and adults, and rehearsals were held in the attic of the central apartment block, which served as the meeting place for various public bodies. How I came to join I do not recall, but I was proud to belong to it. We sang in Yiddish, Hebrew, and Lithuanian, and the songs and melodies we sang then accompany me to this day.

We appeared in public several times, for certain holidays and special events. The biggest performance that I remember took place in the formerly famous yeshiva building, which had been made the center of the ghetto's cultural life. Before the event, the house was cleaned and reclaimed, having been used first as a temporary storage place for the confiscated books, and later as the collection point for concentrating and destroying the ghetto's dogs and cats. On the raised dais of the synagogue we stood, dressed in our best clothes, arranged in rows by height and voice; in front of us was our conductor, Boris Gerber, who had an artificial left arm. All his life, Gerber had presided over the choir of the large synagogue in our city; now, he had to make do with much less. In spite of the special circumstances, he kept up an optimistic front, and with a wave of his hand succeeded in banishing—if only for a short while—the shadows of current events. I was in the alto section, second row, first from the left. The audience this time was very special—it included the ghetto dignitaries, its leaders and captains, as well as several German officers who had deigned to accept an invitation and boost the morale of the ghetto residents—the chief hunters come to hear the song of the deer.

I felt as though the audience was looking only at me, not at the soloists and not at the conductor. I sang, full of self-importance, enunciating clearly with mouth and lips, standing straight and tall, as Father had always instructed me to do. We sang, among many others, "There in the Glorious Land, in Our Brethren's Dwellings." We finished our repertoire, to a great deal of applause, with humorous songs, such as "Spuds on Sunday, Spuds on Monday."

Both with and without the choir, a string orchestra also staged concerts, bearing the name of its conductor, the violinist Misha Hoffmekler. This was the first orchestra I had ever listened to, not counting the orchestral accompaniment in the operas I saw with Mother before the war. Sometimes they played chamber music in smaller ensembles. I heard that, later, the remnants of this orchestra greeted newcomers at Dachau. After the war, Hoffmekler's daughter was one of the sobbing toddlers in our orphanage.

Study Groups

Study groups met in secret. They were started, with the tacit approval of the Komität, by parents and teachers who took it upon themselves to renew studies in place of the schools, which had been closed by order of the Germans. Lessons were held several mornings a week in various homes, and pupils were placed in them according to their level of knowledge and their preferred language of instruction, Yiddish or Hebrew. Mother no longer objected to my studying in Hebrew, perhaps because the study group in this language was held close to our home, in Arke and Maimke's flat. On a regular day, we had three or four lessons, with recesses of about fifteen minutes to allow teachers time to arrive from their previous classes. I do not know who was responsible for the overall coordination of the classes or the number of courses offered throughout the ghetto but the system functioned with great efficiency for nearly two years. I assume that it was the work of Dr. Haim Nahman Schapiro, a professor of Hebrew literature, who for two years had been in charge of the educational and cultural activities of the ghetto. One day Schapiro and his family were taken away without any warning to the Ninth Fort. It was said that his American relatives, with the help of the Red Cross, had been overzealous in trying to discover his fate.

Through the windows of Arke and Maimke's flat on the second floor, one could see relatively far, and we were able to see our next teacher making his way through the sown fields, taking a shortcut to our place of study. We were thus able to keep up our play until the very last moment, when the teacher would arrive and take off his coat.

Our group consisted of six to eight pupils of about the same age, seated around a big dining table. Most of us had once studied together in the lower grades of the Hebrew gymnasium. Here was Mishka Kapulsky, in whose grandfather's flat we had sought refuge on the first day of the war, as well as brown-skinned Abrashke Klavansky, whom we called Tsigayner (Gypsy) for that reason. Abrashke, the only one from this study group besides me who survived, is now a dentist in Chicago.

We had two main teachers in our group—Vetrin, who had been our teacher in the first and second grades, and Kapit, who taught mathematics and geometry. Vetrin had been the coauthor with my father of *The Hebrew Primer*. Vetrin had taught us to read and write in Hebrew. Now our paths crossed again for a while. He probably taught us Bible, literature, and grammar. Kapit had written many well-known textbooks in mathematics. His face was as angular and precise as the laws of his discipline, but his manner with students was correct and amiable. He always wore high black shoes with a pull-on strap attached to their backs. It was he who took me aside one day and, as if whispering a secret and with the discomfort of a man of intellect being forced to deal with material matters, asked me to inform my mother that as the child of a teacher I was exempt—like Arke and Maimke—from payment of a loaf of bread, the weekly fee.

One morning when we were having our lessons on the prophets something happened that is now forever a part of my memory of those lessons—Mek's hanging. A gallows had been erected in the ghetto. From the moment the hammer blows reached our ears, it was impossible to concentrate on our studies. The gallows was erected in an empty lot next to the Komität building, near our house, and all the residents of the ghetto who were there at the time were ordered to come and watch the hanging. From Ruchamah's flat we half looked, half avoided looking at the terrifying sight.

We already knew the main points of the case: a few days before, in the evening, a sentry had tried to stop someone seen slipping through the fence; the person had drawn a pistol and fired. This had happened near the main, western gate, near the section of the fence facing the river.

The German was unharmed, but Mek was apprehended. His accomplice, who at the time was crawling under the fence, managed to slither back and disappear safely in the ghetto. A wave of anxiety spread through the entire ghetto, and the public held its breath—a Jew brandishing a gun and firing at a German! Although he was questioned with blows and torture for several days, Mek never gave his friend away. The two of them turned out to be a pair of petty smugglers on their way, with no combative intentions, to trade jewelry with Lithuanians. Perhaps for this reason the Germans had decided, to the ghetto's good fortune, not to impose a collective punishment on the entire community; they were content to sentence Mek to public hanging inside the ghetto at the hands of the Jewish police so that all would see and be afraid.

Where did they find such thick trees, and how did the builders know the dimensions and shape of a gallows tree? I had seen such gallows in Father's history books. We couldn't see many details from the flat's windows, but we were able to make out the rope dangling down, and the wooden platform. Were they indeed about to hang a man there, in full view of the public? There were those among us who could explain how the rope would jerk up and choke the hanged man, while others claimed that the floor would open its mouth and the man's neck would be broken in an instant. One way or another, it was clear that our next lesson would be an extraordinary one.

By eleven o'clock the lot was full of people. A limousine full of Germans arrived, then another; chairs were set up for the viewers as if for a play or a choir concert. From out of nowhere the doomed man suddenly appeared and was escorted to the platform. From Ruchamah's windows we could see how short he was, how wretched his appearance. With his hands bound, he was led forward, tottering like a drunkard, lost, wandering. People later said that he was nearly out of his mind from being beaten and tortured. All the same, they added, he seemed quiet and restrained, acted with dignity, and managed to whisper some words of pardon to the Jewish policemen surrounding him. Some even claimed they heard "Shema Israel" (Hear, Israel) escape his lips before he was hoisted up and silenced.

From our window we could not see all the details of the episode. One instant, we saw a diminutive figure standing on the platform under the beam of the gallows with his hands behind his back; the next, as soon as we opened our eyes again, the same figure was now swinging on the rope high above the gathered people. Nothing seemed to change—his head, which had already been bowed, now seemed to tilt somewhat more to the side, and the body seemed somehow superfluous, spinning in circles at the end of the rope like a scarecrow in a garden, in puzzled search of something left on the ground behind it.

That was that; thus people die. So simply. All was quiet. No voice called out, no crying was heard. Only a German officer made a short cautionary speech. The Jewish policemen stood at attention, and the German cars began to leave. The crowd dispersed slowly. But we could not return to our studies.

It was ordered that Mek's body be left hanging for twenty-four hours, and policemen were left to guard it. Were the Germans unsure as to whether his soul had indeed departed? That afternoon a few of us went to take a look at the hanging body, approaching as near as we dared. I was content to look from a greater distance. Whether because of the piercing November cold or the blowing winds, Mek's body continued to spin endlessly around on the rope, its legs kicking lightly in the air, as if this additional penalty had been imposed on him and he had not yet grown weary of paying it. Over the next several hours his already small body seemed to shrink even further.

That night I found it hard to sleep, thinking about the corpse outside being covered with thin white frost, gleaming in the distance, its head tilted slightly to one side. Was he really feeling nothing anymore, as Mother explained? Was he really there no longer?

The next day, exactly twenty-four hours later, his body was lowered and taken to the cemetery. By the time I got there, the gallows had just been taken down, as if it had been the backdrop for a theater production now leaving for another show elsewhere. The Jewish policemen were quarreling playfully over the hanging rope, which had been cut into pieces. I was told such scraps were considered lucky. From what I know today of the fate of our ghetto policemen, I am in a position to cast some doubt on the magic power of those pieces of rope.

Mek was buried without a funeral or eulogy. He was denied even a tombstone. Yet several days later a small sign appeared in the mound where he was buried with a single word on it—Mek.

On the day of his burial, the Gestapo came to his flat and took his mother and sister to the Ninth Fort. The study groups continued for nearly another year. Thanks to them, thanks to our teachers' silent toil, I can call this period of a year and a half, however inaccurately, the "quiet period."

STAMPS

Just small pieces of paper, after all, but how they occupy my mind!

One day I will write to the Soviet Union. (I've been thinking about this for many years) Mikhael Sergeivitsch—I will begin—you who opened up your great country, as well as the hearts of its people, both to one another and to the whole world, please lend your ear now to the modest request of a former child: command, please, that his album of ghetto stamps be returned.

This is how it happened.

There were various offices in the ghetto, and each had its own rubber stamp. Oblong, round, triangular—even under the harsh ghetto conditions, there was no difficulty in producing varied rubber stamps. Children took up collecting the marks made by these stamps, competing fiercely. Some stamps were easy to get hold of—an official document past its expiration date, the torn corner of a stamped certificate—and others were rare and much harder to obtain. Some of us did not disdain rummaging through the rubbish outside the Komität building, and some were even bolder and would circulate through the various offices asking for a piece of paper to be stamped. Some clerks obliged with a smile; others were mean and stingy. Naturally, it was precisely the stamps controlled by the scowlers that had a higher value on the exchange market. Special value accrued to stamps that were valid only for short periods of time, or those that had indubitably legal validity.

Police stamps belonged to the latter category. They were diamond-shaped, with rounded corners, and inside were inscribed words of great magical power:

JGP—
Judische
Ghetto
Polizei

My fingers would tremble when I succeeded in obtaining some part of a certificate with this stamp on it to paste into my collection—at times this stamp brought tidings of life or death. I felt as if I were handling an amulet of inestimable value.

Like me, the album survived the war in a unique way. During the last stage of the ghetto, Mother began soberly preparing for evacuation. She placed various family documents in a washtub, which we buried in the ground, and, in answer to my entreaties, she added my album of stamps, which she put at the bottom of the tub—although it was hard for me to part with it even temporarily. Did I take the act seriously? Some time later, I repeated the ceremony in another yard further up Grinius Street, near the fence, together with my tall friend, as a children's game. We made a shallow pit, strengthened it with bricks, and inside it we placed a children's toy—a tin zeppelin, in whose elongated cavity we inserted a note with both our names.

What happened, happened, and the ghetto was consumed by fire. When I returned after the war, I cleaned away the soil and ashes, and discovered the washtub where I thought we had left it. I took off the cover only to discover that most of its contents were baked and charred, looking much like the paper that covered the pot of tcholent I used to bring home from the bakery. But I dug inside the brown container and found that the deeper I went, the papers were less and less damaged. And there, below the many brown or singed documents, lay, incredibly, my album of stamps in all its light-greenish glory, whole and sound as on the day I placed it there, light years ago.

Later, when I tried to cross the border of the Soviet Union—I may get to tell that story some day, too—the album of stamps was one of the few things I took with me as I prepared to be smuggled out. That story did not end so well, and the album, having survived the trials of fire and ash, fell into the hands of my captors, and it probably remains in the vaults of the KGB to this very day.

Is it only for the loss of the stamps that I continue to grieve? When I rescued the album from its hiding place and browsed through its pages, I found a surprise. On the back side of one of the scraps of stamped paper I came across a few lines in my mother's hand: "Children, there's soup in the pot. Heat it at noon with the porridge. Hearty Appetite. Mother." A short, ordinary note, one of Mother's daily messages, scrawled in haste on the back of an item in my collection.

THE OGG

It was all a matter of four summers: the war started in the first summer and ended in the last. Between them were two full summers in the ghetto. And during those summers, there was also the "Irgun Shomrim Laginot." Let's call it "the Order of Garden Guards," or OGG for short.

During the spring before the first summer in the ghetto, the authorities decided to make the ghetto population supplement their food by growing their own vegetables. Seeds were distributed, and everyone was ordered to cultivate vegetables in their gardens. That summer the program failed, both because people did not take to it and because many didn't know how to go about it. By the following summer, the program was strictly enforced. Police inspection patrols, accompanied by Germans, made rounds during the day through the houses, driving out everyone they found indoors to work their gardens. We were once surprised during our Bible lesson by a fat, well-known sergeant-major, and we scattered in all directions like frightened chicks. It was a cat-and-mouse game with very little practical purpose, although in the end a few vegetables did grow in front of our house.

The wide fields in the empty lots between houses at the edge of the ghetto were a different matter. These were prepared and sown by authority of the Komität, and the ghetto police was responsible for guarding them from damage and theft. Then someone had the idea of using children as guards, thereby also providing the youngsters with an educational framework of some sort.

The OGG gradually recruited adolescents and began giving them guard duties. The response was enthusiastic and many joined up. The activity aroused much envy among us younger children, since at first we were refused admission into the order. By the following summer, the scope of the OGG had grown, and so had we. The next summer (the third summer in the ghetto)—I was approaching the age of ten—I applied, encouraged by friends who had already been accepted, and to my joy I was not rejected this time—I was signed up as a candidate. A young guide, sixteen or seventeen years old, interviewed me, tested my knowledge on various subjects, including Hebrew and Lithuanian, the OGG's official languages, examined my physical ability to perform various exercises, and enrolled me in a group to which I would henceforth belong.

After several weeks of preparation, which we completed with much solemnity, the guide tested our knowledge, and we were ready for certification. At the initiation ceremony, we were each issued a white linen sailor's hat—the guard's cap. On its left-hand front corner, where the insignia appeared, was a triangular purple stamp with the characters "OGG" in Hebrew. This cap, our crowning pride, was to be worn while on duty, and only then. Any transgression would result first and foremost in returning the cap to the order.

With fear and trembling, with emotion and anticipation, I looked forward to the day when I would first set out to perform the important task of guarding the gardens.

Around every vegetable plot three or four guards were stationed for a watch lasting three or four hours. Watches were during daylight hours only, since at night there was a general curfew in the ghetto anyway. We were stationed in different sections each time, perhaps to vary the routine. A few policemen served alongside us, each responsible for several plots. We were to turn to them with any question or problem. They also kept guard there themselves during the early hours of the morning and toward evening.

During our watch, we had to march around the edge of our plot, ensuring that no one approached it or stole its crop—potatoes, cucumbers, tomatoes, cabbage, beets, and more. If someone attempted to steal from the garden, we were to alert the policemen nearby, perhaps with a whistle or a shout. In addition, we were forbidden to speak to friends or passersby, to lay hands upon the fruit of the field, or to abandon our post before our shift came to an end. We were also required to show up for all prescribed duties. Anyone who transgressed these laws paid a single penalty—expulsion from the order.

What the poor ghetto residents thought of us when they saw us passing along with our silly goose-step, or when we accosted them to keep them off the edge of the plot, one can only guess. Jeers and insults, which I endured more than once while standing guard, made no impression on me—I was proud to be relied upon, to be entrusted with responsibility.

The OGG got me out of the house and out of the first bloom of youth into a new, more mature world. I was entranced by the hierarchies, the orders, the discipline. I felt satisfaction at belonging to an organization that had strength and power.

Two things, seemingly unrelated, combined to bring an end to my OGG activity. As the second summer season of vegetable growing came to an end, the effects of routine became apparent in the performance of guard duty. We seem to have become tired. We were no longer rotated among the fields, and the once-punctilious changing-of-the-guard at the edge of the field ceased—the framework became looser and looser. Again and again I found myself guarding the same cucumber plot opposite the workshops. This was convenient for me, because here the plots were large and fairly remote. Thus there was a chance for a little mischief and even a little furtive book reading. Moreover, like others, I began committing the sin of the unmuzzled ox, tasting the juicy fruit of the garden we were guarding.

In these larger fields, children and policemen guarded together, and occasionally an officer would arrive for inspection. One day toward evening when I was on duty, after the officer had finished his inspection and walked away, I noticed him, to my surprise, return and enter the field from the other side, bend over, and gather vegetables, which went into his backpack. Agitated, I called this to the attention of the policeman beside me, but he showed no particular interest. For several days I was troubled by a feeling of unease. Should I report it, or pretend that nothing had happened? After thinking it over, I reported at headquarters what I had seen. In the command station I was praised for my alertness, but this brought no relief—reporting an officer of the police, a representative of ghetto authority, was no small matter—who knew where it would end? Several days passed, and with some relief I thought the matter had been forgotten. But one day I was invited to police headquarters near the apartment blocks. With trembling knees I entered the investigator's office. A sheet of white paper lay on his desk, and he began, in an amiable but serious tone, to read the details of my complaint and question me about it. Again I described the details of the incident, and he diligently wrote down everything I said. Was I certain of the man's identity? Was it perhaps someone else who entered the field from the other side? How could I be sure it was the officer? He was obviously taking the investigation very seriously, even though it was a ten-year-old child sitting opposite him. Although

I kept to my story, I gradually began to feel as though I was being accused in this incident. At the end of the inquiry, he read to me, as was customary, the protocol written in Lithuanian, had me sign the report, and remarked that my testimony implied a serious accusation. The man would most likely stand to trial, and I must be ready to bear witness. Heavyhearted, I went home, worrying even more than before that I had overdone it this time, that I had taken the matter too far.

During the following days I waited in much suspense for the summons to the court. The summons failed to arrive, however, and I continued to guard the same plot. I began noticing that the policemen around me were not content with simply tasting the fruit; they were also concealing some of it in their bags—it was impossible to separate the guarding network from the sad reality of the starving ghetto. Sin is contagious; over the next few days I, too, at first with much embarrassment, began bringing the fruit of the field home. Mother asked no questions. She thought the cucumbers were being distributed to us at the end of each shift. As a result, the urge to take grew ever stronger until one day I decided to imitate someone—whom we had once caught red-handed—and brought along a cloth bag that we had at home. I remember the bag well—it had white and orange alternating stripes and white cloth handles; in former days, we had used it for outings on the riverbank at summer camp. Now I hung it by its handles from my trouser belt beneath my long coat. During my shift, whenever I found myself removed some distance from the policeman with me, I would bend down and furtively place a few vegetables in it.

It was the last days of autumn. The policeman on duty with me was amiable and kind. Twilight descending early made it easier for me to add another piece of fruit to the bag, and another, and yet another. I was so satisfied with my initiative that I must have overdone it with the number of cucumbers I took. The bitter result was that at the end of my watch as I was leaving the field, my cumbersome gait raised the policeman's suspicions, and he called for me to return. What have you got there, boy? He ordered me to undo my coat buttons—and I stood there exposed.

My shame, my disgrace, my embarrassment knew no bounds. The policeman paid no heed to my excuse that this was the first and only time I had ever done such a thing. He confiscated my bulging bag and sent me home, but not before preaching me a sermon—the shame of it!—for betraying my duty and the trust that they had placed in me.

My return from the fields, all along Grinius Street from the river to my home, was very long this time and paved with bitter weeping. I was beside myself. I had wanted so much to be a "provider," a partner in feeding the family, deserving of my parents' praise. How could I tell Mother now? How could I show my face among my friends in the street? And—most of all—what would they say of me at headquarters? What shame, what disgrace! I would certainly stand trial; I would be denounced in public. Great darkness descended upon me. Only once before this during my short life had I been in such a disgraceful situation, unpardonable and unatoned: one Shabbat I had hung on the back of a Gentile's carriage in the square at the shtetl of my grandfather the rabbi.

My path brought me home nonetheless; this time, against all hope, Mother had returned early from her brigade, not having been delayed long at the gate. Choking with tears, I told her some of what had happened, and what I left out she no doubt understood. To my relief, she did not scold me outright for my misdeed and tried to calm me. She even promised to go to the police and attempt to retrieve the confiscated bag.

For a few days I didn't leave the house. I was sure that I was facing an investigation and expulsion from the order, if not worse. Then I remembered, to my dismay, that I was still waiting for the summons to testify at the officer's trial. How could I look the judges in the face with the same transgression on my hands? I had done exactly as he had done; my wretchedness knew no bounds.

Another day or two passed, and nothing happened. Cautiously, I began appearing among people. The sun shone as before, and the brigades continued to leave for work at dawn. With much embarrassment, I met one of the OGG seniors; he greeted me and innocently asked why I was no longer coming to stand guard; had I been ill? And thus I discovered, to my surprise, that nothing had been reported of me, that they knew nothing at all of what had happened. Nevertheless, I decided I was never going back to the OGG.

And the officer's trial? Within a few days, the little Aktion occurred. Once again everything was shaken up and destroyed, and nothing ever was as it had been. When several days had gone by and no summons from the court arrived, I understood—with childish relief—that there would be no more dealings with officers who had stolen cucumbers.

And thus ended the episode of my participation in the OGG; the OGG itself came to an end, and the "quiet period" was sealed.

6

Another Fall and Winter

CLOUDS

Mother Doesn't Come Home

One day Mother did not come home from work. The stream of returning workers at twilight dispersed into the streets and disappeared into houses, and Mother wasn't among them. At that time, mothers had to work four or five days a week and we were on our own most of the day. But even when she did return, worn and weary, she would sometimes be late, having been delayed on her way home, stopping here and there to barter. After a long time, another worker from the same brigade came and gave us a message from Mother not to worry—she would be back later that night or, at the very latest, the next morning. She had been stopped at the gate and put in detention.

Immediately I took my sister's hand, and we went to look for her. We may have been encouraged to do so by the people around us, as a means of pleading with the ghetto police. We may also have stopped on the way at Izzia and Shulamit's house to tell them what had happened. I am not sure that we even reached the gate that evening; I don't remember much of the next twelve hours. Maybe it all happened the following morning; the curfew on the ghetto began at nightfall, so how could we have gone to the gate and back?

Yet I have a dim picture of two small children holding one another's hands and standing beside the jail near the main gate of the ghetto. It was a two-story stone house on a corner; behind it was a yard with a gate at the back. Along the inner walls were long balconies overlooked by small latticed windows, and from one of them we thought we noticed the wave of a handkerchief or a weak cry.

We were two children alone beside the locked gate, trying to locate our mother, with no one to speak to. No one was waving at us through the window. We turned around and went home, still holding tightly to each another. That night, we wrapped ourselves up in Mother's bed, shedding tears and worrying very much indeed. As the big brother, I tried with all my might to be brave and consoling and to not think. We felt like helpless chicks whose protection had disappeared, now exposed to the merciless sun and every menacing danger. Never before had we felt so abandoned, so alone.

My memory betrays me—why exactly was Mother arrested? She was freed the next morning and sent home. Perhaps her papers weren't in order, or they had found more smuggled goods in her bag than usual. Perhaps she had exchanged a few sharp words with one of the people in charge at the gate, and he had decided to teach her a lesson. I deduce this from fragments of a picture preserved in my memory: that morning, as we returned with Mother, we met Luria—a tall, smiling man who was in charge of the work schedules for the Komität, and hence the object of a good deal of rage and resentment. One of the ghetto's songs was specifically about him, sung to the popular Soviet tune of "Captain, Captain": "Tall man, tall man, give us a smile."

He obviously had some long and special relationship with Mother, perhaps because of her directness and spunk. That morning he greeted her with a teasing, admonishing smile: So, was it worth it? Clearly, he knew all about the incident. Mother replied with a taunt and we went our separate ways.

I do not recall that I ever asked Mother how she felt that night, her first time in jail, separated from her children. Or perhaps if I did, her answer may have been more than my memory could bear.

Wolf Luria. Some months later, as the vise squeezed harder and harder, this strong, smiling man distributed poison to his family and all of them together tried to commit suicide.

My Sister Falls Ill

One day as I was helping my little sister get dressed, I noticed some small red spots on her left foot near her toes. That evening I told my mother about them, and she found, after a systematic search, similar spots on her lower abdomen and back. My sister wasn't complaining, and she had no fever. As soon as possible Mother consulted the doctors, and they ran some blood tests—such things were apparently possible even in the ghetto. Their conclusion was that she had the symptoms of anemia, a result of improper nutrition. I learned a number of new concepts as a result of her illness: leukocytes, erythrocytes, thrombocytes. The initial blood counts for my sister were too high for some values, too low for others.

During the following months Mother increased her efforts to bring my sister healthy food from outside—chicken liver, meat, butter, and yeast. The high blood counts continued to rise, the low to fall, and my sister became weak and pale. Some years ago I spoke about this with Dr. Gurvitch, who had been one of the doctors in the ghetto. She confirmed for me that vitamin deficiency had a wide variety of symptoms among the younger children in the ghetto, including those I described.

I have almost no memories of Mother's involvement in the ghetto as a nurse. Perhaps she avoided practicing so as to keep her ties with others flexible; perhaps she was afraid of exposing her profession since the Germans had burned the hospital and all its inhabitants. Even so, when an Aktion or other disturbance took place, she would wear a white band or a nurse's headdress, both to gain the trust of the German military and to ensure herself a measure of freedom in her movements in and out of the house.

On ordinary days she would sometimes set out to give an injection in someone's home, or apply suction cups to one of her friends— suction cups and leeches were common folk remedies used in the ghetto. To my sister she gave shots of vitamin B, which she obtained with considerable difficulty. I remember the stainless steel container, holding needles boiled and ready for injection, little glass bottles, and the tiny saw used to open their necks.

All of us had to practice dressing fast to be ready for any emergency, and my sister usually let me help her. More than once she exasperated me, her responsible older brother, by teasingly making a mess of things. I would slap her bottom or complain about her in the evening to Mother. My sister did not let the matter go when I was mean to her, and when Mother came home from a day of backbreaking labor, she still had her work cut out for her making peace between us. My sister was only six and a quarter years old, after all, when she was moved across the fence. Some day I may have the strength to tell about it.

Mother may have avoided talking about her problems so as not to betray the extent to which she relied on the profits of barter and smuggling, which she conducted persistently and enterprisingly. Her dealings took considerable effort and caused her no small amount of trouble. She had to find buyers and suppliers; to negotiate with each one separately over the price of the goods, while ensuring a reasonable commission for herself; to smuggle the items unharmed through the ghetto gate; and to deliver the goods to the buyer. The buyer had to pay her in currency or food—and these, too, had to be smuggled back into the ghetto. Both parties had to put their full trust in their intermediary—the Lithuanian had to trust that Mother was delivering good-quality products, with no hidden defects; the ghetto dweller had to trust that Mother was getting the most she could for the item he gave her, and that she would not fall back on stories of confiscation of goods or payment while crossing through the gates.

It was a multifaceted business requiring initiative, negotiation, and persuasion; she had to know how to improvise, and needed not a little courage. To Mother's credit, she won the trust of all sides, and I never heard of any trouble.

More than once Mother came home frustrated, with the smuggled goods still on her—the deal had foundered, either because negotiations had failed or because the anticipated person had thought better of the bargain or perhaps had simply not come to work that day. A good deal of physical effort was also required of her, thin as she was, for her kilometers-long walk carrying heavy goods—coats and suits one way, food hidden in her clothes on the way back.

Thanks to Mother's efforts, we were never without a slice of bread and a little something to spread on it. The enhanced nutrition left its mark on my sister, who gradually grew stronger and healthier, even though she never fully regained the health she had before her days in the ghetto.

How did Mother bear such a heavy burden? Where did she find the strength to be forever vigilant, with sole responsibility for the fate of her two children? I do not know. She must certainly have received some moral support from her few friends. But I believe that what supported her most, aside from her own natural fund of inner strength, was a group of people into whose circle I was not admitted—the underground.

The Underground

For some time I had been aware that on Sunday evenings and sometimes on weekday nights after work Mother would attend meetings, but she remained perfectly silent about them. At a certain point she began sharing with me her knowledge, for instance, about the situation at the front, very important knowledge, which, it was clear to me, did not have its source in mere rumors. Although I was only ten years old I was a loyal listener, the family member closest to her. And although she never divulged the sources of her information, I gradually made the connection between her mysterious meetings and the knowledge she had.

A communist in principle—and perhaps formerly a member of a secret organization, for I found among her things a badge labeled MOPR (a secret communist body)—she also found comrades in the ghetto who shared her thoughts and ideals. These people were active in a complex network of underground cells, and Mother belonged to one. It was dangerous to do so, because it was well known that the Germans were on the watch for any secret organizations, especially communist ones.

I do not know what Mother's underground organization did. I know they met regularly and exchanged information that had reached them from various external sources—from radio broadcasts, newspapers, and people who came in from outside. I believe they also gave lessons in first aid. They helped friends in distress and engaged in other social activities. Did they also get training in arms? Apparently not.

Little by little Mother shared more of her secrets with me. Why did she do this? Perhaps out of her own oppressive sense of loneliness, and perhaps because she wanted to give me some little hope, the courage to look ahead to what was in store.

I was proud of the trust she had in me, and of never disappointing her by betraying her secrets, and I loved the sense it gave me of being one of the adults. I pitied my poor little sister because she could not share the knowledge of secret matters. Occasionally, I hinted to her that I possessed secrets that had bearing on our chances of rescue. My sister was content with that, and went back to her play.

One day Mother came home, her eyes sparkling—there was a way out. She made me swear again to keep the secret and told me that there was talk of smuggling people to distant forests to join partisans fighting against the Germans. The first candidates for such treatment were members of the underground and their families. Suddenly the horizon expanded, and hope was born.

It was a possibility replete with all the most wonderful elements: deceiving the all-powerful Germans; a journey to distant, mysterious places; a chance for us, human dust, to join partisans who fought with weapons in their hands, taking revenge on the evil ones. And all of this in the forest, in the magical vistas of my childhood memories. Under the circumstances during those days, there could not have been a more marvelous fairy tale than the one now on Mother's lips.

The scrap of information that I thus picked up enabled me, in time, to understand something of the underground's ways without having to ask direct questions. I understood that at the head of the organization in the ghetto stood our family friend Haim Yellin. I also deduced that Mother belonged to Dr. Golach's cell. She was the doctor in the children's ward at the little hospital that had been reopened. It was to her house that Mother hurried every Sunday afternoon.

Meanwhile, the preparations for moving out into the forests increased. Emis-

saries sent there returned optimistic in spite of failures and setbacks. Several li-
aison agents and scouting parties fell prey to the Germans, and the Lithuanian
partisans were less than enthusiastic about accepting Jews into their ranks. In
spite of this, the members of the underground kept their spirits up, driven as they
were by the hope that sooner or later they would flee to the forests, both to fight
and be saved.

Scene: Sunday afternoon. I am with Mother making her weekly round of
errands. We are still near the house, on the edge of the vacant lot across
the street, when we see Haim Yellin coming toward us. Here in the flesh,
in broad daylight, is the mysterious man of the underground, he about
whom so many stories are told, whom few had seen lately with their own
eyes. I gaze in admiration at the wonder-working man, who comes and
goes without fear, who passes through the fence like an invisible man, who
reaches the forest and, what is more, even comes back from there.

At the time I did not know that even in those circumstances he had
the strength, in his various hiding places, to fashion a literary account of
his daring experiences. I was amazed to see him anyway, because I knew
that at the time he was supposed to be on one of his secret forays into the
woods, and that the Germans here were constantly searching for him.

With a broad smile and a hearty handshake he greets my mother.
Mother, I see, reacts hesitantly, as befits a member of a conspiracy. My
heart swells with pride to see the glorious Haim Yellin paying attention
to my mother, and in public. Later that day, my neighbors tease me, their
voices full of meaning—"Nu, so your mother knows Haim Yellin, eh?"

And all the leader of the Jewish resistance in the ghetto does is ask,
"Nu, Leah, are you still writing poems?" "No," answers my mother with a
sad smile, "not as long as we're in this barrel" (in *dem kessl* are her words).
"I can't. When we get out of here, then I'll write again." Then we part. *End
of scene.*

Not long after, Haim Yellin was no more than a legend.

Among the survivors of the ghetto there must certainly have been those who
were in Mother's cell. With their help, I might have discovered more about my
mother's deeds in the underground. When it was possible to ask, I refrained from
doing so, and now it is too late.

And one day I nearly dealt the underground a serious blow, not to mention the chagrin I caused my mother. Among the many who came and went in our room on Sunday afternoon, there was a certain young man whose face I saw several times; he would take a large envelope from my mother's hands and leave without a word.

One day Mother had to be out of the house during the evening, so she asked me to help—could I give the packet to the young man? I agreed, after Mother made sure that I would recognize him. At the appointed hour, about four o'clock it seems to me, a trading partner of Mother's, a nice man and a friend of hers, came to ask about her. Then he asked if she hadn't left something for him. I told him no, but then added, hesitantly, and then only because the man was always pleasant and friendly with me, that there was a packet that I thought belonged to someone else. "Show it to me," he said, "I'll take a look and if it's not for me I won't take it." Although his suggestion was a reasonable one, I hesitated; something within me whispered not to do it. In a moment of weakness, however, and with much uneasiness, I gave him the envelope. He peeped inside, and seeing that its contents were indeed not for him, he handed it back to me and left.

Only a few minutes later the other man came, and the error I had made was clear to me. I persisted in my folly by explaining, while handing him the envelope, that I had just about given the things to someone whom he very much resembled. The man showed no emotion and went away. When Mother returned I told her, in an offhand manner, what had happened while she was gone. Her face darkened and became serious as she raked me over the coals—how could I have given something to someone it didn't belong to? I went over every detail of the chain of events; I told her how unsure I had been, and even went so far as to add, so I had shown the envelope to a good friend of ours, and he didn't take anything—what was so terrible about that? Mother only bit her lip and said no more. The very depth of her silence persuaded me that I had failed in a way that I did not fully understand. It reminded me of the times when I had drawn furious looks of chastisement from Father.

Several days went by before Mother spoke and let me know a little about the damage I had unwittingly done. The envelope had been a secret bulletin, a compilation of news clips and radio announcements that circulated through Mother to the contact person of another underground cell. I had made two mistakes that afternoon, the lesser of which was trying to justify my act of babbling to the second man. But the graver error was showing the material, even for an instant, to the wrong person. Because of me, my mother had been called and questioned closely—and for all I know, also seriously scolded. Limits had been placed on her membership, and an important responsibility—cell leader?—had been taken away from her. She had nearly been thrown out of the resistance movement.

Fortunately for us, the wrong man, Mother's trading partner, behaved honorably and with tact. He continued to visit us with his own concerns and never so much as mentioned the glimpse he had had of the material that didn't belong to him. More important, he never passed on what he knew; had he done so, the results could have been disastrous for the entire underground resistance movement. As for me, I was profoundly sorry for my blunder. I had betrayed Mother and had caused her great distress. And the concealed wish of my heart, to be considered a full and equal partner, suffered a severe blow.

Yom Kippur

An autumn afternoon. We are playing soccer on the lot to the south of the apartment blocks. We play half-heartedly, with a kind of lassitude, until one of us says, "Let's go to the synagogue." The suggestion is made simply, and simply agreed to; we all know why. And so, in the same natural manner we had played but a moment ago, we all turned to the shack at the bottom of the mounds that cut between us and the river.

We came to the house of prayer, which was full to overflowing. All were wrapped in prayer shawls, looking pale and dejected. It was forbidden to pray in public, but it was a decree that the people simply could not obey.

We stood in the doorway, peering curiously inside. In a moment we were seen by the worshipers, and a tremor seized the crowd. Here were the boys, come to the closing prayers for the Day of Atonement—the same boys who had never stopped making noise most of the day beneath the synagogue's windows. They surrounded us, as if embracing us and taking us into their bosom. Some of us found relatives; others were joined by friends who took them in. Our friend Eliezer the writer recognized me, took me to his side, and gave me a prayerbook. As in years past, when I stood beside Father in the big synagogue with the choir, or with my grandfather in his shtetl in his corner at the eastern wall, I now stood with Eliezer until the end of the closing prayer, Ne'ila.

There was much weeping, embracing, and heartfelt entreaty. There was something sobering in the air. The verdict, as every year, had been written "in heaven" and sealed. But there was a feeling this time that the expected sentence was heavier than usual, and that in spite of the sincerity of the prayers, the appeals and petitions for pardon had not been heard. We ended, as usual, by making the traditional wishes for the next year to be in Jerusalem and by blowing an improvised shofar. Outside, they closed with the blessing for the new moon and "Shalom Aleichem" ("Peace Be Upon You"); then they scattered to their homes.

Yom Kippur, the Day of Atonement, 1943.

WINTER

September

September came, and suddenly everything changed. The ghetto was declared to be a concentration camp—KZ (Konzentrationslager) Kauen—and was put under military rule. SS soldiers with black lapels and the skull and crossbones on their caps took the place of the brown-lapelled SA forces, and the change went far deeper than the color of their uniforms. Goecke was appointed chief commander of the ghetto, a high-ranking officer whose name became from then on indissolubly linked with everything that took place in the ghetto.

Decree followed decree. The Ältestenrat was abolished and with it our semi-autonomy; Dr. Elkes was now appointed to be the "Jewish elder," and he had to continue representing the public with much-restricted authority; and SS men took away roles and areas of responsibility from the senior members of the Komität. The number of jobs outside the ghetto was reduced to increase control over the brigades; supervision increased at the passage through the gate and along the entire fence.

Although we heard harsh stories about what was happening in other places where Jews were still alive, we began to believe we were special. They needed us; we were very useful to them and were consequently immune from the calamities that befell other ghettos.

At the end of September, we heard the first news of the destruction of our sister ghetto—the Vilno Ghetto. Those among its inhabitants who could still work were sent to labor camps in Estonia; the old and the young were taken to the Ponar Forest, the killing site for the Jews of Vilno. A few weeks passed, and we were subjected to the Little Aktion.

In its first hours, when we heard that the gates were locked and the brigades were not being sent out, we did as we had done before in such cases—we hurried to the cellar. Between one emergency and the next, we had practiced hiding under the piles of junk. Mother even spread a few blankets and dark coverings in case we needed them.

On that day, after we had spent a few hours waiting quietly in the cellar—I in one corner, Mother and my sister in another—and nothing happened, Mother decided to go up and check things out. After finding out that they were indeed removing people from the ghetto but were using a list to do so and that the ghetto police rather than the Germans were in charge, Mother concluded that the situation was not too serious. Only a few days before, the Komität had published announcements calling for families to enlist for work and residence in a new camp in the country, not far from our city. It was said that the Germans were establishing a camp of 3,500 people that would be an independent body, somewhat along the lines of our ghetto. They needed skilled workers of various kinds, as well as a few clerical workers. Registration was slow—people wavered, hesitating to leave their familiar surroundings. Mother guessed that now they were rounding up the people for the camp. Since we had already, to our sorrow, suffered the loss of the head of our family, we had nothing to fear this time; moreover, the Aktion was being conducted by members of the Komität, and she relied on the strength of their ties with her through Father. Accordingly, she gave us the signal, a series of short knocks, to climb back up to our room.

While we were still adjusting to the rest of the day's stay at home, two Jewish policemen came in, asked us our names, and ordered us to come with them. Mother argued with them, claiming that there must be some mistake. We were not a whole family and did not meet the criteria for being transferred; furthermore, we were still planning to join the head of our family, who was now in Riga. But the policemen were adamant—our names were on the list, and the list was what counted; any clarification had to take place on the selection lot. As we had no choice, we gathered a few clothes, just in case, and left the house with them.

I remember that we were not especially panic-stricken, merely confused, and we children stuck close to Mother, one on each side. We were sure this was a mistake and that Mother would certainly put things straight. What bothered me most was being dragged out publicly into the street, accompanied by two policemen—there may even have been a German soldier—with everyone looking on and seeing us in our distress—"They're taking them, too." As we were going up Varnių Street on our way to the Komität, we happened to meet Izzia Rabinovitz, who was appointed by the Ältestenrat to be in charge of manpower and labor-related matters. Surprised to see us in custody, he confronted the soldiers and asked them to explain. After hearing them out, he gave a brief command to let us go. At that moment we did not understand—at least, I didn't—the full meaning of this command. Wasting no time, we hurried back home and spent the rest of that day in our hiding place in the basement, in case someone came back to get us.

We discovered later that the Komität had failed, using its own lists, to collect the required number of people, in much the same way they had failed during the Riga Aktion; nor did the pace at which people were being rounded up satisfy the Germans. They had consequently begun to bring people using randomly chosen lists. By the end of the day they had removed three thousand men, women, and children from the ghetto. Had they taken us half an hour later, Izzia would have been powerless to save us, for by then the Germans themselves had spread out, together with the blood-hungry Ukrainians, and had taken enough people by force to fill the quota.

In direct contradiction of their previous announcement about the new camp in the province, the authorities now announced that the captured people would be sent to labor camps in Estonia and that letters would arrive from them over the next few days. And indeed, for the next few weeks, a number of brief, noncommittal cards did arrive. At the same time, a few notes thrown out of the carriages at train stations were brought to us by good people. Judging by the rail route, our people had indeed been transported north. In the ghetto chronicles, this event came to be known as the Little Aktion.

That same night, true to their methods, the Germans ordered the evacuation of part of the area of the apartment blocks.

Today we know that during the same day, in a train station across the river, they separated the old people and children from the rest and put them into railroad cars for a few days. The old and the young shared the same fate. In those days and for a long while afterward, my heart went out especially to the children. Today, as I approach the age of sixty, still in possession of my faculties and feeling like a man in his thirties, the terrifying thought strikes me that, at my present age, I might easily have been numbered among the elderly.

I cannot stop asking myself what might have happened if we had not met Izzia at that fateful moment. And this question, too, invades my mind continually: Was another family sent in our place to fill the quota? One could quibble and say that when we were allowed to return home, families were still being collected according to lists drawn up in advance. But in any case, they later began taking whomever they could lay their hands on, but even so they managed to collect only 2,800 people, not the 3,500 required. And those who escaped the curse, escaped.

Izzia was one of the few members of the Ältestenrat who managed to keep his good name, toeing more or less successfully the thin line between fulfilling his public function and remaining human. I escaped from the ghetto laden with debts. Mother is the only one to whom I am, in some respect, perhaps, finding a way to repay what I owe. But I am hard put to find a way to repay the many others who lent their aid at various points in my rescue. In addition to Izzia, there were at least five Lithuanians to whom I owe nothing less than my life.

Barracks and Evacuation

Autumn ended and winter came, this one more depressing than the last. Its horrors had already begun transpiring in other places around us, and there was nothing for us to do but wait for them to reach us.

People were still recovering from the Little Aktion when Goecke's order came for "Kasernierung": the Germans decided to distribute workers and their families into four or five camps adjoining their place of work in the outskirts of the city. This way, they claimed, they could eliminate the time spent marching to work and back, labor sites would have steady workers, and overall production would increase, the latter of course their top priority. Barracks residents were promised that they would not be cut off from the "main camp," the ghetto, and that the general Jewish appointees would represent them as well. A few weeks were allotted to complete the gradual transition to the barracks.

In spite of the ominous terms "Kasernierung" and "Konzentrationslager"—barracks and concentration camps—this time the Komität had no trouble filling the lists with those who were willing to leave. The anxious public cast about blindly for any way to survive. They guessed that by living in the satellite camps that were tied to a few vital plants, they and their families would be somewhat immune from events like the Little Aktion.

During the move to the barracks, the ghetto was ordered to reduce its space once more. This time, people were ordered to leave the westernmost part of the ghetto beyond the bottleneck—that is, the old Jewish quarter, hundreds of years old, the historical roots and trunk of the Jewish presence in the city.

I imagine that the Germans had good reason to evacuate Slobodka, of all places. By doing so they were able to remove the Jews from the main transnational road. In addition, they would be uprooting them from their ancient abodes, a shtetl, with its convoluted blocks of buildings, one piled against another. From now on, the ghetto consisted of a much-reduced square with nearly straight sides, crossed by straight streets lined with simple, fairly modern houses, many of which were separated somewhat from the rest, making them easier to control. Goecke was indeed tightening the noose.

Once again people had to leave their homes. Among them this time were the last of those for whom this was their first move—the original residents of Slobodka. Once more they had to search for a corner to live in—to crowd in among already crowded and embittered neighbors, to snatch up the spaces left by those who had been taken to the barracks. There was scarcely a household that did not take in new members.

In the end, several thousand left for the satellite camps, while in the ghetto there remained only eight thousand, a mere shadow of the lively original ghetto with a population of thirty thousand three years before.

Ruchamah, with Arke and Maimke, were among those who were moved to the barracks. I do not remember how or even whether we said good-bye—in those days, and even before then, each family tended to withdraw into itself. Later, I saw Ruchamah several times in the ghetto, when she came on various errands. She said they were fine; they lived in long barracks that had been out-fitted with wooden, multistoried bunks. Although the men were separated from the women, the children were sleeping with her in a lower bunk. During the day they stayed alone in camp, playing undisturbed. Ruchamah seemed to be reconciled to these conditions.

One act of Mother's in particular during this period revealed to me, perhaps for the first time, how low her spirits had fallen—or perhaps this was the first time that she didn't hide her feelings from me. She had always nursed a hope that Father would one day be returned to the ghetto. And would Father's return have improved our lot? It would at least remove from Mother the sole responsibility for her children and relieve her of her deep loneliness—a loneliness she had never discussed with me. But as time passed, the chance that Father would return became slimmer and slimmer. The Little Aktion had shown us a glimpse of the danger we were in. Mother felt her strength giving out. In a moment of despair and hopelessness, she decided to request a meeting with Dr. Elkes, head of the Jewish ghetto.

What did Mother hope to gain from an audience with Dr. Elkes? What could the Jewish elder do for her? Perhaps she believed he could bring about the return of her husband from Riga, or had some hope that he could help her financially so that she could improve her daughter's nutrition, who was suffering from a blood ailment. Perhaps she was already laying plans for my sister's escape from the ghetto, which would require a great deal of money. Perhaps her hold on the position in the Pilz-Fabrik brigade had weakened and she needed to ensure that she kept her job. I have no clear memory of her motives for wanting to see Dr. Elkes, only that her need to see him was great. And perhaps, like anyone else, my mother, weakened or feeling weary, simply felt the need to cry out her bitterness on the fatherly shoulder of someone in authority—to say to him, enough is enough, I can't go on anymore. When she was younger, she had relied on her even-tempered and always optimistic father, Shalom Zvi the tinker, as an unfailing source of encouragement.

The offices of the now deposed Ältestenrat had already been moved to a new location on the other side of Varnių Street, close to Goecke and the German headquarters. Mother brought us two children with her, perhaps to lend weight to her complaint, although she left us on the porch and went in to see Dr. Elkes alone. For a long time she stayed inside, and when she came out she looked serious and had tears in her eyes. Dr. Elkes accompanied her to the door and patted our heads.

Always pale, slow of gait and refined, Dr. Elkes had the uncommon courage to stand up to the Germans and speak with them face-to-face; often they listened to what he had to say. More than once, I am told, whenever he was about to meet Goecke, he parted from his family as if he would never return to see them again. I always imagined that the pallor of his face, which reminded me of the synagogue cantor during the closing prayer of the Atonement Day, or of the face of Mek hanging from the rope, was caused by his meetings with the Germans. I never heard it said of him that he showed partiality or perverted justice.

Whether Mother felt better after her talk with him I do not know. She did, however, leave his presence with a note for the Komität warehouse stating that she was to receive new shoes for her children. It appeared he still had some kind of authority left after all. I do not recall Mother ever again asking for help. After seeing that the establishment had no power to save, she turned to other sources.

Goe—ke. Like Rau—ke, S—S, ghet—to: pairs of syllables that send shudders up and down the body.

From our perspective, Goecke was the sole ruler, the supreme power. Parents who had no patience left with their children would threaten, "Goecke will come and get you." He was a paragon of deliberation and cleverness, from his point of view, hard-driving in his dialogue with Dr. Elkes, but never losing his temper and showing no signs of personal cruelty. I remember his name better than that of any other German, perhaps because he was commander of the ghetto at the end, when he put into effect the most dramatic measures the ghetto had ever seen.

I feel a kind of ambivalence toward him, something like the dependence of a hanged man on the hangman. For so many years he has been with me, till I have split and become two; he seems to be already a part of me. Do I hate him personally? I wonder, every time I meet a young German.

How ironic fate can be—later, Dr. Elkes and Goecke, in spite of their vast differences, met their end on the same date. The following autumn, Dr. Elkes finally succumbed to fatigue and illness in the Dachau camp, and on exactly the same day, according to our ghetto chronicler, his nemesis was killed on the Italian front.

Gas

That fall people began speaking of gas.

Sunday, a sunny day: Mother, my little sister, and I were taking an afternoon walk while Mother was giving us the news. Suddenly, my sister asked, "Mother, does it hurt to die by gas?" Mother—a registered nurse—answered with the same directness she always did when explaining health-related topics. "No, you feel nothing; you go to sleep and don't wake up." And I, in the fraternity of adults, added, "No, it doesn't hurt at all; you just go to sleep and that's it."

The words of a mother to her daughter during a sunny afternoon stroll in the ghetto.

It was a time when the question of dying and the ways I could expect it to happen were always on my mind. Where were the people being taken, what happened to everyone in other ghettos around us, who, according to rumors, were one day loaded onto freight cars and taken who knows where? The memories of the old folks sunk in their sleep in Democrats' Square or of Mek swinging on the rope were always before me whenever I dwelt on death.

My imagination tended to avoid conjuring up another possible image of death, that of killing pits like the ones at the Ninth Fort. And I had visited such a fort during a class outing one spring before the war—a huge stone structure sunk into the ground, surrounded by a deep moat, with large gates of rusted iron. When we began speaking of gas, I pictured to myself how they might force masses of people into the huge halls of such a fortress, lock the gates, and turn on the gas.

What is the best way to die? It was an important question that recurred with increasing frequency in our conversations.

Mother would reply—she loved reciting—from Lermontov's "Metsiri."

Death does not discomfit me
There, they say, one's troubles melt.

For years I translated this to myself, not entirely, perhaps, by accident: "There, they say, is an eternal sleep."

For the three years we spent in the ghetto, we were always on the verge of being forced into one of these two deaths—to stand at the edge of a pit or be carted to the gas chambers. It was only a question of time before we knew which scenario would prevail. At times I feel as if a part of me is still in a state of waiting.

Mother Seeks a Way Out

The feeling that liberation was approaching in a matter of days motivated people to dare to search for ways of escaping. Although the Lithuanian public remained on the whole openly hostile and unkind, the number of humane people grew who, in light of the tremendous changes on the front, were now more willing to take risks and give shelter to former friends. With them were greedy swindlers who saw a chance to make money—were not the Jews immensely rich? And there were also Lithuanians who reckoned they should try to improve their image in the eyes of the advancing Red conquerors.

There was great danger of being turned in, however. Death awaited not only the trapped Jews—usually at the Ninth Fort—but those who hid them as well. Hiding was likely to be easier in distant villages where there were fewer houses, where there was less supervision, and where the ties between neighbors were friendlier. However, few Jews had such connections any longer, and were usually those from the country whom the war had forced into our ghetto and now succeeded in renewing contact with their former neighbors.

Could one escape to the forests and hide there? The forests I remembered from my childhood were in fact small ones, situated near settlements. One could hide in them for a few days, living off berries, as Dr. Gurvitch and Ettele did during the last days before the Russians arrived. But prolonged concealment in winter was impossible in such places. There remained the fabled forests in the east, surrounded by swamps and crawling with partisans fighting against the Germans. At great risk and with heavy losses, it was there that those of us who were organized headed, led by Haim Yellin.

Anyone whose escape meant moving from one place to another, or living somewhere with a borrowed identity, depended for salvation first of all on their external appearance, on how Aryan they could look. Failing this, they had no chance of surviving, and people with dark hair or the typical Jewish nose were doomed. Women began bleaching their hair with hydrogen peroxide to face the coming days. But my mother, with her long nose and curly dark hair—in spite of the gray shining through it more and more—nevertheless dared many times to venture morning and evening into the streets of the city, well wrapped to conceal her Jewish appearance.

Then there was the barrier of language. Ah, language—fluency in Lithuanian was a matter of life and death, in particular how well it was pronounced. The rolling "r" that most of our fellow Jews could not control could make the difference between life and extinction. In the end, escape from the ghetto was feasible for only a very few. Common folk, simple people without connections, money, and language, had no choice but to huddle together and wait for the end decreed for them, like sheep for the shearers. Mother, however, did not give up; she decided to look for a way out. As for herself, she relied on her membership in the underground resistance and its plan for gradual dispersal to the forests. Her primary concern was for us children. At that time, rumors were afoot about a new kind of Aktion that would target the old and the young exclusively. We began to hear stories about parents smuggling their children out and delivering them to Lithuanians. When Mother first heard of it, she said, "We'll never split up. We'll stay together, for good or ill." Secretly, she hoped she would be allowed to take her two children into the forest with her. In time, as she came to realize that the chances of doing this were slim, she still hoped that I, who was a ten and-a-half-year-old, could stay with her. Accordingly, she decided to start looking for a safe place for my little sister.

At first the idea seemed absurd and completely unrealistic. Few Lithuanians would agree to house a Jewish child. There seemed, on the face of it, a better chance in delivering children to a priest or a monastery—the clergy were generally considered to be more compassionate, at least as long as the children could be baptized. Of what importance was baptism, in light of the other likely alternative? Nevertheless, some parents were put off by the idea that their child would grow up in all respects a Catholic. When the time for my own escape came, I, too, found it hard to imagine participating in their rites, taking the communion wafer under my tongue, praying and making the sign of the cross like the acolytes who had passed mutely by our house before the war.

Stories were passed around about complex operations to smuggle children out, mostly babies, sedated in a bundle or knapsack. First it was the children of a high official in the ghetto, or the son of previously wealthy people who was entrusted to a former nanny in return for a large sum of money, precious stones, and promises of goods, most of it paid here, the rest across the ocean in the days to come.

Such is the way of the world. Often when I hear stories of miraculous rescues, my trained ear picks out, almost between the lines, such key sentences as, "Luckily, we had possessions in the village," "Mother managed to hide a few rings with precious stones in her clothing," and so on.

Mother had no connections, possessions, or money, but she didn't let it stop her. She stubbornly began inquiring among Lithuanian workers in the factory and acquaintances about the possibility of hiding children. It appeared easier to find shelter for a girl rather than for a circumcised Jewish boy; and the younger the child, the better the chances, since the child would arouse less attention, would adapt faster, and grow accustomed more easily to the ways and the foreign language of her new family. All of these reasons strengthened my mother's resolve to transfer my sister first.

Preparations

How does one deliver one's child to strangers under circumstances of extreme danger? How is it done? There are so many arrangements to make. Even if the people seem friendly and decent, will they be nice to your child, and can they keep a secret? Is their house sufficiently isolated? Do they have hostile neighbors or a policeman living next door? Do they have relatives in the country where your daughter can be safe when danger is near? How sagacious will they be in devising a credible cover story that will arouse no suspicion? How swiftly can they react if they need to hide your child in an emergency, and will they keep their presence of mind? Do they have enough composure to refrain from demanding that your daughter return at the first difficulty they encounter? Are they likely, perish the thought, to become fed up and deliver your daughter to the Germans? And are they, after all, merely cynical crooks, doing the work of the Gestapo?

Many were the details that Mother had to gather and check before she could make up her mind. She then had to consolidate all of this vital information. A Jewish mother, alone and frail, bending under the physical burden of work in the brigade, had to sum up and weigh all the factors and all the alternatives—none of which was certain—and arrive at the fateful decision: whether to trust the Lithuanians, to give up into their hands her own daughter, or to forego the entire enterprise, the daring deviation from the norm, to succumb to the temptation to "sit and do nothing" being forced upon her and leave her daughter where she was.

And she was alone with these uncertainties, without a helpmate, with no one to share the responsibility or the decision. Certainly she confided in me, her ten-year-old son, telling me quite a bit. I was her sounding board for some of her worries, or what she was ready to share with me. In the end, after many hesitations and grueling negotiations that included money and payment arrangements, Mother decided to deliver my sister to Martha's family.

Martha was one of the workers in the felt-boot factory. The opinion of her fellow workers about how decent and honest she was—most of them were also neighbors—was by no means unanimous. Furthermore, one of her or her husband's relatives was of German extraction. That she had no children was important, although this could be either an advantage or a hindrance. On the one hand, she might show special interest in raising the child entrusted to her care; on the other, she might be too strict with her or fail to show enough affection. The absence of other children in the house would prevent idle chatter in the street on the one hand; on the other hand, the sudden appearance of a little girl in such a family would draw the attention of neighbors. As far as money went, the family made a good impression, appearing to be neither overly demanding or greedy. They were satisfied with a modest sum up front and monthly payments that were not too high, most of which covered actual costs, including nutritious food for my sister. They stated repeatedly that they were not doing it for the money.

Their house was in a neighborhood of simple laborers on Green Hill, across the river from the ghetto. They, too, had reservations about taking my sister. It seems to me that there was even some difference of opinion between the couple, but in the end the demurring side gave in. I believe it was the husband who was initially against the plan.

There were three in the family—the couple and their elderly mother. To this day I am unsure which of them was German. Mother stayed with them once overnight to get to know them better. They seemed humane and sympathetic to her in spite of the German background, which at this point even seemed to give them a certain advantage in terms of security. Now the child had to be prepared, final details needed to be worked out, and a means of getting my sister out of the ghetto had to be found.

I have heard many stories about parents who, at great risk to themselves, succeeded in arranging a hiding place only to have their child either refuse to go or fail to hold up against homesickness in the new place and return. Mother had spent a good deal of time preparing my sister even before she knew what was going to happen. Mother explained the great danger facing children who stayed in the ghetto and the need to take any opportunity to escape; like my sister, I, too, would be leaving soon, and all of us would meet again before too long, as soon as possible. At this point in Mother's talk, I added my own assent, nodding in approval, and to this day I am troubled by the memory. In the meantime, Mother added, my sister had a nice place waiting for her with people who loved children, in a house with a yard where she could play all day without fear, where she would have plenty of good food to eat.

Mother gave my sister her solemn promise that as soon as the danger passed—as it was expected to do as soon as the Red Army arrived to free us all—she would immediately come to take her back home. My little sister understood. With full trust in Mother's promise, she accepted her fate. She was a wise old woman at the age of six years and four months, having spent a third of her life in the ghetto. We can only imagine how much longing, fear, and sorrow her little heart had to bear.

Perhaps that is why my friend Ruti, who was taken out of the ghetto at about the same age as my sister, does not remember a thing.

My Sister Leaves

Toward the end of December, on the shortest day of the year, my sister left the ghetto. How do I know the date? Because another event occurred that day that is recorded in the ghetto chronicles—the final day of evacuating Slobodka.

In the dark, cold evening, Mother and my sister went through the gate, hidden inside a brigade. Once outside the ghetto, they immediately broke rank, slipped into nearby alleys, and slowly and cautiously made their way over the bridge and along the other bank of the river to Martha's house.

Mother stayed with my sister in Martha's house for two nights and a day before parting with her, and I cannot remember her ever being so furiously angry at me as she was the night she returned, alone, to the ghetto. I remember trying very hard to keep my spirits up that evening. Of course she would be angry—she had just left her daughter in the hands of Lithuanians. In an act of defiance I got up and fled outside into the darkness, into the curfew and the cold, wishing I would be caught and arrested. And just then the sirens sounded, the few lights around were extinguished, and I found myself in pitch-darkness—an air raid was approaching our city. I could hear the soft buzz of airplanes through the heavy winter clouds. Confused searchlight beams started up like a pack of hunting hounds from different parts of the horizon, converging on a certain spot in the heavens. It was terrifying. Until that evening, I had almost never seen an air raid developing, since we were usually ordered to go inside under such circumstances. I will stay out this time, I thought to myself, I won't go in, and let a Russian bomb fall on my head, then Mother will be sorry.

Two days before this, at four o'clock in the afternoon, the other kids and I were still gleefully looking for gold from house to house, flat to flat, in the area that would be turned over the next day to the Germans. An entire quarter lay free for the taking, and there wasn't a door behind which all the treasures of Ophir were not waiting for us to root through and claim. Even though people had completed the evacuation several days before, from our point of view the houses were still packed with all manner of goods. I had promised Mother I would return home on time. It was four already, and I knew it was getting late, but it was hard for me to recover from the seductive giddiness that had seized me since morning.

When I finally returned to my senses, as from a deep dream, I realized I could no longer make it home in time. Instead, I ran straight to the gate, hoping to meet my mother and sister on their way there, or at least meet them before the brigade left for work. But I was too late—the space around the gate was empty.

My little sister. I had tried to teach her things—reading, arithmetic, a little geography. She could already identify the dog of Scandinavia, its bone, Denmark, and its peninsular tail, Kola. Sometimes when I tested her and she couldn't remember one area or another, she would point sweetly and slyly to the Kola Peninsula, just to placate her demanding older brother.

Several days before my sister left the ghetto, she developed a small sore near her upper lip. I believe now that it was herpes, caused by deep stress. A yellowish scab peeked out from under the olive-colored woolen hat that Mother had knit for her; no doubt she wore it on her head on the day she left. And I thought to myself, I hope the Lithuanians don't change their minds because of the sore. "Why isn't he here? Why didn't he come to say good-bye?" she cried—so Mother scolded me when she returned.

And I came too late. Dear little sister, I cannot pardon myself for not coming on time to part with you; I cannot forgive myself for being the one of us two who remains alive. I would crawl on my knees like a pilgrim, I would go to the end of the Kola Peninsula for solace and forgiveness.

I ruined all the preparations of that day, the last few hours that we three could have spent together. What she wore on her way; which toys she took with her; the words my mother used to soothe and encourage her, and the replies my sister gave. Without a parting hug or a kiss from me she went through the gate. How she felt the rest of that day and in the days to come; how well the yellow scab on her upper lip healed—I go wild when I think about these things.

Broken and grieving, Mother returned to the ghetto. Upon her return, she encountered a new and painful reality—in her absence, they had moved another family into our tiny room, a family with a baby who occupied precisely the corner that had belonged to my sister only two days before. For this, too, Mother blamed me—why couldn't I have put them off at least until she had returned from the city? The strong odor of kerosene—for killing lice—and urine filled the room. We were crowded to the point of suffocation, and I hated the new roommates who had been forced upon us from the moment they first came. They were a young couple, congenial and accommodating by nature, but they came at a bad time for us. They took up the inner half of the room and spent all their care on their baby, Motele. From then on Mother and I shared a single bed next to the north window.

In her bitterness, Mother made no effort to remove the tension that had grown between us during the days since she returned. And I, like a stubborn calf, refused to talk to Mother for several days.

From this point onward, the news at home focused on what Mother heard from work about my little sister and her Lithuanian family. In spite of false starts and difficulties, it appeared that things were beginning to go smoothly. My sister cried a lot for the first few days, refusing to be consoled. She yielded slowly, however, and her ties to the Lithuanians improved. She began saying words in Lithuanian and trusting the grandmother in the family. But even so, we heard during the days to come of occasional outbursts of anger, of sudden fits of crying, and of capricious stubbornness. Mother could only pray that Martha and her mother would be tolerant and wise enough to understand the distress of a little girl cut off from her home, and not rush to regret their actions.

For seven whole months my sister stayed in Martha's house, eating at their table, drinking from their cup, and being their daughter.

My sister was taken out of the ghetto on December 22; on December 26, members of the corpse-burning squad of the Ninth Fort, availing themselves of the Germans' laxity on Christmas, made a daring break. Their escape, a brilliant operation, meticulously planned, prepared painstakingly over a very long period, took them through locked iron gates, forgotten dungeons, and cavities in the depths of the ancient fortress until at last they were outside. A few of them succeeded in returning to the ghetto (where could they escape to and hide in such a short time?), but it was impossible to hide them anywhere near humans, in part because of the indelible stench of rotting corpses that stuck to them.

A NEW YEAR

It was the beginning of 1944, reminding me of the number 44 of our house on Vigrių Street.

Depending on the circumstances, Mother tried to spend one night a week with my sister. This is how she did it: at the end of her work shift in the factory, she would slip into the Lithuanian locker room, change her clothing, and leave at dark through their exit into the street. After about half an hour's walk uphill, I imagine, she would reach Martha's house and cautiously slip inside, taking care not to be seen by anyone in the nearby houses. In the morning she would either return to the factory the way she had come, or she would go down by the river, which was not far from Martha's house, and blend in with the brigade as it came up the bank, carefully donning the yellow patch as she did so. And so it was each time. It was an act of real daring to cross the city each way, not to mention the risk she took of being cut off from her main base, the ghetto. Anything might happen during her absence, and the brigade might change its route on any given morning or be canceled entirely. I would rather not think about what my fate might have been had anything happened to Mother while she was in the city. The underground conspiracy was also at great risk. If, God forbid, she were trapped there, not only would two or three of us be lost, but many of the underground's secrets and the fate of its leaders would be jeopardized. It was only through my mother's courage, however, that my sister had a chance of living.

It relieved Mother greatly that she was able to meet Martha nearly every day—or at least to see her, even from a distance—at the factory; few indeed were the parents who had given up their children and could enjoy such a privilege. Such contact was certainly also marked by pain, like the pain of a mother who continues to meet the people who have adopted her baby.

I lived in the city for a year and a half after the war, and never once did I try to find the factory where my mother worked or reconstruct the path she took to walk to Martha's house, let alone go up to the house—any more than I thought of visiting the Ninth Fort.

During her nighttime visits Mother did her best to smooth ruffled feathers, to put people in good spirits, and to radiate optimism—she, from the ghetto. On the whole, she managed throughout the entire period to maintain a relatively good and trusting relationship with the Lithuanians. At a certain point they started hinting to her—perhaps she understood it on her own—that she ought to visit less frequently to help her daughter adapt. She may even have taken the initiative to appear less, at no small emotional cost to herself. Martha sometimes complained that following Mother's visits my sister was more "difficult." It was certainly to the advantage of both sides to reduce the risk incurred by frequent meetings. So during the next few months, Mother's outings were less frequent. I do not know when her last visit to my sister took place; when summer came, in June 1944, it seems to me, about half a year after my sister went to live with them, Martha informed Mother that with the war front drawing ever nearer, or perhaps because summer resorts were opening, they were leaving with my sister for their family in the country—and no one ever saw them again.

Friends

Who were Mother's friends at the time? On whom did she rely when the burden on her own shoulders was so heavy? I occasionally amused myself with adolescent suppositions about the people Mother might be seeing whenever she was out of the house. I knew that on Sunday evenings she would be at Dr. Golach's. I cast a certain suspicion on the polite and generous merchant who used to visit us on Sundays. And another of my candidates for her romantic relations was Eliezer, the author, one of the regular visitors at our house.

Eliezer and his wife, Zipporah, were our loyal friends. Zipporah had black hair gathered a long braid and brown eyes, and she was beautiful. Father does not know how large a place they had in our lives during those years. My father met Eliezer's elderly father in Dachau, but Eliezer and Zipporah did not survive.

During the last winter in the ghetto, people of letters were concerned not only with their personal survival but also with what would become of the fruits of their spirit. One day Mother returned from a conversation with Eliezer and declared that she had decided to bury our manuscripts and family documents in the ground. This was no simple matter—after a day of hard labor, or during already full weekends, in addition to all the disturbances in the world and growing fatigue, to burrow through the large amount of paper that my parents had dragged with them from place to place and decide what to keep and what to discard was a huge task. Mother took this on with the discerning practicality of a person writing her will: she chose her diplomas from the Vilkomir Middle School and her nurse's training at OZE, and Father's diploma from the Teachers Seminary in Vilna and the University of Kovno, together with a photograph of the graduating class. In addition, she took Father's personal diaries, his writings, and her poems. All these she gathered, wrapped, and placed in the tin tub meant for boiling laundry. She also placed there, as I have already told, my album of stamps and seals.

Now we needed to decide where to bury the treasure. We considered hiding it in the double wall of the room, in the attic, or in the basement. But Mother's inclination was to bury it in the ground, as far as possible from the house.

Did she anticipate burning or destruction? There was always the possibility that possession of the house would return to the Lithuanians, who would doubtless throw away anything they thought had no value. Burial in an open field was also problematic. It would be difficult to dig there undetected, and there would always be the question of locating the spot after the passage of time. So we decided to dig a hole in a hiding place. We ruled out the cellar in our house for some reason; perhaps its floor was tiled or too hard, or Mother was put off by the piles of junk down there, which would have had to have been moved. Furthermore, it was important not to disturb the natural look of the pile that served as our permanent hiding place. So the lot for the tub's burial spot fell to the floor of the storage shed that stood in our yard.

After a few evenings of digging, taking care to scatter the dirt on the edges of remote vacant lots, Mother and I gradually dug a hole deep enough to hold the washtub. Before covering it with a layer of dirt over the top, Mother went inside the house, brought out a small plank that she had prepared, and, using a chemist's pencil (which cannot be erased, and which turns purple when moistened), wrote down a few lines. I can still see her writing something like the following lines:

> Here are the family manuscripts and papers
> of the poet Leah Greenstein and her husband,
> the author Israel Kaplan, who were incarcerated in
> the Kovno Ghetto with their children,
> Sholik and Yehudith, from 1941 to 1944.

She may have added other lines, and she probably wrote the same message in Russian.

Mother placed the board on top of the buried papers, and then we put the tin lid on. Above that we placed another board or flagstone, filled the top of the hole with dirt and tamped it down, and smoothed the surface so as to leave no trace.

Winter's End

We were a diminishing population in an ever-tightening noose. The chance that the next blow would not fall directly upon us became smaller every time one fell. Many who saw no means of escaping began preparing hiding places for themselves near and beneath their houses. These hiding places were called *malinas* (forest berries), perhaps because of the way wild berry seeds are hidden within the fruit or their capacity for camouflage among the foliage in the forest. In every second house they began digging burrows, concealing doorways, blocking hidden passages. Some excavated passages from their houses into other structures in the yard. If anyone spoke of them, it was to say, in secrecy and without adding unnecessary details, "They are making a *malina*," and there the matter dropped.

The young couple in our room did not stay with us long. No sooner had they moved in than they began lengthy negotiations with a peasant in a distant village, a friend of their father's, about hiding their baby, Motele. The farmer was willing to take the child, but the baby's parents, lacking the strength to part with him, kept delaying the separation. Their conversations on the subject and their tears and sighs at night filled our tiny room and sapped the rest of our strength. The peasant came to the city every few weeks, and each time they had to make arrangements for the baby's removal later, during the next visit. Twice or thrice the parents regretted their decision at the last minute, after the man had already brought his wagon with a cradle hidden inside, close to the fence. Motele was finally taken out of the ghetto, wailing and heartbroken. His parents abandoned our room shortly thereafter. Without their baby, perhaps it was easier for them to find a more convenient place for the two of them, or perhaps it was simply too hard for them to go on living in a room where their baby's cradle had so lately stood.

When did the plan for my leaving the ghetto begin to take shape? When Mother came to realize that there was probably no chance of my joining those leaving for the forests. At the same time, the inquiries she had made about finding concealment for my sister had left her with several strings to pull for me. Mother didn't rush to make arrangements, however, because among other things, those who were willing to take me demanded a lot of money. And since it was relatively quiet in the ghetto, Mother continued to pursue other alternatives. Her assumption was that if the situation worsened, there would be signs that they were about to evacuate the ghetto, which people began to suspect more and more as the front once again threatened to reach us. When that happened, she would take the necessary steps to have me smuggled out. It was odd to imagine myself leaving here, all alone among Lithuanians. There were so many questions, so many qualms and dangers, that it was easier for Mother and me to leave the issue of escape from the ghetto in the preliminary stage only.

And I have said nothing yet of Mina and her nanny.

Mina was a girl my age, pale, delicate, quiet. She was usually called Mineleh. When I came to know her better, I discerned a seriousness in her thought, a clear-sighted sorrow, that belied her age. Her father had been a teacher, a colleague of my father; her mother was chronically ailing. To help look after the daughter, they had hired, even before the war, a young girl from a small village to live with them in their home. Together they had entered the ghetto, living in a room in the old Slobodka quarter, in an old house made of unplaned wood with a moss roof, like all the houses in the shtetl.

There was a great deal of loyalty among my father's friends. Hadn't it been his fellow teachers who came to help us on that chaotic day we were evacuated? For as long as Father was with us, he kept up his visits to this family; sometimes I would go along. Both fathers were taken to Riga, and both families suffered the loss. Mother continued to pay them calls as much as she could. I never saw Mina's mother when she wasn't in bed. Quiet, weak, but with a welcoming face, her long hair gathered like a pretty frame that became progressively darker around her fine, pale face, she was embarrassed by our visits each time anew. Ever grateful, she apologized repeatedly for being unable to return the kindness of our steadfast interest in her and her daughter. One day I learned she had died. Mineleh stayed on alone with the nanny, who never abandoned her. When the residents of their quarter were ordered to clear out of their houses, Mother saw to it that the pantry adjoining the kitchen in our house was partitioned in two. The others in our house weren't keen on the idea, but they gave in; after all, Mother argued, the Komität was bound to crowd someone in with us anyway.

From then on, from the beginning of the last winter, Mineleh and her nanny lived beside us, their lives mixing with ours. Their presence probably made it easier for my mother to visit my sister. The nanny was a young girl, somewhat provincial, conservative in manner, full-bodied and bright-eyed, consciously pleased at the praise her devotion to her task brought her. What the two lived on I do not know, for the nanny was not on a work brigade; perhaps her health was bad. Instead, she worked at crafts or sewing.

The nanny's manners began changing rapidly after she moved to our neighborhood. She lost some of the restraint and inhibition that had characterized her behavior while Mina's mother was alive. She now threw herself into the river of life. Gold rings adorned her fingers, and unsuppressed laughter issued from her room. As it happened, a goldsmith had begun singling her out for special attention, and her countenance showed that she enjoyed not only the secret pleasures that were not entirely contained by the thin walls of her bedroom but also her newly gained status. As if by magic she changed from a backward girl into a woman who was always well dressed and radiant with alluring feminine charm. Wonderstruck, I would watch her lying about the house for days on end with fine silk stockings on her legs and fur-trimmed green slippers on her feet. Without a trace of embarrassment she would emerge for a moment from her chamber, dressed only in an open robe, asking for a match to light a fine cigarette, before shutting herself back in with the man who was adorning her with jewelry. The light smell of perfume, blending with the atmosphere of sin, filled my nostrils, turning the head of the eleven-year-old boy that I was.

Half a year later, when I went to see the ruins of our house, I was surprised to see another object—a green fur-trimmed slipper, on which I thought I glimpsed traces of flesh.

Thus ended, perhaps, the sparkling life force of Mineleh's nanny.

7

Spring

Sunday

It was an ordinary Sunday in spring between Purim and Passover. Many things awaited Mother's attention on the weekly day of rest. But Sunday was also the only day we could see one another a little, so I had taken to staying in our room rather than going outside with my friends.

The day began with our lying in bed awhile, talking. We had so much to tell one another—impressions of what was happening in the work brigades and outside the gates, conversations with Lithuanians, and chance remarks overheard from Germans. We were examining the crumbs of information that came our way from every angle, about the war front—so slow in coming—about what might await us in our ghetto in light of fragmentary news from other ghettos, always in the complete absence of any reliable measure to determine exactly what was happening around us. Locked railroad cars had been seen standing on a side rail; black-lapeled officers had been seen surrounding the fence as though they were planning something; a high official had let slip a remark that swept through us like fire through a dry field. How were we to deal with these waves of information—and to remain sane and not abandon hope? On this particular morning, Mother was filling in the details of her last visit to my little sister and the results of her latest inquiries about a possible hiding place for me.

But there was no point in stalling; it was time to get up. There was cooking to be done for the coming week, as well as laundry, sewing, and attending to many other matters.

It was a pleasant day that Sunday. Mother finished her housework early, put off going out until later, and sat down with me for the only meal in the week that we ate together. At that hour, my sister was probably coming home from church with her Lithuanian family. Mother was at ease that day, although you could never be sure you really understood the meaning of her wise and silent looks. We were talking away about this and that, and had come around to a subject she was very fond of—opera. Mother must have been in an exceptionally good mood, perhaps because her migraine wasn't bothering her that day. She may also, after four months, have begun learning how to deal better with the pain of having turned her daughter over to strangers. At any rate, she began humming parts of her favorite arias, just as she used to do a long time ago—perhaps the aria from *La Traviata,* or from Halevi's *The Jewess,* or the one from *Carmen,* which we had seen during the last year before the war.

Mother had wanted to be a singer. That same Sunday she told me—for the first time, which is why I remember it—that she had taken voice lessons, a field of study that I hadn't known existed. Not content merely to know that there was such a thing, I begged Mother to show me what kind of exercises she did with her voice. So she sang several scales for me—the door of the room was closed—some rising, some falling, the way singers do when they are warming up, and I even pitched in, mimicking her and doing my best to follow.

At a certain point I had to go to the bathroom. I opened the door to go out, and there in the adjoining kitchen were our neighbors, Rayah's parents, just finishing their meal. On their faces were looks of wonder, ridicule, and amusement all mixed together—the idea of letting oneself go in the middle of the day like that, and in the ghetto, too!

Later that day, Mother finished her errands and attended the meetings about which it was best to keep quiet. When we met again after the curfew had locked everyone in their houses, she was still relaxed. She told me the latest news she had picked up from her underground cell, about the preparations for a large exodus to the forest in the near future. We went to bed early that night, with our clothes laid out, as usual, for quick dressing. In the light of the oil wick I watched from the shadows the fatigued body of my mother as she arranged her clothing for the next day. Her extreme thinness was an advantage whenever she needed to wrap up in a sheet, a tablecloth, or a fine suit beneath her tattered clothes. She rearranged her smuggling corsets, which she had made herself. They were made of white linen, and their deep narrow pockets could hold flour, sugar, butter, and even eggs, one beside another. She wore this corset above her undergarments, which were those, I noticed with a certain sadness, of a man. Perhaps they had been my father's.

It wasn't late yet, and Mother took something to read in bed; the two of us were alone in our little room. It may have been Gogol, an author she liked. She would read me his stories, translating freely from Russian. She especially loved reading the story of the lonely clerk who had dreamed all his life of owning a new coat—"The Overcoat." Or perhaps our imaginations roamed that evening to more poetic vistas. At my request, she may have recited, with pathos and poetic diction, the measured verses of Goethe's "Lord of the Forest" ("Erl König"), one of her favorites:

Wer reitet so spät durch Nacht und Wind?
Das is der Vater mit seinem Kind.

Who rides so late through the night wind wild?
That is the father with his child.

My heart would race each time I heard the repeated attempts of the Lord of the Forest to entice the fever-ridden child from his father's bosom. The father cannot comprehend his child's cries of distress, and when he reins in his galloping horse at the doctor's house in the village, he holds the boy's dead body in his arms. And perhaps the words "wer . . . so spät" raised echoes within me of another kind, the memory of a father's rebuke as he scolds his wayward child, evoking latent feelings of guilt. Shuddering, I snuggled close to my mother's side.

German words. How entwined is the language with my sense of self, in spite of myself, how it grips a part of me even today. In this language I first heard Mother say the words of the "Lord of the Forest" and the words of "Oh Tannenbaum"— the same language that now directed at us a salvo of Achtung! Los! and Halt!

The wind wailed outside. The last gasp of winter struggled against the approaching spring. Our eyes were nearly shut in sleep. It was a blessed evening, the end of a long day and a good one, a day of closeness. Holding one another, we fell asleep. But even as we slept, our ears remained alert, ready to receive and sift through the sounds of the wind to hear other sounds, too, sounds of threat or danger.

The night was short this time. By dawn, perhaps even before then, a new era had begun.

MONDAY

It was still dark outside, and we heard the sound of a motor. For many nights I had been lying in wait for an unusual sound and now it had come.

Before I could even wonder what it meant, loudspeakers blared that everyone in the ghetto should remain in their houses. From this moment, we did everything automatically, although our hearts were pounding and our hands shook. In a tremendous hurry, we threw on our clothes, adding extra layers just in case—Mother may have managed to grab a few items of food—and we bolted for the shelter.

Ever since the Little Aktion, we had practiced going down to the cellar, although I always felt there was something artificial about these drills that Mother insisted upon, as if they were a game of hide-and-seek; I found it hard to imagine that something would ever really happen to us. Now we rolled in among the different pieces of junk, the pots and the rags, as deep as we could, careful not to move anything more than necessary, so as to leave everything strewn about just as it was. Mother covered herself up with an old mattress, while I crawled under a big washtub beside her. We heard motors running and soldiers marching outside. We held our breath—ready, listening, waiting.

The cellar had two openings: the main doorway, descending steeply from beside the house's stairwell, which we did our best to leave as neglected as we had found it, its door partly open and stuck deep in the dirt slope, and a small window near the ceiling, facing Grinius Street at ground level.

The dim light that came through the window was no help in distinguishing night from day. I shut my eyes so tight it hurt. The day became a succession of sounds only, sounds sweeping over me in waves. I tried to make my body take up the least possible space, at the same time expanding into a gigantic auricle, a listening device that filled the entire space of the cellar, wound around its openings and nearly spilled outside.

Before long we heard footsteps approaching. It was frightening to hear them come so close. Singly, in pairs, in threes, they stepped together, firmly, sure of their goal. At first they went past our house, as if hurrying elsewhere. The experience reminded me of being at the dentist's, thinking maybe that's it, it won't hurt anymore today; but they returned. Now we heard them in our yard, then on the stairs, ascending into the house.

The first wave of steps ended after a quick pass through all the rooms; the ones who came after turned over beds, moved furniture, rummaged through closets. When they were directly overhead, I curled up as tightly as possible, trying not to breathe. A wooden floor is so very thin; might it not also be seen through? Now I was no longer only a great ear but also a great heart whose pulses echoed like the bells in the basilica beside our old home. How was I to keep its beating from betraying me?

The searchers left just as they had come, and we had not yet divined their intentions. A tense silence fell over us, through which we heard cries and shouts from a distance. They were not only searching for people but taking them away as well. By lists, or all of them? Suddenly a bloodcurdling cry broke through the window, like a close explosion—Moyshele! We heard short breaths, as if someone were struggling, and grunts of resistance; with furious curses and abuse the shrieking voice was silenced, until all that remained was a thin unending wail like that of a mortally wounded animal, and we knew—they were taking the children! What had happened in other ghettos was now happening to us.

Again and again the thud of boots returned, combing our flat, passing from room to room, overturning and moving, never stopping, as if they had come with lists and refused to give up. Each time we turned once again to stone—if only they don't come down to the cellar, if only they stop searching the flat, if only they would go.

Then we heard footsteps in the yard, suddenly making a sharp turn, heading straight for the door of the cellar.

Two voices. They tried pushing through the narrow opening between the door stuck in the dirt and the door jamb. At first they did not succeed.

Wer Reitet So Spät

Wer Reitet So Spät

Wer Reitet So Spät

Wer Reitet So Spät

I do not breathe. My heart does not beat. All my strength is focused on curling up, shrinking in size, being smaller than an unborn baby, tinier than the head of a pin. The door is shoved with force, and gives. They grope their way inside. I am a stone. My eyes are shut so tightly I doubt they will ever open again. I try to vanish, to vaporize, to become nothing. And suddenly, something falls on them or in front of them, blocking their way. They apparently have no flashlight. One of them curses and says out loud, "Wie am Negerarsch" ("It's darker here than in a nigger's ass").

They turn around. Their footsteps climb the slope, leave the house, and fade away.

Wer reitet so spät durch Nacht und Wind?
Ein Negerarsch!
Ein Negerarsch!

It took a long time for our breath to return, for our hearts to start beating again.

Mother broke the shock of silence first, explaining to me in a whisper that what they were saying, those vulgar words, meant life for me at the moment. Immediately, she decided to act. If she had been the rider in the forest, no doubt the fate of the child in the fable would have been different. Now that it was clear to her that this was an Aktion directed against children, she would leave our hiding place and go up. An empty flat would raise suspicion and invite trouble. If more searchers came, Mother could use her good German and try to divert them.

I was afraid to remain alone and feared losing her, as well, but something had to be tried. Cautiously, Mother extracted herself from her hiding place and left the cellar, and I spent the rest of the day there alone, huddled up as before, and fear lay beside me as before. Yet I had a glimmer of hope—Mother was guarding me. Further waves of searchers came and went, never letting up. Through the floorboards I heard my mother's seemingly calm voice explain politely and directly, "No, there are no children in this house. The other people preferred to join their relatives in the next house over."

All around, the hellish Aktion continued. Wave after wave, punctuated by short silences, would break anew, sending through the window the sound of energetic marching, heart-rending screams, vigorous cursing in German or Ukrainian, and the broken cries of mothers as their children were wrenched from their bosoms. In a strange and inexplicable way, because of the window at street level, I felt like I was in the midst of the whirlpool outside. Again and again I heard the groans of their futile struggle, cries that were suddenly cut off, frighteningly, for no clear reason. These voices outside, together with unending anxiety, remain in my memory as the essence of that day of terror.

All the doors and windows were open to avoid suspicion. Although I could only listen, Mother could peer out from deep within the flat to see what was happening. What did she see? Where did she get the strength to watch? Did she stand or sit? She never told me, nor did we ever again have much chance to talk about it. All day, she never came to visit me even once. I believe that one time only did she call to me from a distance, perhaps from the yard, to give me a word of encouragement.

And during all that time I hoped and prayed that the next wave would not reach me, that the day would end, that they would stop looking here; yet this day was especially long, refusing to come to an end.

However, they never came down to the cellar again. A few days later, when it became possible to look, I found a chalk mark on the doorjamb. And so the means of my deliverance that day had been a chalk mark on the door and the angels of death who had not had a flashlight.

Yes, I had prayed that day. I made the prayers up myself, using a special pattern, praying them in a specific order that I did my best to repeat conscientiously. I had begun saying these prayers before this, perhaps during my sister's illness; they reached their highest pitch later, in a far-off village. I murmured them faithfully and obsessively, and they gave me a certain measure of comfort.

Evening came at last; night arrived. A heavy silence descended everywhere. At nightfall the Germans seemed to disappear, and people began carefully to leave their holes. Like bound captives groping to feel their limbs, everyone began asking around, finding out what had happened, who had been taken.

The calamity was horrible, inconceivable. Names began circulating from all sides—hundreds and hundreds of ghetto children and old persons had been removed, as many as they could lay hands on. Children were torn from their mothers' arms, clawing and wailing. The Germans had not refrained from using brute force and had availed themselves of whips and dogs; no one escaped their clutches.

How fortunate we were—no one in our household was harmed. Mina and her nanny hid in a small chamber with a camouflaged door; Rayah's parents stayed in the Gafanovitches' dirt cellar in the yard; one child in the other wing of the house lay all day under some blankets piled with seeming carelessness on a bed without being seen. By contrast, the children from the house next door were all taken, including the toddler Yankele. More than a year later, their father, Leizer—I was living with him then—was still mourning, moaning at night, refusing to be comforted. And what happened to my various friends, those my age? That night, I had no way of knowing.

And as many as the children taken, so were the number of stories about how they had been taken and their struggles, their efforts to escape, to beg, to plead for life—all in vain. The search of the houses had been thorough and complete—they were ransacked remorselessly. And even though most efforts to hide had been unsuccessful, it was hard to understand why some had waited in their houses, as if paralyzed by shock, not even attempting to hide, while their children were collected like abandoned eggs. The lesson of my mother's deeds is with me always—take action, do not wait around, and do not just ape the behavior of the crowd.

What was next? What would happen tomorrow? Were the calamities over, or would they continue? It was good that my little sister was no longer in the ghetto. She still had a chance of surviving. It was said that they transported the children in buses with windows shut with wire and painted white. Some remembered seeing vehicles like these several days before, parked in the outskirts of the city. Someone else knew enough to add that the children were transferred to a train waiting for them on a side track. Where did the train go?

To this day when I see a long line of empty buses along a street, my heart sinks.

Meanwhile, we had to be ready for anything, even at night. Accordingly, Mina and I were fitted out with a folding camp bed that had been widened by laying a door atop it. This improvised bed was set next to the entrance to the little room, whose camouflaged door had passed the test that day. Were something to happen during the night, we could slip quickly into the room. Everyone in the household looked for ways to help us—adding a blanket, straightening the sheets. I could feel the care and concern focused on us from all around. Fully clothed and shod, ready to jump up at any moment, we lay down together to sleep. But in the end, not only did I find it difficult to fall asleep beside Mineleh, but I also permitted myself, even in this dire time, to imagine myself—I even tried it, a little—hugging Mina in her sleep. For some time I had been looking for ways to draw her attention to my feelings, without daring; what is more, I hoped she would show signs of returning my affection in some way. Surrealistic madness which now, when I recall it even after all these years, embarrasses me greatly.

Even after these days had ended and half a year had gone by, and I was wandering about like a stray dog in the liberated city—even then, my fantasies focused in part on the possibility that Mineleh had, like me, survived. I imagined the excitement of meeting one another again, the two of us all alone but for one another; our hands would clasp and never let go; we would remain together for the rest of our lives, like brother and sister, like a pair of lovers, forever.

Tuesday

Morning came, and there was no need to wake us. At the crack of dawn we heard the sound of a motor and immediately we leapt into our hiding places. Mother hesitated—should we go back to the cellar, which was so easy to enter and search, or should we hide in the little room that had proved itself only yesterday. Mina and her nanny, who had been in the little room yesterday, went to the Gafanovitches' shelter in the yard, while Rayah's parents, who had been in that shelter yesterday, went somewhere else. There wasn't much time to make up our minds, and in an instant, Mother decided upon the little room and even joined me there. Why did she come in with me, when it was clear that this time we would have to stay there all day at least, with no chance of leaving in the middle as she had the day before? Apparently she did not want to leave me alone again for so many hours. Moreover, Rayah, who spoke German, decided this time that she would stay in the flat and be the one to meet the Germans. It strikes me that Mother may have preferred to stay with me as a means of avoiding the difficult hours that awaited her had she stayed outside the hiding place. Did she perhaps feel an instinctive need to be with me, like a bird with its chick in the hour of danger, in case, God forbid, these might be our last hours together? I had never dared raise these thoughts until I wrote these words.

I rushed into the little room. We probably took some food with us, too, bread and jam to last through the day. They shoved the large, four-door cupboard over the opening to hide it, and we were alone. The room was very small—it was Rayah's, apparently—and had a good chance of being overlooked, especially since it stood next to the rooms in the other wing of the building, so that its window, which we were careful to keep open into the street, could easily be mistaken as belonging to the other entrance. Inside the room, to the left of the door, was a bed; beside it stood a two-doored armoire with its back toward the outer wall of the house, next to the window facing the street. We spent most of the day there, each of us crammed and folded in one half of the armoire, whose doors, like the window, were wide open—or perhaps the armoire had no doors, only curtains. I spent a whole long day in or beside it, yet I remember almost nothing about it.

If I try to compare the feelings of dread of those two days, the second day was harder. On the first day, the terror was instinctive and things happened almost before we realized what was going on. On the second day we went into hiding much better informed—and anxious. The Germans, too, knew more—most of the ghetto's children and old folk had fallen into their hands the first day; as they started the second day, they had a good estimate of how many they were missing, and accordingly they returned with redoubled rigor to complete their mission. Once more they came through, this time more thoroughly and systematically, wave after wave, from house to house and room to room; with them were more Ukrainians, and some said some Latvians as well.

While we were still getting settled in the little room and there was no movement around us yet, I heard the noise of engines from far off. For the only time that day, I dared raise my head and peek out of the window. I saw a convoy of three or four military vehicles covered with tarpaulins, slowly proceeding down Varnių Street. With a stifled cry, perhaps my only one during those two days, almost fainting and choked by terror, I began burrowing further and further inward, down into the depths of the farthest corner under the bed, curling up into the darkest recess there.

To hide, to disappear. As at a summer resort during thunder and lightning storms; as once under my grandfather's bed when he, the rabbi, caught me one holiday wearing flashlights on the buttons of my best clothes, or after the errant Sabbath ride on a peasant's wagon in the village square. Just so I ran, breathlessly, some months later, between the lines of fire at the front in a field being sliced by bursts of gunfire; just so when escaping from Russian patrol dogs between mounds of snow in a thick forest. To escape, to get away, to survive.

Mother, from her place, tried to calm me a little, to boost my spirits, but it was to no avail. Much time passed before my body stopped shaking and I dared move a little from my hole in the corner, to crawl like a half-paralyzed animal out of the bed area that sheltered me, to hide in my half of the armoire on the side that was farthest from the window.

The window was open, and the noises in the street washed over us, much louder than the sounds that had penetrated to the depths of the cellar the day before. Waves of shouts, orders, speech, and screams sometimes made it seem as if the armoire was in the middle of the street and for some reason no one had seen it yet.

From time to time Mother had the courage to peep furtively through the window. I preferred to stay curled up and seated most of the time, with my eyes shut. Even so, at times we exchanged whispers or chewed on something. Then we heard them coming. Footsteps sounded in the different rooms, furniture creaked; there were sounds of beds being overturned, furniture being shaken. They were in our flat, searching it and getting closer to us. Through the partition of the wall I heard their voices as if we were trapped in a mine under an avalanche of rock, hearing the diggers approach us—although here it was a death squad making its way toward us.

To shrink down, to become smaller still; like a mouse, like a ladybird beetle. Striving to be an entity no larger than a point, a nullity. Only the pounding heart to tell, only the held breath to betray us. Again the eyes shut tightly, the teeth clatter as in a dead man's skull, the brain dry of all thought. Only to pray without ceasing, to beg of the supreme power of the universe that a miracle might happen, that the threat about to materialize any instant be thwarted before it overwhelms you like molten lava, like a whirlpool in the river.

At one point they turned to the cupboard that hid the opening to our little room. I heard them checking inside it, then trying to move it without success. Then came combing sounds from the space between the cupboard and the wall, scratching sounds. Though the sounds were weak, they reached me with unbearable loudness; the room seemed flooded with light as strong as that of the burning bush—it was unbearable. The point of a bayonet scratched lightly at the wooden door of our room—then the Germans turned and went away. At that moment I could define what stood between me and my destruction in precise units of measurement, the several millimeters of thickness in a door slat, within hearing of a single scratch.

The Germans were not stupid in their search. By that hour of the day they likely had grown tired. Their continual struggle with mothers and children fighting for their lives seemed to have dulled their sword-sharp alertness. It is not merely lip service to say that, thanks perhaps to those who were carried to their death, some of us survived.

Two of my friends, brothers who lived up Grinius Street, once invited me to go on a wonderful adventure in front of their house. They blindfolded me, stood me on a board, and slowly began lifting me up, gently swaying, while whispering hypnotically, saying that I was soaring through the sky, sailing among stars. I was overcome with dizziness; I begged them to put me back on the ground.

Now, so I was told, the boys had begged not to be loaded onto the truck as it stood in front of their house. But their pleas went unheeded; although they tried to resist and clung to the doorway, they were hoisted by force and taken away.

And as for me, it seems that even today I can hear the kind of wail that would have escaped my lips had I been caught. Sometimes it comes back and haunts me during nights filled with bad dreams.

I remember little of the rest of that day, even less than I remember of the day before—only the hazy traces of a very long day that wouldn't end. Because there were not many children left in the ghetto to trap in the first place, and because those who remained were well hidden, it took a long time for the Germans to conduct a meticulous search for them. For this reason, apparently, there were long, nerve-racking pauses between the waves of searches, pauses that became part of the looming terror of that day.

The few children who were hunted down that day, it is said, were not sent out on trains but were taken to somewhere nearby—perhaps to the Ninth Fort, and this was true of others captured during the coming days.

On one of those days, Mother told me of other moments of dread that she had during the second day of the Kinder Aktion, which she didn't mention earlier. At a certain moment she had looked out the open window and, to her surprise, her gaze met that of a German officer who happened to be going by the house. Losing her control for an instant, she sprang back in fright. Immediately afterward, she heard him turn into the path that circled our house and come inside. For a long while he poked through the flat without discovering either the meaning of Mother's frightened look or her whereabouts. It was extraordinarily lucky that he saw Rayah, which perhaps abated his suspicions. And Mother, who understood perfectly why he circled the house, kept the knowledge in her heart and said nothing to me at the time.

The day gave way at last to evening. With dusk, the sounds of activity died down and, as on the day before, we gradually began crawling out of our shelters, not believing it was over.

We were still stretching our limbs and exchanging our first words with one another when we suddenly heard a vehicle racing through the streets—they were coming back! Was it a sly trick designed to surprise those in hiding as they emerged? I was quickly sent, to my great relief, to Grandmother Gafanovitch's hiding place; I didn't want to go back to the little room. In a deep pit, I now discovered the riddle of our neighbors' shelter, a secret kept until now among the members of their family: a dry well in the backyard near the door of their house, its opening hidden by thick boards overlaid by bricks. On top of these they had added, as if carelessly, firewood and perhaps a heating range for doing laundry. We descended into the well by means of a long ladder; there was a stool at the bottom for the grandmother. Beside it, on a blanket, there was room for another child or two. Mina had stayed here all day, and now I joined them, too. The place was deep and sealed off, close and moist, like being under a warm quilt. Here it was almost impossible to hear what was going on outside, which was an enormous relief.

We were not alone—Mrs. Gafanovitch's sons did not forget her and would occasionally send her words of encouragement through the piles of junk. The look on the grandmother's apparently calm face—she never stopped knitting even for an instant, whether in the dark or by the light of a weak candle—was soothing and comforting, in direct contrast to the tremendous tension of being in the little room above ground all day. A calm came over me; I had felt nothing like it for two full days at least. How different those days would have been, I thought to myself, without sounds coming in from outside; I wished I could stay forever in this womb, breathing peace like this.

When we emerged, we discovered that the sudden return of the Germans was brought about by a tip that had led them straight to a nearby pharmacy. There, behind an apparently sealed wall, many children and adults had spent two days in a large shelter. Now, at precisely the last instant before their salvation, the destroyer descended upon them all, adults and children alike. One of them who tried to escape was shot on the spot.

WEDNESDAY

That night I slept at the Gafanovitches', near the well. At dawn we reentered the shelter—Mina, the grandmother, and I—and stayed there all day. Nothing special happened near us, but I know the Germans came back to the ghetto that day. After discovering the hidden shelter in the pharmacy the night before, they concentrated on searching certain locations, this time using trained bloodhounds. And so a string of hidden and well-camouflaged shelters that had stood up under the searches of the previous two days were uncovered on the third day of the Aktion. They took away the children and blew up the shelters. The dull sounds of explosions reached us even in the depths of the well.

And that was the end of the cleverly hidden *malinas,* most of which were discovered through tip-offs. There were wretched parents who gave away likely locations in return for the empty promise that their child would be returned to them. There was a story about a former Jewish policeman who pointed out certain houses, and another about a mother who covered her crying baby daughter's mouth when Germans were heard near the shelter's opening; when the danger had passed, the baby was no longer alive.

During the coming days, in the face of mounting rumors about the imminent destruction of the ghetto, many still preferred to prepare shelters. Even my mother, I was told, stayed for several days in Dr. Golach's *malina.* In the end, when the Germans came to destroy the ghetto in earnest, having learned from the children's Aktion about our *malinas,* they brought a special engineering platoon, accompanied by Special Police and SS forces from Vienna, Riga, and Hungary, to carry out the work of destroying the ghetto. They went from house to house, exploding and burning each one, sparing none. A municipal Lithuanian firefighters unit was also involved in the effort. So it seems that the Aktion against children—the Kinder Aktion—encoded and prefigured the manner of the ghetto's destruction.

The Coming Days

My memories about the rest of the days of that week are hazy.

The Aktion seemed to be finished on Wednesday. Above the ghetto and among the houses a great lament remained, frozen and unheard. People moved about in a mixture of hysteria and apathy, feeling shocked and beaten. How did parents handle the blow? How did loving children deal with the loss of their elderly parents? What did surviving family members do with the toys, the clothes? I am never able to think too long about this, let alone understand. People were paralyzed by pain and sorrow, and no one went to visit. Not a few insisted on believing that their children were still alive and had merely been moved to another camp—anything else was unthinkable. And the rapid advances of the Red Army, which took place precisely during this time, did not provide any encouragement.

Events had happened rapidly during the Kinder Aktion, but we learned about them gradually, or perhaps we were capable of digesting them only slowly. Thus, on Monday when the Aktion began, the Jewish police force was ordered to muster in their best uniforms for a joint air-raid drill with the German units "so as not to be a disgrace," they were told. They showed up, about 140 strong. After a rigorous inspection, they were marched, left-right left-right, into trucks that transported them straight to the Ninth Fort. Some of them were executed that very day, perhaps to prevent an uprising of the Jewish police like the one that had occurred during the Aktion against the Vilno Ghetto. The officers were investigated and tortured—they were required to disclose the location of hiding places, without being told of the Aktion taking place at the same time in our ghetto. Afterward, we heard of the bravery and revolt among those who were executed, together with acts of debasement and betrayal on the part of a few policemen. Ninety of the policemen remained alive and were returned to the ghetto a few days later. The same Monday, members of the Ältestenrat were also taken to the Ninth Fort. In this way, the Germans prevented any possible formation of organized resistance.

And Motele, the baby—the child of the young family that was placed in our room during the winter, whose parents decided after many hesitations to deliver him to the peasant friend of the family—had been returned to his parents; his mother had regretted the decision and wanted him back. He, too, was taken in the Aktion.

Once again, the ghetto was not as it was before. Without children, without the Ältestenrat, without the Jewish police force—which was abolished—the ghetto took on the well-known form of the concentration camps in Germany. The area of the ghetto was reduced yet again. The trap narrowed; the sand in the hourglass was running out.

Not much time remained for the ghetto to hurt and to mourn—only about a hundred and ten days more. The ghetto was torn down and its people were moved west. Another six to nine months of concentration camps and gradual death awaited them; only a small number would survive. Perhaps fate was being kind to the bereaved parents, who perished several months after the Kinder Aktion.

Years later, while I was writing my thesis on viniculture under the desert-like conditions of the Aravah, I came across an article in the semiannual proceedings of the American Horticultural Society. It was by a scientist named J. P. Kenworthy, who described the following experiment: on March 27 and 28, 1944, he went through a vineyard and nipped the buds of all the young grape shoots to measure the influence of this action on the level of minerals in the new leaves. I was struck by the curious fact that, ironically, on the very days of the Aktion, Dr. Kenworthy was eliminating young buds in the sun-filled Imperial Valley in California.

This is how things often are with me—every year I make horizontal and vertical grids on the calendar, stumbling at dates that remind me of certain events during those years. I never stop comparing and matching.

INTERMEDIATE EPILOGUE: A FOLLOW-UP

The Aktion against children did not, in fact, ever stop. As the days went by, either through planned forays or whenever a lone child was spotted, children were pounced upon and taken away. Never before had the Germans targeted members of a certain age group, except for the very old, saying: you must all die; none among you shall live. There was in the Aktion against children a kind of total, unequivocal decree denying Jewish children the right to exist.

Who were the children who perished, who were executed there? How much life force was cut down during those few days? Each deserved the right to live and raise a family. Even among the small number that survived one can count professors, engineers, scientists, educators, and even a president of the Supreme Court of Israel.

With the help of an expert in statistics and demography of Eastern European Jews, I once tried to measure the relative rate of survival among children in our ghetto. According to his estimates, there were 5,060 Jewish children under the age of fourteen in our city before the war.

> Of these, I estimated that about 150 survived.
> Therefore, about 4,910 perished.
> Thus, about 2.9 percent remained alive.
> About 3 in every 100.
> And I am one of those three.

INTERMEDIATE EPILOGUE: ARKE, MAIMKE, AND THE 131

For years I thought that Arke and Maimke were taken during the Kinder Aktion because all the children were collected at the same time even in the satellite work camps where they were staying. It was said that the Germans enticed the children with candy and, pretending to play a game, tied their hands and took them out of the camp that way. When their parents returned from their work, they found no one home. Recently I discovered that the two boys made it through that day unharmed. Arke was working with the adults; Maimke, the younger of the two, had stayed in the camp because he had a cold. He was saved by the man in charge, who was fond of him both because of his infectious mischief and because his son, the "Tsigayner," and Maimke were friends. Accordingly, he hid them together in the morning in a tool cabinet and they were saved.

From Ruchamah I first learned that my friends had survived the Kinder Aktion and that when the ghetto was wiped out, they were sent west with the men. Details of how this happened remain wrapped in mystery: when, after the selection, she and her two sons were left on the train platform in Stutthof, Prussia—I might have stood there, with my mother—they suddenly heard a sharp cry behind them, coming from the cars into which the men had been loaded. "Kaplaniukes!" someone unfamiliar shouted to them. "Come here quick!" Arke and Maimke, whose last name was Kaplan, got up, left their mother, and, at the very last moment, jumped on the train as it started its long journey. To this day Ruchamah wonders who the voice belonged to; she has no idea who it could have been. The cars were already closed, if not locked, and she did not see the man's face. Like the rest of the women from our ghetto, she was left in the concentration camp near Stutthof, where she was liberated with the last few survivors.

The men and the children of Kovno Ghetto were moved to Landsberg, to a satellite camp (Lager 1) of the Dachau camp network. Several weeks after they arrived there a selection took place, and the youngest children—131 of them—were sent to Auschwitz.

Ruchamah was fated to remain alive only because her children were separated from her; otherwise, during the next selection, she would have been sent with the other women and children to the other side.

Nor is this the end of the story. Once I drove my father to visit one of his elderly friends on a kibbutz in the west Negev. On the way, I told him what I had heard from Ruchamah about the fate of her children. Father smiled as if he were about to reveal a secret: it was he, it turned out, who had told Ruchamah what she knew. He had been in Dachau Satellite Lager 2, where he happened to meet the boys' uncle, who told him that the boys had been with him at first, and were later taken elsewhere. Since they were separated for deportation to Auschwitz, the fact was kept from him for several days; he was told the children were ill and had been taken to another camp.

"I can add something else," Father suddenly said, "something I haven't told anyone since I found out." In Auschwitz, he continued, they had taken the boys, as usual, to a rope stretched out at a certain height. Everyone who passed under it had his number taken down. Arke and Maimke took the initiative, organized a group of delegates to accost the man in charge of them, the Überkapo Albert, with a suggestion and a plea: they would work very hard, with all their might, even harder than the boys who were taller than they, if only he would cancel the expected decree and leave them here. The Kapo laughed good-naturedly, so the story goes—and even went so far as to clap one of them amiably on the shoulder—and answered to this effect: "Meine kinder, aber ein Gesetz ist ein Gesetz" ("I'm sorry my children, but a law is a law"). A few days later, the children were gone.

Ever since he had heard this, said my father, he had wanted to write about it. He had wanted to call his story "The Delegation," but hadn't felt up to writing it; perhaps he would still do so one day. I wryly thought that if a delegation had been appointed, Arke was certain to have been one of its members. As I said before, my friends were good at following regulations and rules. A kind of calm came over me, as if suddenly my affiliation had become clearer for me—I am in fact the 132nd child of this group.

I did not rest with this knowledge. Years later I found out that the twenty or so survivors of the group of 131 held a reunion every May 4, the day of their liberation. One time I went to their meeting. With obsessive solemnity they immediately sank, as during their previous meetings, into a repetitive, never-ending discussion about the reasons that they were not sent straight to the gas chambers but were allowed to live on for several months in the camp. They guessed that there had been mistakes in the Germans' schedule of execution or that thousands of Gypsies and Hungarian Jews were in line before them, but mainly they emphasized the impressive display they made upon entering Auschwitz. At the urging of one of the grown-ups among them, they arranged themselves for a march in neat rows, left-right, left-right; when they saw the Germans one of them cried out, "Mitzen ab!" (Hats off!) It is this, most agreed, that impressed the Germans so much that they decided to leave them in the camp for a while.

I began asking questions. In Auschwitz they underwent two selections, at the end of which only thirty-one remained. During the first selection (on the Jewish New Year), the Germans went through with a stick of a certain height, recording the numbers of any who were shorter than the stick (a few managed to survive this selection by inserting cloth and stones in their shoes). The main selection, which took place on Yom Kippur, of all days, was conducted by Mengele himself: they were all ordered to strip and stand naked in rows, their arms stretched out at their sides, so that Satan's eldest son could pass among them and identify which of them still had hairless genitals and armpits. These he ordered to leave the ranks and station themselves in front of the recording officer. All of them disappeared the next day.

As for the story of the "delegation" that Father tells, they hadn't heard of it. However, some of them remembered a nine-year-old boy who, at the end of the selection, ran about offering his ration of bread to anyone who would change places with him.

Danke, my friend from kindergarten, visited Auschwitz recently, and brought from the archives a detailed list of a "transport of children from the Kovno Ghetto, 1 Aug. 44" that had a note attached: "two killed on the way." There are 129 rows on the list. Each row contains the number tattooed on the arm, and sometimes the name of the child beside it, the name of his father, and his date of birth. And in that list—black on white—I found the names of my friends, Arke and Maimke. So that everything is correct, lawfully recorded. *Ein Gesetz ist ein Gesetz.*

8

Escape

On that morning I didn't want to leave at all. I really didn't want to go.

But I had to.

When Mother and I got dressed, it was still completely dark outside. We grabbed something to eat and out the door we went. This time we took the narrow lane between our house and the one parallel to it, along Grinius Street. Perhaps Mother thought this would draw less attention to us, or slightly shorten our route to the riverbank. It was from this path that, two weeks earlier, the German officer had entered our house.

We left quietly so as not to awaken others in the house and without having said good-bye to anybody the night before. I wore a long, black, man's coat, long riding pants (a *galifeh*), a large cap pulled down over my face, and a large muffler around my neck. This was my second attempt that week to join Mother's brigade. The time before, I was already standing in the lines when I was given a signal to leave immediately—the dangerous guard had appeared unexpectedly.

I was sleepy this time, somewhat groggy from interrupted sleep, turmoil, and tension, trailing along after Mother without too much joy. The possibility that today I would succeed in slipping out of the ghetto seemed remote to me—I did not believe it would happen.

A few days before, around sunset, and for the first time since the Kinder Aktion, I ventured a long way from the house. Camouflaged then as I was now, and with great care—German patrols continued to police the ghetto—I went to the gate facing the river at the end of Varniŭ Street and waited there for Mother and to watch her brigade coming home from work. By that time Mother had already made arrangements for me outside, and had spoken with a Gentile woman who, in return for a considerable weekly sum, was willing to hide me in her house. Now I had to be taken out as soon as possible. The route Mother's brigade took seemed made to order for this purpose—rowboats were anchored on the opposite bank, not far from the woman's house. While we were standing there talking, I heard a loud and bitter voice behind us; two women were sitting on a stone or a mound of earth. One of them was saying to her friend, in a grieving and plaintive voice that she made no effort to disguise, "My Chaimke is no longer alive. Why is that boy still here?" I clearly understood that I could not stay in the ghetto anymore.

On the morning that we left a gray dawn had already broken, and we were still in the narrow alley between the houses when a puppy came running after us. A puppy in the ghetto? Surprised, I stooped to pet it as we hurried along; it responded by wagging its tail. Keeping a pet had been officially outlawed ever since all the dogs and cats in the ghetto had been destroyed, but from time to time an animal like this would slip through the barbed-wire fence and immediately find a warm welcome with someone. I hadn't had a dog since Belka disappeared. My heart sank—did I have to leave today of all days? Had the puppy come straight from the other side of the fence? Or, what was more likely, did it belong to one of the children who had been missing for two weeks now, and was it still looking for his master? I wanted it very much. I suggested that Mother wait a moment so I could take the pup back and shut it in our room—that way, if I failed to get away this morning, at least a puppy would be waiting for me at home. I was a child, and a worse possibility than that I might be retracing my steps in a short while apparently never entered my mind.

As could be expected, Mother did not countenance my vagaries at the time. It is easy to imagine how heavy of heart she was that morning. I didn't give up, however. For the rest of our walk through the gate, I played with the amusing thought that if my escape fell through this morning, the pup might still be hanging around the house when I returned. It was apparently so important a matter to me that during the next few days, with all the upheavals and dangers, the question continued to preoccupy me—would I have found the puppy if I had gone back home that day?

We lined up in rows. I was in the middle of the inner row; Mother was beside me. We heard an order, and the lines moved forward. With officious noise, and with no interference from the guards standing to one side, at least as long as the German officer was absent, our people conducted their own rituals of giving orders and reporting. It was apparent that there was an understanding between the brigade workers and the guards, thanks to the steady bribes that came their way.

The body tense and alert, head bowed, empty of all thought. Without a word being said to them, people walked close on either side of me. A few steps more, without any further inspection, and we had already made it to the bank of the river. A few rowboats were waiting there, bobbing in the shallow water as at summer camp. They divided the passengers among the boats; Mother and I were in the first one. A few minutes later, and the boat was pushed out into the deep water.

Mist rose from the water; the boat began moving, pointing itself in a certain direction. One bank receded and fell away; the other came closer. Was a Lithuanian paddling the boat, or were our people helping? I didn't dare look.

Vistas opened up, views that were not of this world. The river seemed endlessly wide to me. I heard the thin splash of oars and people talking in whispers. I saw no Germans; perhaps they stayed on shore with the other half of the brigade. All was quiet; it was spring, and I had not seen the river up close like this for years. Is this how things had been, then, only a few minutes from the ghetto, for the last three years?

Softly spoken words in Hebrew caught my attention: "You have to remove his patch," a wife says to her husband, with reference to another child that was also being smuggled out in their own boat. I imitated them, and before long we were at the other bank. Many people stood bunched together there, as though waiting for the riverboat to take them back in the other direction. They were Lithuanians waiting for the brigade, ready to conduct hasty business with them until the other half of the brigade arrived.

As the bank drew closer, my anxiety grew. Mother soothed me—contrary to my fears, the presence of so many Lithuanians was a good sign. Mother's instructions were clear—stand up, get out of the boat, and go straight through the waiting crowd, looking neither right nor left. While people were getting into lines, more or less, I was to go forward without hesitating, go past those gathered there, cross the street, and turn into the path leading into the hills just across from us. There, after several minutes of slow walking, a blond woman would join me and tell me where to go.

The prow of the boat hit the shore. My heart pounded like a drum, and my eyes were dark veils. Moist gravel was under my feet. Seeing but unseen, I left the people, not looking behind me I went by and approached the street. No Germans to be seen, thank God. The road across looked empty, too. I started up the path, getting farther and farther away.

I walked on as if in a dream, going deeper into the gorge. Though I had no idea what the next moment would bring or where my steps were taking me, I was soon engulfed in the green slopes, and tall trees stood all around, holding crowns of deep purple; my eyes were unused to the sight. An immense joy began swelling in my breast—I had not seen such sights for years. The trees were so tall, so abundant was the greenery; my mother had not prepared me for this at all.

I kept going and no one came toward me or caught up with me from behind. I began to worry—had we considered this possibility? I had no address and no name. What was I supposed to do if no one met me? Should I retrace my steps and join the brigade as it trod to the factory? And what would I do there? I did not recall that we had ever discussed such a situation. In the meantime, a figure approached me. Her face revealed nothing, and I was filled with dread at my first encounter with a strange person. I averted my gaze and held my breath as I passed her when suddenly she said, in Lithuanian, "Keep going and turn into the second gate on your right; I'll catch up in a bit." Doing as I was told, I discovered a wooden gate covered with vines and a broken mailbox lying on its side. A steep path rose from the gate. When I was halfway up the slope, after a slow climb, the woman caught up with me and directed me behind a little house on the top of the hill.

Wagon loaded with books during its delivery to the Germans. Kovno Ghetto, Lithuania, February 1942. Photo: Zvi Kadushin. © Beth Hatefutsoth Photo Archive, Zvi Kadushin Collection.

View of smoke rising from the burning Kovno Ghetto. Lithuania, July 1944. Photo: Zvi Kadushin. © Beth Hatefutsoth Photo Archive, Zvi Kadushin Collection.

The ruins of the ghetto after liberation. Photo: Zvi Kadushin. © Beth Hatefutsoth Photo Archive, Zvi Kadushin Collection.

The author's first day of school.

Enjoying sledding in ghetto. Photo: Zvi Kadushin. © Beth Hatefutsoth Photo
Archive, Zvi Kadushin Collection.

The author near the "Central Committee for Liberated Jews" in Munich, March 1946.

The author, seated beside his father, departing for Palestine. Munich, April 1946.

Ona Pečkyte, Kaunas, ca. 1970.

Mother, Yehudith, and the author, 1940.

Vincas Daugela and Ona Viesnauskaite, near their house in the village of Liepynų, district of Marijampole, Lithuania, 1950.

The author, his father, and the *Unzer Veg* newspaper team, Munich, March 1946.

Magda Diener, Paris, 1960.

Nahum Diener, Paris, 1960.

קאָוונאָ

KAUNAS

In front of the memorial of Kovno, the Memorial Valley of Jewish communities, Yad Vashem Hill, 2000.

9

On Green Hill

J̲ULIJA G̲RINCEVIČIENE WAS AN ELDERLY WIDOW WHOSE ONLY SON HAD been jailed for theft. We didn't talk much about it for many days because she was ashamed of it. It occurs to me that her son is probably still alive. He might know the identity of the blond woman who led me to Julija's home.

The blond woman introduced me to the old lady, and both of them listened to me attentively, all the while nodding their heads and expressing sorrow and disbelief over the cruelty of the Germans toward the Jews in the ghetto in general, and over the Aktionen against children in particular.

They tried calming me, telling me that I was now safe, that there was nothing to worry about, and before long the Russians would arrive and the villains would get their just desserts. They fed me a thick slice of fresh bread and butter and gave me a hot drink. A great fatigue settled over me, as though I had not slept for many days. The old lady offered me her bed, as she might to a guest, and the blond woman went to work in the factory to tell my mother that I had arrived safely. Surrounded by icons of the Virgin Mary and other saints, I fell into a deep sleep, unable to believe that I was at last outside the ghetto.

My memories from that day, April 12, 1944, are of two distinct kinds. I clearly remember every second of the first hours of the day—our early rising, the puppy, crossing the river, trudging into the unknown by way of the green path—but from the moment I entered Julija's house, all seems shrouded in darkness. How did I feel? What did I do all day? Where did I sit? What did I look at? I do, however, clearly recall the next day's dawn after my first night's sleep. I remember a deep hush to which I was not accustomed, mixed with a faint light that filtered through fine curtains like those we once had in our old house; the light was unlike any I had ever seen. I heard the barking of a few dogs, and scattered voices of a different kind here and there, all at a different volume.

During the coming nights Julija continued to insist that I sleep in her bed while she slept in a makeshift bed in the middle of the room. There was another bed next to the table under the window; perhaps it had belonged to her late husband, and no one slept in it now. We never talked about him. It may also have been a clever ruse, not to keep linen on two beds. If someone should visit unannounced, she could quickly gather the sheets from the floor and stuff them into the closets, leaving no sign that there was anyone else in her house.

And indeed, as soon as I arrived we began speaking of safety measures. I was instructed to be very careful, to stay out of the yard and the street, to stay away from the window, and to keep my voice down. If we heard footsteps or saw someone through the window, I was to dash into the clothes closet; half of its shelving had been removed to make room for me. This would be my temporary hiding place until the pit under the kitchen floor was finished, the digging of which she had already begun, perhaps with the help of the blond woman's husband. They also considered digging an alternate hiding place in the yard, but excavation was more difficult there and hard to hide from the neighbors. Most of my instructions were delivered in a firm, authoritative tone by the blond neighbor, perhaps because my hiding here was her doing and because she was the younger of the two and more attuned to everyday reality. I imagine they both thought they were dealing with an ordinary boy of eleven on whom they had to impress, in spite of himself, the importance of caution so as to prevent disaster.

The house was perfect for our purposes. Little Workers' Street 59a was the last house in the lane, somewhat isolated from the others in the same row, as the letter in its street number indicated; it was situated at the top of the part of the hill that overlooked the river. The lane itself, bordered by a number of scattered wooden houses, meandered unofficially in curves that joined Darbininku gatve ("Workers' Street"), itself an extension of a thinly populated suburb on the northeastern edge of the city, in the direction of the river. No other house faced ours directly, which was a huge advantage for me. The house had another access from the river: the steep path I had taken to get there—a path that branched off from the lower route.

There were two dwellings inside the wooden house. The blond woman and her family lived in the one on the northern side of the house, facing the lane. My landlady, the Lithuanian woman, lived in the southern one, with its entrance from the yard. This, too, was an advantage for me, because I could both see an approaching stranger through the window and hear his footsteps as he approached. The flat itself was small, containing a single living room with an entrance through a glassed-in porch. From the entrance, you turned left into a dark kitchen with a large, heavy, black stove. It had four or five openings above the flames that could be enlarged or reduced in size by using metal rings that fitted one inside the other, reminding me of the kitchen in our house before the war. The stove was for both cooking and heating, and was fueled by wood logs stored in a small adjoining storeroom; during the third year of the war, it was hard to find coal. In the center of the kitchen was a large, thick-legged table; under it, covered by a carpet, were a number of sawed-off floorboards that camouflaged the pit where I was to hide.

The bathroom adjoined the living room, and I believe it served to store the large chamber pot that was emptied each morning into the outhouse, which stood in the backyard.

When I arrived, the pit was very small—apparently the good neighbors had only just begun digging it, and I could not squeeze inside. So during the evenings, I scooped away the thick clay on the pit's sides and bottom, widening and deepening it, with only a small degree of success.

Julija carefully scattered the excavated soil about the yard at night. She spread a blanket in the bottom of the pit, and I was able, in the end, to sit hunched in the pit for an hour or more. It had none of the spaciousness of the Gafanovitches' shelter, but I was here now, and these were the conditions. Fortunately for me, I seldom needed the shelter. I doubt in any case that it would have saved me during a careful search.

Julija had no relatives in the city, and only a few acquaintances who visited infrequently. Every such visit, even when I knew about it in advance, was a major upheaval for me. I suppose that as long as I was there, she discouraged visitors. She tried to dismiss unforeseen guests as fast as possible or would linger with them in the doorway without inviting them in.

When guests did arrive, I would dart into the closet, do my best to sit still, and listen patiently to the slow and tiresome conversation of the old woman and her friends. I prayed that the visit would soon be over. It was hard to remain calm when there were only a few steps and a thin board between me and a stranger. It was no less difficult to shake off the associations with previous periods of hiding. The closet was old, and it was all I could do to keep it from creaking with any small movement I made to scratch an arm or leg. I was also plagued by the fear that she might suddenly need something from the closet. When the days grew warmer and I had gained a little more confidence, I would slip into the darkened yard before her guests arrived and wait there until they left, gazing at the stars, listening attentively to the voices rising from the nearby houses, and trying to imagine what was happening there.

Julija was a practicing Catholic—morning and evening she recited her prayers.

There was a tacit understanding between us that she knew clearly just who had crucified Jesus, but under the circumstances, we avoided the topic. For her part, she familiarized me with her prayerbook and showed me how the beads of the rosary around her neck helped her recall the prayers in the correct order. My interest in these details, as well as in the act of communion, was not merely academic—I took into account that I might need this knowledge in the days to come.

She was a simple and unfortunate woman. She had been living alone and in poverty for years. Her son was a petty criminal who had brought her little comfort. She was alert and had a store of life experience, but she often preferred to rest in a wise silence. In return for hiding me, she demanded of Mother a large weekly sum, 250 Deutsche Marks, as I recall, most of which I suppose she spent on improving her son's conditions in prison. She visited him regularly. I do not know if she told him how she came by her money. She told me she had not spoken about it to anyone. We were together day and night for about ten weeks, but I remember no special conversations with her. And while it is true that she profited materially by hiding me, she was still a good-hearted woman for having agreed to hide a Jewish boy in the first place—only for a few weeks, they had told her. For her part, Mother hoped the Russians would soon arrive, thus sparing her the need to find another shelter for me and making my placement in hiding affordable until then—no small gamble.

The key to my situation was in the Lithuanian lady's neighbors. They were the go-betweens and supporters, and without them I could not have been hidden. Because the blond woman worked with Mother, she could send and receive daily greetings and letters, sometimes even small packages. On the first evening I was invited into the flat of the blond woman and her husband, and they took a great interest in what was happening with me. My words contained nothing new for them—because of their vantage point above the river and rumors in the city and factory, they already knew a lot. Along with their own fond feelings for us, the Jews, they had things to say about the harsh attitude of the Germans toward the Lithuanian population. Lithuanians in general were no longer as amiable toward the Germans as they had been during the first years of the war—jailings, executions, and conscription into the army and the auxiliary corps were now their lot. They made no effort to conceal their fervent hope that the situation would soon change.

I saw before me a Lithuanian couple of the kind I had scarcely known existed: humane and concerned for the persecuted merely because they were persecuted.

The nature of their empathy indicated, in the impression I formed of them, that they were enlightened and educated, made of the same stuff as the conscientious members of the underground resistance movement, although I knew nothing of their jobs before the war or their political past. When I went back to see them after the liberation, they had already moved to new living quarters in a flat that formerly belonged to German officers, testifying perhaps to a certain connection with the new government. They were glad to see me then, and very pleased with the way things had turned out

They had no children. They had adopted a girl, a war orphan, from the region of Minsk, one of the abandoned children the Germans distributed at train stations to anyone who was interested. She was three or four years younger than I, with curly blond hair, a round Slavic face, and smiling blue eyes. I believe her name was Maya, or perhaps Katya. They raised her as their daughter in all respects, a fact that also testifies to their kindness. When I think about good Lithuanians—and this is not easy for me to do—I remember this couple, whose names, however, I have forgotten. I hope that Stalin's regime did not do away with them.

Further up the lane, at a distance of only a few hundred meters, was my sister. But Mother's injunction was clear and absolute: there was to be no contact between us and neither my sister nor her Lithuanian family should ever know of my presence close by. Aside from the need for caution, her rescue depended on her making a clean break from her former world. (All this was logical, but what about longing, the trembling heart? What do I know of the emotional world of a girl of six and a half years, of the strength she needed to suppress the secret of her own identity, of the loneliness and sense of abandonment that must have gnawed at her?)

Julija and the blond woman, for their part, knew about my sister and where she lived. From time to time they would tell me they had seen her or one of the members of her foster family, and I in turn would tell Mother.

Nearly every evening—excluding Sunday—I would receive a letter from Mother and send her one of my own, which was delivered to her the next day. Sometimes I even managed to respond to whatever I had just read in her letter; she, with inexhaustible patience and forbearance, read and absorbed, replied and encouraged. I was not abandoned and forgotten; I knew she was watching over me; her fingertips touched mine; I was not alone. As a security measure I burned her letters in the kitchen stove as soon as I had read them.

The loneliness and oppression of hiding bred wishes and longings that Mother did her best to grant and that I did nothing to restrain. Books in Lithuanian, a postage stamp album, a Lithuanian-Russian dictionary, and various other things. I now believe that these items, which the blond woman faithfully relayed to me, constituted an unnecessary risk, jeopardizing my concealment.

Early in my period of hiding, I dreamed of keeping, right there in the old woman's home, a dog, "like all the neighbors"—it was an attempt to enjoy—already!—the fruits of my escape, the flight to another planet.

I rearranged all my postage stamps and made a detailed catalogue in which I described each and every stamp in my collection, just as in the catalogued sketches of Johann of Innsbruck. The first stamps in the album were from Australia, with the figure of Florence Nightingale leaning over the wounded; after Australia came Albania with its unique national name, then Belgium, Bolivia, and so on—I can still recall them in order according to the Lithuanian alphabet. Every once in a while I would come back and improve the catalogue or rearrange the stamps—innocent attempts to bring a little order into my upset world. I read a great many books then, too, all in Lithuanian. Some of them came from Mother; my neighbors gave me others, perhaps from a public library in town. Thus I came to know about the famous detective Arsine Lupin. For practical reasons I had asked for the thick Russian-Lithuanian dictionary, one of the few books that still remained in our house. I tried memorizing a few phrases in Russian, such as "What's the way to—," "Give me something to eat, please," and "Please hide me in your house."

Although Mother seemed to be careful not to send things that would arouse suspicion, had a search party in fact reached the old lady's house and found the stamps, the books, the newspapers, and all the rest, I doubt they would have had any question about the identity of the fugitive in her home.

The first days with the old woman were overwhelming. The change, the differences, were so great and beyond my ability to grasp.

On the one hand, there was the wonder of my successful escape from the ghetto. As if by a miracle I had passed through the eye of a needle, through an impenetrable screen. As in the adventure stories by Jules Verne, I was thrown into a new world, where people lived upside down in the bowels of the earth, eating different food, wearing different clothes. Sounds I had not heard for a long time reached me in my new place—the creaking of a well while drawing water, a rooster proclaiming its virility, children laughing—and between each sound there was a tranquil silence, a stillness that was also unfamiliar to me. I had trouble believing that this world was real.

On the other hand, there was a deep anxiety, more immense than that I had felt most days in the ghetto. Had I reached this place before the most recent Aktion, I probably would have been more at peace. As it was, every rustling sound and flickering shadow seen through the curtain made me snap like a wound-up spring. I seemed to have escaped from the ghetto, but in fact I remained trapped in a drawn-out Aktion, chained to a reality in which my existence was no more sanctioned than it was in the small room or cellar during the Kinder Aktion.

There at least Mother and other people of my own kind had been beside me. Could I trust the old woman not to deliver me deliberately, or not to lapse into gossip? Might she not have shared her secret with her son in prison, who could use me as a bargaining card to gain his freedom? Had this consideration escaped my mother's sharp eyes? Or perhaps the Germans would find me by some other means and suddenly appear and take me away. The threat maintained a strong hold on me, and on my dreams, for many years afterward.

Small wonder that I remember little of the first days. I poured my feelings, my fears, and my suspicions into my daily letters to Mother. Their importance in keeping my condition tolerable should not be underestimated. Some were beautiful enough for Mother to take to Izzia and Shulamit and read them passages, so they told me once.

Izzia and Shulamit. The fates of our families were at one point woven together. Muki, their youngest son, one year ahead of me in the Hebrew gymnasium, would accompany me home on days when no one came to get me. Now Izzia and Shulamit preserve the memory of Mother as they saw her during the three and a half months when I was no longer by her side—if only I could transfer to myself something of their store of memories.

During my correspondence with Mother I remember particularly the period before May 21, my much-anticipated eleventh birthday, an annual event for which Mother always managed to create a festive atmosphere: a present at the foot of the bed in the morning; a Napoleon cake with a special taste for which I continue to search in vain; decorations on the wall; and birthday wishes. Now, in hiding, a month or so before my birthday, in my letters to Mother I began writing beside the date the number of days remaining until my birthday. From day to day I announced the countdown to my birthday more elaborately, and I wrote in several languages—not only Yiddish, in which my letters were written, but also in Hebrew, Lithuanian, and Russian. I can only guess the pangs I sent through my mother's heart with this innocent countdown.

My memories of being at the Lithuanian woman's house rely on small landmarks, such as the daily routine, being bent at the table over a book or stamps with my ear cocked to the window, scanning the street and the green slope; or being absorbed for hours at the windowpane and curtain, gazing dejectedly at a fly trying to get outside. In the ghetto, between calamities, I had enjoyed a good deal of freedom to wander and snoop, moving here and there without restriction. But now I was in strict confinement. For ten spring and summer weeks I was shut in a one-room house. Although I cannot remember the details of this oppressive period, writing about it is difficult.

Then there was my close surveillance of Julija Grincevičiene, to whom I was attached twenty-four hours a day. What did she do all day but attend to the minutiae of her life? She cooked and cleaned, darned socks and mended nightgowns. She went out to the yard to draw water from the well—at night, I helped her with this—and every few days she went downtown either to exchange food stamps or to trade in the black market for things that were hard to find. She was a decent woman who felt obliged, in exchange for the boarding fees she received for keeping me, to find good food. At my request she also brought home a daily newspaper, either in Lithuanian or German. We ate together, and above all I remember slices of bread spread with a layer of butter and a generous sprinkling of salt—a treat I came to enjoy.

On weekends, before going to church, she would have a bath. She put a large tub in the center of the room and emptied into it kettles of hot water from the kitchen stove. She bathed me here, too. Her old white body was of no interest to me. I liked watching her as she finished washing her hair. She would fashion a long gray braid or two, which she then gathered into a bun and hid well under a colorful kerchief that she never went without. She smelled of fresh clean soap and exuded the tranquility of the old, a wholesome calm that had no parallel in the world I came from.

One day I dreamt I helped guard the ghetto fence.

The years since then have somewhat obscured my memory of this dream and I cannot tell whether I was stationed high in the watchtower or, more likely, merely stood on the ground below like a guard, inside the fence. It is an important point in my attempts at reconstruction, because at a certain moment I raised my eyes to the sentry, who stood diagonally above me in the tower. The look I exchanged with the German had a certain complicity and secret understanding.

A moment later I shifted my gaze forcibly to where it belonged, from the fence to the people in the ghetto, and to my surprise I saw my mother's face. I smiled, proud that she should see me doing my duty, but with a look that said: just between us, even though I seem to be one of the guards, we both know whose side I am really on.

I opened my eyes and there was my mother's face. A week after we had parted she managed to visit me. Mother, I asked in wonder, have you been looking at me long? Did you know I was just dreaming about you? She told me once that such a thing could happen. Since then I have often asked myself, when I look at our sleeping children, whether I, too, am sometimes woven into their dreams.

Many times have I returned to this strange dream, one of the dreams whose details have remained within me for years. Each time I try to digest anew the discomfiting fact that, in my dream, the victim reveals an affinity for his persecutor, is willing to cooperate with him and deliver himself up to him, all in return for a feeling of belonging.

And it is in this embarrassing dream that I find my mother's face so realistically woven. I would willingly risk many more chilling night visions if I could receive in exchange, upon opening my eyes, the living face of my mother.

My last day with Mother began, then, with a dream. She slipped out of the brigade and came to the Lithuanian lady's house at dawn. She stayed with me the entire day. We talked and talked. She sewed on buttons for me and mended my clothes. She had an air of calm, unlike her manner of late. It reminded me of the Sunday three weeks earlier before everything had changed. Mother heard my impressions of the week that had just passed and told me about hers, got to know the old woman, whom she now met for the first time, and laid down a few security measures with her concerning me.

Mother brought chilling news with her, although she must have filtered out many of the details. Among other things she told me that the day after my departure, surveillance over the gates had been made much tighter; it was doubtful whether I could have attempted an escape afterward. As the front line approached, rumors began circulating about a plan for moving the ghetto westward. In addition, there was talk about the possibility of the Riga deportees being brought back to our region, even to our ghetto, Father among them. Mother was thus hesitant about joining the partisans in the forest, especially since many of the escapees were caught on their way to the forests. In addition, a week before my escape, Haim Yellin had been cornered in the city. During the chase, he had wounded and killed some of his pursuers, but in the end he was trapped in a basement, where he was apprehended with his wrists already cut but still alive. He was now no doubt being tortured in some Gestapo dungeon. Some said they had seen him being taken through the ghetto, perhaps for investigation, bound in chains and his face already changed. His friends were confident in him, but they suspected he might be publicly hanged, like Mek had been. He certainly had no hope of remaining alive. And unfortunately, a group had just been caught in the city as it was escaping to the forest—the truck driver had turned them in. Our people had succeeded in killing him, but the ambushing Germans had fired on and killed most of the escapees. Four of them had managed to return fire and get away. Jews fighting and killing Germans was thrilling but upsetting news—what retaliation might the Jews of the entire ghetto expect?

Toward evening, when darkness fell, Mother got up and left. We parted, thinking we would see one another again soon, at her next visit. In all likelihood she went from my hiding place fifty steps further to my sister's house to spend the night with her before going back to join the brigade at dawn.

It was not strictly speaking a parting, and for many years I expected her to return. There was no doubt in her heart as she put it, that we would meet one another "after the storm." I tended to believe her, even though she had also promised me long ago that war would not break out.

Even if she had had a place where she could have hidden, or had escaped to the forest, she could not have left us far behind—she owed weekly payments for our hiding places. I do not know how she got so much money, even with her buying and selling. I tried to find out from Izzia and Shulamit whether there was a fund for helping out in such cases in the ghetto; the answer was no. Later, when I left the old woman's house, the burden of payment was reduced, but by that time the path to the forest was closed.

During my first days at Julija Grincevičiene's I feared the Germans would come to get me any moment. Little by little I grew calmer. I saw that the place was out of the way and that no one was watching it. I gradually grew used to the noises around me and to everyday sights. At the same time, any innocent passerby asking for directions would raise waves of disquiet in me, like a stone thrown into a lake leaving ripples.

When I first arrived at the old woman's house the weather was cool and in the evening the stove had to be lit. In May, however, spring came. It was pleasantly warm, and plants turned green and began blossoming. My spirits, too, seemed to lift a little. By chance, Julija needed help retrieving something from her attic. To get to the attic I had to go through an opening in the outside wall of her house on the side facing the river, and thus I discovered an unexpected source of diversion. From then on I often climbed the ladder that stood permanently under the opening, taking with me a blanket, a book, and food. I would stay there most of the day. The disadvantage was that I had to climb up in the open, from the outside. I hurried to climb as fast as I could and promised I wouldn't dally in the opening but would move farther inside.

For the first time I was able to see the entire area, which I loved doing; it was like going with Mother to hang laundry on the rooftop of our old house, or perch on the wide sill of the window. Now a jumble of rooftops and corners of yards spread around me, and a strip of street stuck to the middle of the slope. Further down, the roofs appeared to drown in the river, hiding the shoreline from my eyes, and, to my disappointment, obscuring the place where the brigade boats docked and the street where the workers marched morning and evening.

But before me I saw the ghetto—the entire territory on the other side of the river laid out as if in the palm of my hand, all the way to the distant hills. I looked down upon it as though I were soaring above it, gazing from a distance with a certain detachment, as spirits might do. The area of the ghetto could be discerned by the grouping of the houses and its main streets. If only I had binoculars; I wanted to go into every house, to squeeze through every door, and especially to split open a large block of buildings that hid my view of the house on Vigrių Street. A flood of warm feelings swept through me, a longing for the people in the valley below. At this hour in the attic, with the sun setting and the last of its rays passing distractedly over the distance, holding in flames one patch of roof or another in the ghetto, a special letter to Mother was born. I tried to describe the sights of this hour—the exhilaration of it, emotionally taking leave of the expanse of life that lay across the river that formed a part of me. I imagine that this letter was among those Mother showed to Izzia and Shulamit.

The days passed without particular incident. My command of the language improved, the "r" sound began rolling much easier off my tongue, and my self-confidence rose. The neighbors complimented me on my excellent Lithuanian and my not necessarily Jewish-looking features. So I conceived my next reckless idea—to leave the house in the dark of evening for a short stroll, first in the yard and then, little by little, outside as well. To my surprise the Lithuanians agreed—my restlessness was not lost on them.

At first I stepped out for only a few minutes; then, with Julija's consent, I gradually increased both the amount of time I spent outside the yard and the distance I went beyond it. After weeks of being cooped up in a room, I had a compelling need for some activity, and I was also curious to find out what was happening beyond the shutters of the window and the fence in the yard. My first excursion was very short—at the first moving shadow or sound of a door opening, I whisked myself quickly inside. During the next few days I went further. Cautiously, I went past the neighboring houses, those that seemed to threaten me more directly; in the low light of the evening they seemed sleepy and peaceful. When I saw silhouettes approaching, I would turn artfully in another direction until the person was swallowed by one of the paths; then I would resume my foray.

As if under a spell, I was drawn into the depths of the lane, closer to the paved streets of the city. There was the house where my sister lived. I had no illusions that I would meet her; in any case it was forbidden. But still I wanted, irrationally, to hear her voice—if only by chance—to see her silhouette in a doorway or window, perhaps to see the face of the Lithuanians who were giving her shelter.

I did in fact get very close to her house once or twice, although the risk was great for both of us. I stationed myself in the shadow of a corner, my gaze fixed on the house prohibited to me. I saw flickering lights; muffled voices reached me from inside, but immediately I had to go, because the closer the lane brought me down to the city, the more often it was frequented, quite naturally, by people. And yet I had stood next to my sister's house; it was real, even though she knew nothing of my presence. I never returned again—and I never saw my little sister again.

Because my neighbors listened secretly to the radio, I heard the main news from the Eastern Front about the major victories in the battles of Kursk, Gommel, and later Vitebsk. These reports, together with poring over the daily newspapers—like an invalid confined to his bed who leaves no corner unread—almost gave me the illusion that I was like everyone else. I began taking an interest in various features and articles. With great curiosity I read pretentious descriptions of the impregnable defenses of the Festung Europa (the European stronghold) along the English Channel. I followed the declarations that no one would ever get through it. What encouraged me most, however, were the repeated announcements of "redrawing the line" of the Eastern Front, the stock euphemism used to describe retreats following military defeats.

In the German army newspaper my attention was caught by a strange story in the literary section of the weekend supplement. It was about a proud and handsome rooster that had been raised in a German family's backyard during the height of the war. It had stayed with them through bombings and want until one day, to mark the end of the year and the upcoming departure of their son from the front, the family's parents decided, after much deliberation, and for want of other food, to butcher the beautiful rooster. In the evening, the family members gathered for the festive meal, but when the main course was served, an oppressive silence fell over the table; their throats became choked with sobs; they were unable to continue eating. This is the gist of a story, awash with self-pity, that stood out in a family German magazine in the summer of 1944.

The days of grace spent in the attic and the evenings spent roaming the neighborhood passed. Perhaps the days turned cold and rainy, or tension had mounted in the area—it was during the first days of June, close to the opening of the second front in the West. In any case, I didn't leave the house again. Even the atmosphere within the house changed, and so did my relations with the old woman. Perhaps we had grown tired of one another, or perhaps she had other reasons for reminding me that shelter in her house was supposed to be temporary and for a limited period only. The chances that her son would be freed from prison had apparently grown, thanks to the approaching front, and he was expected to return to his mother's home. For my part, I may have complained to Mother, asking her to consider changing my housing. This fit in with my mother's scheme to find a rural hiding place for me, if only she could arrange it, far from the big city. The high weekly sum she was paying for me was also a burden, and she could not afford to keep me there.

So Mother began looking for another place. One day she informed me that she had found a new place in the country. Before long, a woman would visit me and tell me about the arrangements for leaving. Years later I received evidence that corroborated this from Ona Pečkyte. After forty years she wrote me (I translate freely from Lithuanian).

Much is forgotten over time, and many things are remembered. Yes, I remember your mother. It was in 1944, under German occupation. I worked in the felt-boot factory in Janova Street. They brought people from the ghetto to work there. Your mother was among them; I hadn't known her before this, but we would sometimes exchange a few words during work. Not a tall woman, she was thin and looked very tired. I was greatly surprised when she asked me one day if I could hide her son. I didn't sleep all night. I wondered how I could help her, whom to turn to, and whom I could trust.

I didn't sleep either the night I received this letter. It was a relief to be suddenly certain, after all so many years, across the distance of seas and continents, that another person existed, a very old woman, who remembered the same details of the plot that I did—it was not all a fantasy, the fruit of my imagination or a hallucination, as I had sometimes tried to tell myself. I had indeed been there!

One evening a short, plump woman with a pleasant face and glasses came to Julija's house. She spoke with the old woman and me, telling us that she would come for me on the following Sunday. I was to be ready at dawn, dressed in good clothes and carrying a small bag. She planned to take me to a village, to some good people who could be trusted, and I was not to worry. Before I left, I was to destroy anything I didn't need. She would bring me any belongings that I really needed some other time; meanwhile, Julija would hide them.

These were unquiet days, the last days of Germany's presence in the area, three weeks after the invasion of Normandy had begun, and the news was filled with hysterical proclamations. With all this, the tumult of war on the Eastern Front grew ever closer, and sirens wailed more frequently by night and by day.

A day or two before I left—it must have been about June 24—the third anniversary of the German conquest and the beginning of the war was celebrated with a great deal of noise. Newspaper headlines overflowed with the doings of the German military rulers and their Lithuanian supporters with parades and other commemorative rituals. Their speeches were full of boasting, dripping with poison and hate directed toward the Allies and their Jewish collaborators. And even though I had recently been planning in great detail how I would go downtown to watch a children's theater program, Pečkyte's plans threw me into a panic because we would have to cross the entire city on foot in broad daylight, reach the station, board a truck with strangers, and travel a distance with them. I was stricken with anxiety.

Then I indulged in a shameful act of childishness: I sat down and wrote my mother a whiny letter of complaint. I may have picked up some of the worries and fears of my two Lithuanian guardians. My poor mother. As if she had a choice, as if she would not want the best and safest solution for her son, as if I were not already uniquely lucky in the arrangements she had made for me.

And because my pen flowed so freely, I let loose with pathetic words of parting and sorrow, even going so far as attaching to my letter, with a dramatic gesture that I borrowed perhaps from one of the novels I had read, a lock of hair from my head as a souvenir. To this day I find it hard to reflect on my foolish, ridiculous action; to this very day I can't forgive myself.

My brave and tortured mother. She was steadfast in her will to save my life in spite of my burdensome and capricious words. In her next letter—her last—she answered me in a restrained and soothing tone. The arrangements for my escape were safe, she wrote, and there was no need to be anxious about them. What else she wrote, how she said it, what means of persuasion she used, what her final words of parting were exactly, I cannot recall. I was too worried and tense that day to retain for long what she said. More's the pity. I am fortunate that I managed at least to reply to her again, making up with a few words of conciliation and farewell, somewhat softening my childish protest. These were the last letters we exchanged.

On the last evening, I went to the neighbors' house to say good-bye. Neither they nor I knew just where I was going next. They fortified me with best wishes and words of encouragement. That night I hardly slept, trying to decipher the indecipherable, to anticipate what might happen to me the next day. In the morning I packed my things, put on my best, most grown-up clothes, and said good-bye to Julija. I thanked her sincerely and with feeling. Now, as I was about to leave, both of us felt the warmth of the bond between us. I promised that when the storm was over I would come back to visit her. We will see each other again, I told her.

10

In the Village

It was another fine sunny day in June, a Sunday morning just like the one three years before when the war had begun. Pečkyte arrived early. With an intense look on her face like the one she had had during her first visit, she inspected my clothing and knapsack. I said good-bye to my Lithuanian lady and we left.

We had agreed to keep the greatest possible distance between us. At corners, she waited a bit to make certain I was following. She had assured me that at that early hour the city would be empty and that I had nothing to fear. If I were stopped, she had reminded me, I was not to say that I knew her, and above all I was not to say where I had come from. Julija had made me swear the same thing, and I made the promise as a thing to be taken for granted.

She set out with me in tow, walking slowly, awkwardly, like a mole blinded by sunlight. I do not recall much of my march across the city. We almost certainly went down the entire length of the little lane, also passing my sister's house. We descended the main artery through which the Russian tanks had rolled four years earlier. At the first opportunity, we turned into a side street that took us to the old quarter. We did not see many people, but I was dumbfounded by every person we passed. And then we were already in Rotushe Square.

We had to wait for a truck next to the former Jewish Ethnographic Institute. A few other people stood there, weekend passengers calmly waiting for a ride. It had been years since I had been so close to strangers, people with no conception of the danger they represented to me. Opposite us still stood the model shelter, expanded and reinforced; it had evidently been put to good use in the intervening years. Nearby were the benches and the garden, the spires of churches, the roofs of cathedrals—all stood here as aloof and haughty as before; nothing had changed. Across from them was the stairwell of the bishop's house, redecorated in bold colors.

Pečkyte bought a newspaper and gave it to me, both to pass the time while waiting and, if necessary, to hide my face. I struggled against the fears that rose and revolved in my mind—how would we get into the vehicle, where would I sit, what would I say if other passengers asked me questions, and, especially, what would happen if sinister-looking people joined our journey? How would I pass through checkpoints on the way? The truck pulled up, and people clambered onto it from all sides; we did, too, after the woman paid for both of us and informed the driver where she wanted to stop. We sat some distance apart and, after waiting again for what seemed an age to me, away we went.

The truck turned south. We quickly reached the big bridge over the river; it still bore the damage of the massive attack upon it that Monday night at six on the second day of the war. Soon we were above the southern bank of the river, leaving the city. Beyond this point, on the right, was where the "Flug-Platz" brigade had turned on its daily march to the airport. We continued toward the expanse past the airport, toward the southwest. The road was straight as a ruler, the fields were full of golden grain. There was no sign of war or of armies. From time to time we met German military trucks with chimneys perched on them—they were powered by wood-burning engines due to the shortage of gasoline. The truck we were in had low sideboards and was full of sacks of grain or seeds; we held onto them as we rode. I sat down in the left-hand corner nearest the cab, stealing glances from time to time at the other passengers, hiding my discomfort behind the newspaper so as to shield myself from their searching looks.

People would get on and off at various locations, but thank God there were no inspection points. We rode for two or three hours, well into the afternoon. I had an apple and a sandwich with me but I didn't eat either of them. Pečkyte and I exchanged glances of relief when she finally motioned to me that our stop was coming up.

The truck turned off the main road toward a village some way off. At Pečkyte's request, the truck stopped just after making the turn, and we climbed down. A wagon was waiting there; beside it stood two men. Pečkyte greeted them and introduced me, and before I knew what was happening I was already on the wagon and Pečkyte had turned back to the main road.

We were alone in the wagon, just the Lithuanian peasant and me. Pečkyte, the last link between me and the world I had just left, stayed behind, promising she would visit me soon at my new place.

Here was the chain of events as I was gradually able to piece them together afterward: Pečkyte had brought me to her native village, where a man named Viktoras Daugela lived. It seems that his wife, Magdalena, suggested I be taken to his brother, Vincas. Vincas lived in another village and agreed to take me in.

This much Pečkyte had arranged during special preparatory visits she had made to her own village.

During a long, slow ride that lasted several hours—a single horse pulled the wagon in which Vincas Daugela and I sat side by side—we got acquainted. The horse was weak but did the job. It was a peasant's caution: I discovered later, on his farm, that he had saved his better horses. Vincas Daugela was broad-shouldered, tall, and somewhat stooped, with a long and very wrinkled face, a pleasant countenance, and merry eyes. Easygoing and good-hearted, he was a heavy smoker and coughed a lot. He was a confirmed bachelor. His farm was in a village on the other side of the town Marijampole, through which we were journeying. Although he could not read or write like many in his village, he was keenly aware of world events.

He asked me about my life and shook his head incredulously when he heard what was happening to Jews in the city. "Here in our town there used to be a lot of Jews. I knew some of them and they were good, decent people, but all of them were killed during the first days of the war." When he was asked to give shelter to a Jewish child he had assented willingly, especially since it was only a matter of weeks before the Russians would arrive. He seemed hesitant and chose his words carefully—perhaps with the shyness of a peasant meeting a city person, although I sensed a certain firmness and decisiveness behind his words.

Heading south, we approached Mariampol, as the Jews called it. The man told me to stretch out in the bottom of the wagon, to pretend indifference, and not to look around too much. If someone stopped us, he said, he would know nothing about me; he had picked me up along the way at my request. I was a mute Russian refugee, looking for work in the area.

We went slowly through the cobblestone streets. On Sunday morning the village was half asleep, with no special traffic. Some people from our ghetto had lost their lives during the previous months in this very town on their way to the forests. We accomplished our journey, though, without incident; there were no roadblocks or guards, and we were soon once again on our way along country roads, heading south toward Liepynų, Daugela's village.

Now the Lithuanian explained the cover story he had concocted for me, as he had worked it out in his head during our journey. Although he was a bachelor without a family, there were a number of laborers and a housekeeper on his farm, which was sometimes visited by neighbors and people passing through. Although I did not look Jewish, my accent when speaking Lithuanian might well be a problem. He therefore hit upon the idea of presenting me as a deaf-mute refugee from Latvia—he had heard that they were sending orphans to this region. He suggested that I help him with chores, not only to pay for my keep but also to blend in with the household and help mask my true identity. I was extremely anxious to please him. I told him I liked to work, that I would try very hard, and that I had even had some experience growing vegetables. Then he told me that he thought my name should be Juodas—"black" in Lithuanian. To my wonder, he explained the logic behind this odd notion—he had once met some Latvians and discovered that their language was quite similar to Lithuanian. He had picked up the word "juodas" and knew that this was at least a real Latvian word, without knowing what it meant in their own language. Juodas was also close to Juozas, a common Lithuanian name. Being identified as a Latvian could explain my understanding of the language being spoken around me, and by virtue of being a deaf-mute, my faulty accent would not arouse suspicion. My host was somewhat like an overgrown child, a good, kind-hearted man, and a dreamer. It was a good thing that, in the end, my concealment almost never had to withstand any serious tests. It was through his innocence that I was saved.

It was evening when we arrived at his home. I was relieved to find that the house was isolated, with no close neighbors. Daugela took his wagon into the backyard and opened the door to the house for me from inside.

No sooner had I put my things down when I was ushered to a large, heavy table, where I sat down to eat with all the members of the household. They sat around the table inspecting the strange bird that the master of the house had brought back with him from a visit to his brother; I was even honored with a meal—so I found out afterward—in the dining room, which was reserved for special occasions. Among the gazes directed at me, the clear and somewhat suspicious look of the serving woman stood out from the first. My city clothes, my foreign ways, the fabulous story of my identity, and my tense behavior were a riddle to them all.

After dinner the peasant hinted for me to join him to go to piss outside, and there, with our backs to the windows of the house, we talked a little in secret. Daugela encouraged me: he was satisfied with the way things were going; judging by the reactions of the members of his household, it appeared that his plan was working.

I was put to bed in a front room, in a nice bed, padded with pillows and cushions that looked like a stage setting that had stood unused for quite some time. The pajamas I wore, and perhaps my ritual of washing my hands and face before sleeping, only added to their wonder about who I was.

The unfamiliar surroundings and the feeble light of the votive candle lit for the holy Madonna in the corner didn't prevent me from falling into a long, troubled sleep. When I woke up the sun was already high in the sky and all was quiet. At first I couldn't remember where I was. I was ashamed of the contradiction between my promise of readiness to work hard and the impression of laziness that I had certainly just given on this first day. With a generous smile, the farmer came in and welcomed me to a tasty, refreshing breakfast. He offered me some of his clothes, which, although not the right size, were at least more like those worn locally. He also decided to cut my hair—it was long, for it hadn't been cut in months, and I hadn't even thought about it. (Where might I have cut my hair in the ghetto? I do not recall.)

Daugela's reserved suggestions demonstrated to me how much my appearance stood out, and yet my behavior was, relatively speaking, quite calm and deliberate, probably because I had spent such a long time with the elderly woman on Green Hill. Even so, it had not been enough to school me to act like one of them.

What happened first? Did we take a walk through the fields and then he cut my hair, or was it the other way around? I find it hard to remember. After years of being cooped up in the ghetto, I was now walking beside a friendly peasant who treated me with respect, showing me with unconcealed pride the extent of his domain. We went through farm buildings that stood beside the house, from there to the vegetable garden, and further out, as in a dream, to an expanse of golden grain. Once again I was walking through country paths like those at the summer resort. A feeling of comfort quickly engulfed me—surely the Germans would not follow me here.

But on the first day I committed my first slip-up; it is seared in my memory.

Evening came and I was once again summoned to the dining room. I found a stranger there who could read and write, that is to say, ostensibly a man of the world. Having heard of the new boy on his neighbor's farm, he had come to take my measure. Bald and red-faced, he began questioning me and refused to be content with my game of gestures. Daugela did his best to explain to him that I was a deaf-mute and that I couldn't be expected to answer his riddles. It may have been then that he took me to the yard to give me a haircut, hoping his neighbor would leave me in peace. We whispered to one another in the process. When we came back into the room, the neighbor was still there, and I heard the members of the household arguing among themselves and with the neighbor, wondering who I was and mentioning that they had seen my lips move while I got my hair cut; moreover, none of my responses or behavior in general was like that of a real deaf-mute. Like a trapped bird, deeply embarrassed, I looked secretly at Daugela, who was hard put to pretend that he wasn't concerned or didn't understand what was going on.

And then the neighbor hit upon the idea of trying to communicate with me by writing. His common sense told him that although differing in speech, Lithuanian and Latvian are sister languages and there was a chance I might understand what he wrote. I took the bait. I began answering the questions he wrote on a piece of paper, and a written exchange soon developed between us. Time after time I answered, in my foolishness, to the great wonder of all present, and in fluent Lithuanian, too. Here Daugela intervened; with growing concern he had watched the correspondence, and he now motioned for me to go outside.

Too late I realized I had unwittingly revealed the subterfuge. I was trapped. My false identity had crumbled and now I was at the mercy of these people. In my heedlessness I had probably brought disaster on myself and perhaps also on my host and savior. My eyes brimmed with tears; I was panic-stricken. What would become of me now?

Several minutes passed before Daugela came out and called to me in the darkness. He told me that he had been compelled to tell everyone in the house that I was indeed a Jewish child. It turned out that they had been suspicious of my identity from the beginning because of my clothes and my city behavior, and they hadn't bought the farmer's simple story for a minute. He was aware, he said, that he should never have hatched the idea in the first place. However, he assured me that they had all promised to keep the secret and not divulge it to a soul, and he trusted them. Even the snoopy neighbor, who was a man with education and odd habits, a single man without family, was fundamentally good and would do no harm to anyone.

Since the incident passed without bringing disaster, it even resulted in a certain advantage for me. Now that my true identity was known, I was able, to my great relief, to behave more like myself with members of the household. To their credit, their loyalty to their master, and perhaps their basic and natural feelings of humanity, were such that they guarded the secret well; none of them gave me away by so much as an innocent slip of the tongue. Even Ona, the housekeeper, who more than any of the others showed her reservations about me, obeyed the wishes of the head of the house. The neighbor, too, kept his lips sealed. We met from time to time and talked a little; he also lent me his books to read. When I left Daugela's house for good, I made a point of saying good-bye to him as well, and in the years afterward, when I sent a few letters to my farmer, I always imagined that the first reader of the letters was probably "the learned neighbor."

As a result of the language incident, even more security precautions were necessary in case something went wrong. Daugela said that Germans came to the farm occasionally, mostly to confiscate crops and livestock and to look for draft dodgers—they used the locals for support troops. And there was always the possibility of a special raid as a result of a suspicion or an informer's tip. It would be best, then, suggested Daugela, if I slept not in the house but in the nearby hayloft, where I would stay whenever I was not needed in the house or yard. The summer nights were warm, and I could wrap up in a blanket and sleep well. The loft also had a gate that led out back, through which I could escape straight into the fields without going through the yard. If escape ever became necessary, Daugela suggested that I go some distance and hide in the tall grain. We decided upon a meeting place, in case it was too dangerous to meet in the yard; it was beside another hay shed, further back. On ordinary days I would do some work on the farm, helping with various chores—not that he needed my help, he hastened to add, but so that I would draw less attention from any strangers visiting the place.

But in spite of the Lithuanian's assurances, I never lost the fear, from the first day of my stay there to the last, that someone who knew the secret of my identity would suddenly turn me in. It was not a concern that was new to me.

Daugela was fundamentally a sensitive man. He gave his instructions apologetically, as if somewhat embarrassed. Yet he behaved courageously; he could not have treated me more humanely than he did. From the time I began sleeping in the loft, he would visit me once or twice in the evenings, even when he had nothing special to say. When I had to stay out there because there were guests in the house, he never forgot to tell Ona to bring me food, or he would bring it himself.

So I went to live alone in the hayloft. The bottom part, in front, was a stable; in it were three horses tied to their mangers. These horses were the apple of Daugela's eye, and whenever there was a threat of confiscation, he would send these horses into the grain fields until the danger passed. A ladder extended into the hayloft, which covered most of the stable. I found a remote spot in the pile of hay, next to the corner where the roof met the outer wall of the building, in a place that received light and air. I could reach the place only by crawling through a kind of tunnel through the hay that I made myself. Daugela suggested that

I pull the ladder up after me whenever I climbed up, since its presence might arouse suspicion. After a day or two, I got used to the snorting of horses and the sounds they made shuddering and chewing, which went on all day and night, and I began to feel somewhat more at ease.

To this day I have no idea what Daugela's village looked like, or how his farm was situated in relation to it. The village apparently spread over a large area, and I know only that his house was one of the outlying ones, standing in the part of the village closest to the province's principal town, Marijampole. I remember in detail, however, what his farm and its immediate surroundings looked like.

North of the farm, beyond the shallow stream on the edge of the town, stood the sugar factory. Its size and its tall smokestack made it the most imposing structure in the area, not only by virtue of its profile on the horizon but because of the noises it emitted every hour of the day, regulating the surroundings with their rhythm: sirens between shifts, the sudden belching of steam, the banging of iron gates as they opened and shut, the whistles of trains coming and going, dragging clanking cars. I was a city boy, and these noises helped reduce my feelings of alienation from the otherwise strange and silent surroundings.

In those pre-harvest days of July it was quiet on Daugela's farm, and I did my best to be useful and earn my keep. As a result of my lack of experience or unclear instructions, more than once I did more harm than good and made people angry. I kept on trying, however. First I was given simple chores, such as feeding scraps to the pigs in their pen or the fowl in the yard, or turning the handle of the churn.

Because I lived in the hay shed, it was also my duty to feed and water my neighbors, the horses, a task I was proud to perform. I did my best to help and to make myself liked by all, but I realized I would never effect much of a change in Ona's reserved, perhaps hostile opinion of me. My presence there was clearly not to her liking, and it was only out of deference to the master of the house—Ponas ("lord" in Lithuanian), they all called him, not by his first name—that she suffered my presence.

During the coming days I slowly came to realize that Ona had a central role in the house, one that went far beyond that of servant and housekeeper. With a wink I was told that she was the lord's mistress, had lived with him out of wedlock for many years, ever since she had arrived, and had had an illegitimate child by him. I was told all this as if it were perfectly natural, but I felt as if I had been told a secret that carried the scent of sin. She was fairly young, blond, and full-bodied, with white energetic arms, and I had difficulty linking her in my mind with the lord, who was so much older than she. I was doubly careful not to make her angry.

From the harsh world around me I would go, like a scolded cat, to my hiding place in the hayloft. There I had a warm, cotton-filled quilt, a bundle of clothes, a few hidden books, and even pajamas. I took care—in addition to washing my face and hands—to put my pajamas on every night.

My hiding place was so complete that even Vincas, who climbed the ladder once or twice to look for me there, was unable to find me except by calling for me several times, and for this he praised me. I was free to do as I wished, not necessarily bound to the house's activities. The opening along the eave of the roof beside which I lay down was important not only for air and light but also as a lookout point. From here, I could keep track of everything that happened in the yard, with a direct line to the kitchen door. Watching through the aperture filled a more important function: it gave me a sense of security and command over my situation.

And even today when I lie down on my side, I sometimes consider whether I am on the "proper" side. To find out, I have to reconstruct the position I slept in up there in the loft, in the space between the rain gutter and the hay; then I know the answer immediately. The origin of this notion lay in one of the few books I found at Daugela's or at his neighbor's. It was a farmer's almanac, a kind of collection brimming with sundry information and advice for peasants, which I read from cover to cover several times. The almanac explained the meaning of the four seasons, the changes in weather throughout the world, the equinox and solstice. The book listed agricultural labors by season and had a key to the meaning of dreams. I was drawn to the chapter on keeping well and sleeping healthily. According to the almanac, the best sleep could be attained only in a well-ventilated room under a light covering, and only by sleeping on one's right side. In the loft it was easy to follow the recommendations for plenty of air and a light blanket, but the question of sleeping on the proper side bothered me. I entered my space by crawling in from the right side toward the left, stretching out at the end of the tunnel on my left side, which left me in a position to look outside. Yet according to the almanac, I should turn toward the hay with my back to the light, destroying my vantage. I hesitated and then concluded that under the circumstances I had to reject the recommendations. Thanks to these deliberations, however, I still remember the formula for "healthy sleep on the proper side."

One morning a German soldier suddenly appeared in the yard, riding a bicycle. No one there at the time reacted strongly, and no one brought the fact to my attention. My breathing stopped. In an instant I was on my feet and fleeing in fear to the far side of the farm, not daring to return to the barnyard. It was so unexpected, so out of place in the daily life of the farm. Had he been sent to ask about me or take me away? Evening fell and from afar I heard Daugela calling me. As it turned out, no one realized I hadn't been told that Ona's son had been drafted recently, and he now wore a uniform and carried a gun like any other German soldier. When I didn't appear for supper, my host realized that I might have been scared by the sight of Ona's son and came out to find me. When he brought me back, he insisted on introducing us—I, a Jewish child and refugee from the ghetto, and he, Antanas, a soldier in the German auxiliary forces. He was stationed in a nearby camp and was therefore able to visit; he was one of the family here. In spite of his proper treatment of me, I found it hard to behave naturally. I was completely unable to get past the barrier of his green-gray uniform and the black weapon in his hand. Thereafter I was warned beforehand when they knew he would be over, sometimes with friends, and I would leave for the shed or spend a few hours in the fields.

Days arrived that were quieter than any I had known during the previous few years. In appearance and speech I became more and more like the local youths, and while I took care not to reveal myself, I was never again so frightened by the appearance of a stranger in the yard. When one arrived, I would walk in a leisurely manner to a distant corner of the farm or head for the fields at a moderate pace. I was at peace with my improvised life and my prolonged stay in the lap of nature.

What my name was then I cannot remember. I believe I was Juodas to the end, as I was first introduced.

Some evenings, after supper, the farmer and I would go out together to urinate in the yard, and it was then that we talked. This was the only daily human contact I had. We would discuss the situation at the front and the chance that the Russians would soon arrive.

It was July, the hottest month of the year. I tried to express the feelings of loneliness that beset me and then intensified, my deepening anxiety, in a daily ritual I found myself performing every evening when circumstances allowed. The sky would be ablaze with a purple sunset, spotted by silhouettes of clouds. I would station myself behind the hayloft on the side facing the fields to the northeast, in the direction of my city. Full of longing, I would pour out my prayers there in a prescribed order that became more and more fixed with every passing day. These prayers were born first of all in the depths of the cellar, in my hiding place in the armoire, from the fear of footsteps drawing ever nearer, from hours of extreme distress and hopelessness. I would mention my distant loved ones, naming my relatives and friends one by one and including the general population imprisoned in the ghetto, praying in Hebrew and Yiddish for their peace, health, and salvation. At the end of that improvised ritual I felt some relief.

One morning when I was leaning over a pile of sugar beets spreading a scorching chemical fertilizer, I looked up and saw Pečkyte standing in front of me. I was so surprised that I nearly didn't react. For a moment, I felt a certain discomfort with this invasion of the monk-like barrier I had raised around myself. Perhaps my little sister felt the same way about visits from Mother. Pečkyte had indeed come to see me on Mother's behalf, bringing greetings. She had little to tell me about how Mother was doing, or about my sister and the community in the ghetto. She brought me several items of clothing—from Mother or Julija—and went back home. I never saw her again, and at the time I didn't even know her name.

Every once in a while Daugela would discuss with me what I should do when the war front arrived. In contrast to his unprepossessing appearance, he was deliberate and cautious. He reminded me that there were large forests to the southeast. If our region should fill up with Germans, whether as a result of the war or a search for me, I should consider escaping farther away, toward the forests that lay at a distance of a day's walk or two. During the summer, I could hide there for a few days, living off berries, which were plentiful.

I would agree with him, but to myself I wondered if he wanted to be rid of me. Daugela was not only a decent man but one with common sense as well. I could have counted on his knowing that the Russians might appreciate his having saved me, and he had no reason to try to send me away before they came. For that matter German propaganda had unintentionally helped my case by incessantly repeating that the Soviet regime was controlled by Jews. Who knows how many Jews may have owed their survival during the last stages of the war to this misinformation?

How long was I with Daugela? A short while only, five weeks in all—the last week of June and all of July—but life there was so different and my experiences so intense that I find it hard to believe I stayed there such a short while, only half the time I spent at the Lithuanian woman's home.

During these very same days, Father was transferred from Kaiserwald, near Riga, to Ponivezh, in the region of our city. The Germans planned to build one of the largest military airbases in the Baltic area there, and there was talk in the ghetto of the Germans having agreed to return some of the exiles to our city. So Mother had reason to stay in the ghetto and wait. When the war front suddenly drew closer, the Germans sent the Ponivezh prisoners, including my father, straight to the concentration camps in Germany; a short while later, they did the same with the people in our ghetto as well.

11

Liberation

ONE SUNDAY MORNING WHILE I WAS PLAYING IN THE YARD WITH THE old dog by his kennel, happy that we were beginning to be friends and that I could already pet him without his being at the end of his long chain, a motorcycle with a sidecar suddenly drove into the yard, and in it were two German soldiers.

I hardly had time to be startled. Continuing to stroke the dog's neck, I managed to half smile at the invaders. I thought they were looking me over as they parked their motorcycle, but they went into the kitchen, and their behavior gave no indication that they were after me in particular. As soon as the door shut behind them I slowly turned around, ambled lazily to the gate of the barn, went through it to the back door—and shot like lightning out to the fields, farther and farther away. Under the circumstances, my regular hiding place in the hay did not seem safe enough.

In the darkness of the second shed out in the fields, where I could hide behind a crack between the thick unplaned timbers, I stopped for the first time. Cool air from the deep pit where the ice was kept rose, the unhurried peace of the day of rest. It was hard to believe that much of anything could happen on such an ordinary day. A good hour passed and no one came near. I simply could not wait helplessly in a closed place, so I went out of the cornfield to look around. Then I heard Daugela shouting from afar, "Juodas, where are you?" Cautiously, I approached him from the side, keeping my distance. As usual, he had a light smile on his wrinkled face, as if to reassure me and put me at ease, for he had understood that I was frightened and he knew that he would find me at the spot where we had prearranged to meet. He had disturbing news: the Germans had come to tell him that because of the approaching front, all inhabitants of the area were being evacuated. They said the evacuation was temporary, no more than a few days, until the situation at the front stabilized. Everyone was to meet in the village with their wagons by two o'clock in the afternoon; they would be led out

in one of the convoys to a more distant village in the region. People were to take
with them only food and bedding. No one was to remain in the area.

Daugela was businesslike in spite of the onerous consequences of the order
for him—abandoning his livestock, leaving his farm without a caretaker, and so
forth. The past few days had been relatively quiet. We were used to the flashes
of light from the front, which had not grown more frequent, and the muffled
rumblings, which brought with them light tremors in the earth, had not grown
stronger. The obvious conclusion was that the front was still far off and approaching slowly and that the evacuation would last quite some time. Shame-
faced, he said he could not take me with him, as I was likely to arouse suspicion
among his neighbors in the caravan, and the longer the evacuation lasted, the
greater the danger. He suggested that I, too, abandon the place because the region would certainly be crawling with soldiers. Daugela said that I should go in
the opposite direction, eastward, to the large forests that he had already discussed
with me several times. In the forest I could hide for a few days, and the Russians
would arrive there first.

Daugela was apologetic as he spoke, but the idea of going east did not appeal
to me. He tried to persuade me that the effort was worth it, and that I would be
able to do it. My outward appearance was now that of a local youth, and I would
not provoke unusual questions if I were seen alone. He would provide me with
some food for the journey and would also leave food for me in one of the stable's
mangers, just in case I had to retrace my steps or arrived back to the farm before
he did.

When I recall this conversation, I cannot help but be amazed by the man's
dedication. A harsh decree had just been imposed upon him, a farmer, yet he
came out to the fields to look for the Jewish boy in hiding with him, and to explain to him—patiently—how to find his way to the forest.

It all happened quickly. Daugela went straight back to help Ona pack, lock
up, feed and water the livestock, hastily harness a horse to a vastly overloaded
wagon, and hide various items of value. There was no point in being a nuisance
to them by asking further questions, and within a few minutes there I was, non-
plussed and confused, leaving for the first time through the front yard of the
house, treading eastward on the main road in broad daylight. What did I take
with me? Did I have on sandals or shoes? Did I climb up to my hiding place once
more to take anything? In my pockets or my bundle I had two or three apples, a
few slices of bread, and a large slice of sausage, from which I immediately took a
few bites. And perhaps I had a few folded banknotes that Mother had sent with

me like iron supplements, and which I in my innocence believed could help me at a time like this.

Half incredulously, I took to the road, walking along it with no idea where it was taking me. To my relief, there were no people as far as I could see; everyone was apparently busy getting ready to evacuate. This was the same road by which I had arrived several weeks before. As I walked along, I began to realize, with rising discomfort, that the road was leading me closer and closer to town. I hoped that the road would fork to the east before reaching the entrance to the town.

Just then, however, an air raid began. One after another, airplanes started diving and strafing the ground. Their principal target was the railroad somewhere ahead of me. A freight train stopped on the tracks and caught fire. Though this happened at a distance of a kilometer or two from me, the sight so frightened me that I jumped into the ditch beside the road. It had been more than three years since I had seen such a spectacle from the wide windowsill of our old house, and my curiosity had not lessened. While lying on the ground, I tried to identify the airplanes and the logic of their actions, but they were soon gone. The train did not look to me like a military one; it looked more like a freight train transporting sacks of sugar from the factory. What was the point of bombing it? I felt insecure in the exposed place where I lay, and there was a grove of trees not far away. Although it brought me closer to the town and the burning train, the noise of which I could hear from where I stood, I was drawn to it; perhaps it would serve as a temporary substitute for the forest Daugela had told me about.

As I got closer to the grove, I realized that it was much smaller than I had thought and that a bewildered family had already taken shelter there. The airplanes, which had disappeared for only a short while, reappeared as if they had forgotten something. This time they hovered suspiciously over our little patch of forest. Once more we crouched in ditches and depressions until the airplanes disappeared.

I realized that this was not a good place for me—because of the people, because the trees drew the attention of the bombers, and because the grove was too close to the railroad. So I got up and moved some distance away, weighing my course of action and waiting for the attack to end. As I looked at the deserted road, I suddenly saw the figure of a lone German soldier riding a motorcycle, climbing the road to our village. It was a strange sight, and I thought immediately that it must be Antanas, Ona's son. I gathered courage and called his name. At first he didn't hear, but I ran toward him and we met. As on every other Sunday, he was given a few hours' leave to visit his mother and had set out, unaware of what was happening. I informed him what had happened that morning and prepared him for the likelihood that he would find no one at home when he arrived. I got the impression that he would try to catch up with the evacuees and perhaps even join them.

The train cars, which before had looked like the broken beads of a necklace, now turned to a skeletal chain of hollow steel from which thick smoke still rose. It wasn't a good idea to return to the grove and the people in it. I had probably aroused their curiosity by talking to the German soldier—after having earlier pretended to be a deaf-mute. Nor did I have a strong desire to go far from the village. I began to feel hungry and decided to return to the barnyard and take the food Daugela had promised to leave for me. The fact that Ona's son had taken the same direction rather than turn around also strengthened my urge to go back.

It was late in the afternoon by then. When I returned to the yard, an odd silence greeted me. This was how the ghetto had been after it was evacuated. I hurried to the stable—the horses were gone. Deep in the manger I found, as Daugela had promised, a wrapped bundle; in it were another chunk of sausage and half a loaf of bread. After some hesitation, I finished them, still in the yard, and then set out again. I feared staying there alone, but I hated to go too far. Now that I knew the stretch of road to the grove of trees and the edge of town, I preferred to take it. I hoped night would soon fall and prevent me from advancing very far. I was an abandoned pup afraid to leave its kennel.

The angry arrival of a couple of airplanes at a fork in the road quickly sent me into a ditch where a Lithuanian couple and their child were already lying. The airplanes turned toward their unknown destinations on the outskirts of town and disappeared, and the couple argued about whether to go away or return to their home in spite of the Germans' orders. "Who are you, berniukas [little boy]?" they asked me. Their words, their manner of speech, and the way they took an interest in me led me to believe they were teachers. I answered them with hand gestures, as I thought a deaf-mute would.

The swooping plunges of airplanes along the road broke up our exchange and caused us all to jump once more into the ditch. Immediately, an argument started between the two good people as to how a deaf child could tell as well as they when an airplane was coming—they concluded that the deaf must be blessed with keen instincts.

Because of the heavy activity in the skies, now increased by rounds of anti-aircraft guns, the Lithuanians decided to leave the main road and the houses.

"Come with us, boy," the woman said. I gladly joined them—the abandoned pup had found a good-hearted passerby and began trailing after.

They crossed the main road and turned down a dirt road to the south, passing a brick granary that stood at some distance in the fields. The structure looked sound and capable of serving as a decent shelter. Opening the door revealed a scene reminiscent of kicking a clod of earth from an ants' nest in a field—the place swarmed with people. Entire families were there, the residents of the neighborhood, crowding excitedly around their bundles and telling one another their stormy adventures—a scene so very familiar to me. I do not know if they were hiding here because of the air raid or if they were trying to evade the order to evacuate that hung over them. Every so often the large doors opened and more people would crowd inside, like livestock seeking shelter in a blizzard.

The day was ending and the crowd readied itself, with much confusion, for a night's sleep. But then the doors opened once more, and there stood a number of German soldiers, machine guns in their hands. They spoke to those who were near the doors, briefly and sharply, without raising their voices, ordering everyone to clear out of the granary immediately—it was meant to house a unit of German soldiers. The announcement spread like a confused stammer through the crowd, accompanied by muttering and protest. In spite of the unusual circumstances, I felt a certain comfort and security in my anonymity within the grumbling crowd, which began moving slowly and with evident reluctance. Clearly they had never been in a ghetto.

The people emerged from the granary, and most of them miraculously disappeared. It was not clear to me what I would do now. And then, while I was trailing slowly behind the others, at a certain moment that was both sharply defined but not at all understood, I followed an inexplicable impulse to turn my head and look back.

In that same split second during the evening dusk, my eyes beheld an unearthly sight: away to the north, the entire sugar factory began, in one massive block, to rise slowly into the air; then during its slow disintegration, as in a slow-motion film, it began breaking into small bits, and the fragments started to float, in equally moderate tempo, down to the ground, piece by piece.

No sound had yet reached us and no flames could be seen. Perhaps a shock wave had reached me; otherwise, why had I suddenly turned around for no clear reason? Perhaps the teacher-couple was right about human instincts.

The sight was so shocking, so spectacular and frightening, that I started an uncontrollable, headlong, and aimless flight to the southwest, casting glances over my shoulder as I ran. All this happened before a loud, rolling rumble reached me, shaking the ground like an earthquake. The noise had not yet subsided when a column of fire began to shoot up behind me. Giant flames burst into the sky from the factory, lighting up the area as though it were broad daylight. They shot up higher and higher through the polished ribs of the steel structure and filled the space with purple tongues that turned instantly into black smoke, shooting out on all sides and engulfing everything around them.

The silhouette of the factory, the mighty and solid foundation of the entire region, crumbled into pieces before my eyes. White plumes of steam, pulsing and whistling like a hundred engines, began hissing in the covering darkness; evidently they were caused by steam engines splitting apart. A splutter of small explosions followed, as if the place were stocked with caches of arms, now being set ablaze one after another. There had been rumors for weeks that the Germans were stocking the factory with dynamite, truckload after truckload, to blow it up in case of retreat.

I ran like a frightened hare, without knowing where I was going. Then, as if timed to coincide with the explosion of the factory, I suddenly heard gunshots. At first I thought they belonged to machine gunners in the granary trying out their weapons, but I soon realized the shots were coming from a different direction. Rockets rose red in the sky, light artillery shells exploded not far away, and rounds of tracer bullets flared with splendid slowness, chasing one another as though trying to impose rhythm and order on the surrounding chaos.

The entire area lit up. Suddenly, inexplicably, bursts of fire issued from behind every mound and stack of straw, and though the shots were not necessarily directed anywhere in particular, the reddish cascades of tracer shells began illuminating my path of escape. Viper-like hisses swept closer and closer to my head, leaving little doubt that they were bullets.

I ran and ran, and fell. Again I saw no one around me—I was alone. Far to the north, the burning frame of the factory continued to light the horizon like a sunset, like the red copy of a sketch whose original had disappeared.

I ran and ran; I ran to save my soul. I understood that the front had suddenly closed in on me, and that I was scuttling through the space between the two sides as they faced off with fiery displays of strength.

Through the changeable, flickering dusk I saw a number of houses, and I fled automatically in their direction. As I drew nearer, I saw a dark stain in the ground—a pit or dugout. I threw myself into this with such force that I couldn't stop it, even after noticing that the place was full of people. One or two other refugees from the granary may have tumbled in after me.

The dugout was narrow, and people lay crowded in it in weary silence. Those near the opening moved a bit to make room for me, and there I stayed on my knees, curled up and cold, until the next morning. Sleep was next to impossible. The noise of explosions grew louder, and people prayed that we would not be hit. It bothered me very much to be so near the opening. During intermissions of gunshot rounds and shell explosions, there were broken snatches of conversation—it was evident that everyone else knew one another and that I was the only stranger. I continued to play deaf and dumb; who knew what tomorrow would bring and who the soldiers around us might be?

For the last part of the night, the sounds of war seemed to grow tired and sleep. All was quiet. My neighbors, who had been talking in whispers, also stopped. Once more I was in a shelter, once more crowded into a mass of waiting people, who strained to decipher the secrets in the silence.

Then human voices broke the stillness. At first far away, then nearer and nearer. They walked around us, calling and shouting. They were evidently working with a certain purpose. Were they more local people searching for shelter, or soldiers looking for something, stationed above us for some unknown purpose?

We heard footsteps approaching, and against the pale sky we saw a man's silhouette. He came straight for the dugout; we held our breath.

Carefully, he groped his way inside; perhaps he had even started to lower his pants when he cursed angrily and went away.

The curse was in Russian.

I was saved.

A flood of words escaped from my mouth. I had to announce my existence, to explain in a few words to the farmers near me who I really was; how I, a Jewish child from a distant city, had come to this far-off place. In their eyes I was like an odd creature who had landed from the moon—all the Jews in the area, from the nearby town, had been killed off three years before.

No, it was impossible to say it all, nor could I express it. In the meantime, we still did not dare leave the dugout. Only later, in full daylight, when quiet continued to reign, did we emerge and stretch our limbs. Mortars were standing all around us, their crews earnestly engaged in cleaning and oiling. They gave us tight-lipped smiles: it was a 3-inch mortars platoon of the Red Army that liberated me—not with a glorious parade or festive songs but with a ripe Russian curse.

It took several days, perhaps even weeks, before I fully understood what had happened in such an offhand way during the twilight hours of the morning, and with what casual simplicity the miracle took place. Everything during the last day had occurred with inexplicable suddenness. Only the morning before I had been petting a dog in its kennel, then the sidecar motorcycle had arrived and overnight the area had changed hands. And it had happened at night, which added a mysterious dimension. The darkness that lifted was like a slowly rising curtain in an opera, revealing rescuing angels in the light of day. Dumbfounded by the tempo of events during the past day, I wandered as if drunk among the soldiers. I felt the need to present myself to them, to tell and tell—my rebirth demanded an endless stream of telling. Some soldiers nodded understandingly; some added that they had "Hebrew" friends, as they say in Russian. One officer perhaps even patted me on the back and tried to speak to me in rudimentary Yiddish. I will never remember all that happened that day. The soldiers were busy fortifying their position and getting ready to move on, and we citizens were ordered to move south before the battle was renewed.

One of the families that had been kind to me in the dugout asked me to join them. At their farm they harnessed a horse to a wagon, fed their animals, gathered a few possessions, and traveled to another village that was farther away from the currently drawn line of battle and where their relatives lived. There was no point, they said, in any other course of action—Daugela's house might very well still be on the wrong side of the front, and it was better not to return to check, especially since he himself had left. So I went with these people.

The trip to the relatives' village took no more than an hour or two, but for me it was a journey as magical as the entire day. Our path wound through remote country roads; we avoided the main roads, which were full of military vehicles. I felt as though I had been thrown behind the scenes of a gigantic play: everywhere we went, army troops were in movement or getting organized—a sleepy rural area had been transformed overnight into a stormy arena of activity. Tents were pitched, telephone lines were stretched, short signposts were erected at every crossroads. From groves of trees tents displayed the symbol of the Red Cross, which I remembered from the first day of the war. The soldiers were friendly and happy, their actions sure; their behavior was free, careless even: cigarettes made of *mahorka,* leaves of tobacco dried and cut by hand and rolled in a strip of newspaper, hung constantly between their lips, and crumpled sailor caps sat low on their foreheads. With their noisy, never-ending bustle, accompanied by vehement curses and friendly interjections on the order of "anu rebiata"—come on, guys—they were like a traveling troupe of tin-smiths. Whenever they stopped us for inspection, they exchanged lively greetings with us and good-naturedly let us go on. I wanted to run from one to the other as I once ran after them begging for *znatchok* (a red star) as a souvenir, embracing them and kissing them, letting each and every one of them know how grateful I was for being saved from certain death. But they were busy, their minds on other things.

We got to the relatives' home. It was a huge, hospitable house with several wings, into which many refugees were already packed. They put food out on a table in the yard and at night spread blankets on the ground for us. It looked as though we might have to wait for an indefinite period of time until the front moved on and everyone could go back home.

Rumors that the Germans would attack to regain their territory never stopped circulating, and I was afraid.

Strange days ensued. Signs of war were everywhere. We were close to the front, but its lines were unclear. Cannons echoed and airplanes dropped bombs, but we could not discern who was attacking whom. During air raids we often dispersed into the fields to distance ourselves from the house and the Russian troops stationed nearby. The planes flew over without doing harm; no bombs fell close to us.

Every day the Lithuanians returned to their farm, which lay inside the front; I went with them. After several trips I knew the route. The Russians camping in the Lithuanians' house greeted us warmly but allowed us to stay only for a short time. The walk to the farm was always packed with adventure. The front was close and the danger of being shelled or bombed was ever-present. We tried to avoid large buildings or encampments of soldiers. Most of the airplanes flying overhead in daylight hours were Russian, on their way to the front. They would pass over us in a low, characteristic formation; in the center, like the head of an arrow, a group of four heavy, slow, double-engine bombers; beside them a pair of light and nimble fighter planes perpetually making seemingly theatrical swoops to the sides, up and down, apparently ensuring the route. When they returned from their mission a short time later, the bombers flew higher and more swiftly, their load visibly lightened. The fighter planes continued to buzz around them like playful pups. One day a pair of such planes loomed overhead while we were walking in the fields. Even though we were safe because they were "ours," we instinctively jumped into the ditch beside the road, and I cut my foot on the rusty barbed-wire fence. Although it bled and even hurt, I kept going and didn't pay much attention to the wound. But on my return to our lodgings, I believe they dressed the wound—I may even have been attended by the military medic. How-ever, about two weeks later the wound, which apparently had not been properly cleaned, gave me a fever and caused me quite a bit of trouble. Today I still have tiny scars on the top of my left foot, and they mean a lot to me, providing me with the only physical evidence I need to prove that my story is true.

The Russians had *katyushas*—female soldiers who bore arms, wore uniforms and insignia, and served in various units in the field. They were equals among equals and were given no special treatment. My eyes were drawn to boy soldiers serving in different units. They were aged twelve to sixteen, boys who had been swept up by the military campaigns, bore arms and wore uniforms, sometimes with medals, spit, smoked, and cursed, tried to speak in a deep bass voice like adults, and filled various soldierly functions. I wanted with all my heart to be just like them and join the Red Army.

A few more days passed and one morning the troops disappeared. The Lithua-nians were free to return home, taking me with them; the front had moved elsewhere. On our return trip, I heard that all the neighboring villages were under Russian control and that their evacuated residents had come back home. Full of gratitude, I parted from my good-hearted hosts and excitedly set out for Daugela's house.

This time I approached Daugela's house through the front gate. At the time, Daugela was closer to me than any other person, my tenuous tie to my true identity and the world where I had once belonged. I went to him, a new self. I opened the gate: chickens were in the yard, the pigs' familiar grunts rose from the pigsty—I had been away only about a week, and nothing had changed. Where was Daugela? Ona met me in the kitchen with an agreeable look, but she did not seem overjoyed to see me. The master might be in the hayloft, she said.

I went out to the stable, my good old shelter. Daugela wasn't with the horses or anywhere I looked. I shouted once, twice, three times, until finally a muffled answer came from the mounds of hay—my master and rescuer was in my hid-ing place under the haystack, fast asleep. I put up the ladder and he descended, somewhat sheepishly. We hugged each other and shook hands. The Russians, it appeared, had begun enlisting workers to pave an airport, and my Goy was try-ing to evade the draft in my former hiding place.

We briefly exchanged news of the last few days. My heart was full and over-flowing, ready to tell the whole story of my exodus, but circumstances didn't al-low it. He said that after gathering the country people together, the Germans had led them by caravan to a neighboring village. There they were kept under heavy guard for a few days until they were allowed to return home, where they found themselves under Russian rule. The Russians tried to confiscate Daugela's horses, but he had succeeded in hiding them in the fields. Now they were after the man himself. While explaining this to me, he asked me for a letter testifying that he had saved me. With the help of such a document, he felt certain they would leave him alone and even help him out in the future. I solemnly wrote him a note in the most official language I could command, both in Lithuanian and Yiddish, stating that Vincas Daugela of the village of Liepynų in Julijampole Province had hidden me in his home from such a date to such a date, risking his life to save me from the Germans, and that I would remember him always for it. I also requested that he be helped in any way possible. I signed the note with my full name, giving my old address in the city.

We descended from the loft and ate a good meal in his house. Daugela insisted that I would not sleep in my customary place that night, as I had planned to do, but in his house. He also suggested repeatedly that I stay with him until the situation on the front was clear. The front might pull back—the Germans were strong and had not yet been defeated. I thanked him again and again, but said I wanted most of all to try to get back to my city as soon as possible. He promised to inquire of friends about the location of the front in that region and about possible means of transportation.

Later that evening, or perhaps the next morning, Daugela informed me that my city was also in Russian hands, and that the way was open. We could get in touch with the military command in the city and find out how to get there. The man entreated me again to stay, and I am unable to say whether his offer to remain with him stemmed from politeness only or a sincere and honest wish for me to stay. But I had already decided to leave the next day. Had I heard then that most of my city had been burned? I cannot remember. I had no patience at the time, and didn't want to stay even an hour longer.

Morning came. I went out to the loft and, groping stubbornly, extracted the few belongings I had accumulated during my stay that were scattered among layers of hay. This time I took leave of Ona as an equal. Once more I left with the man, as in the beginning, by wagon, but this time I sat up straight at his side with a secret joy in my heart, and we were going in the opposite direction—toward the city. And even though he feared that his horse would be confiscated, Daugela insisted that he bring me to the local military command.

In the city, they directed us to the military post. The commander greeted me very cordially, with a broad smile. He listened to my halting Russian and clapped

Daugela on the shoulder. I can imagine that Daugela expected a more ceremonious acknowledgment. The officer gave me a note for the military policeman who was directing traffic at the northern exit from town, and Daugela took me there. We shook hands and said good-bye. It was clear to both of us that our parting was temporary and that we would meet again. I thanked him again and again, using all the words of gratitude in my vocabulary. A military truck arrived. I was hoisted up, and the truck pulled out, heading north.

RETURN

Once more I was on the road, only six weeks since my previous journey over the same path. Two or three Lithuanians were with me; they, too, were returning to their homes. The roads were loaded with military vehicles traveling in every direction. Occasionally we cast worried glances at airplanes passing in the sky—certain anxieties were not easily alleviated. What if the Germans suddenly came back, bursting in upon us and cutting off this narrow road stretching like a slender thread between yesterday and tomorrow, turning the wheel back? This latent fear would hover over me for many years to come.

After an hour or two of travel we were close to the city, and the truck stopped for a rest in a village along the main road. I took a short stroll. I soon found myself looking at the single remaining wall of a building with a splendid Hebrew inscription on its side—the burned facade of a synagogue. A pile of bricks and iron behind the wall was already beginning to blend in with the surrounding rubble, wordlessly telling me of the terrible fate of the Jewish community there.

For years I didn't fully understand why I was so impressed by the image of the ruined synagogue in the village of Gudleva. Perhaps it was because, except for the sugar factory, it was the first glimpse I had of war's destruction on my return trip and of the destruction of the Jewish world everywhere. In this synagogue, too, like the one in my grandfather's village, they had imprisoned the Jews of the surrounding towns before killing them. From here on, through my future years of wandering, the reality of half-bombed buildings never ceased to accompany me like a permanent backdrop, depressing my spirits.

We got back in the vehicle and before long found ourselves approaching the city's suburbs. Here the driver turned left, and we had to get off. Only a few kilometers lay between us and the city itself, and I started to cross them on foot.

I was following the daily path of the airport brigade. It was a hot day in the first part of August. My backpack was getting heavy, and I grew thirsty. Slowly we made our way to the slope that descended toward the confluence of the rivers. From there we could see the entire city, which looked quite undamaged, even though a few of the river's bridges lay askew like unwanted children's toys.

The other passengers went off to their destinations, and I was soon alone. The road I was on dipped down toward the riverbank and turned into the main thoroughfare of one of the suburbs. I noticed a rifle-bearing soldier walking with two people, a young man and woman. Their hair was thin, and they were dressed in a patchwork of ill-fitting clothes. I must have heard snatches of their speech as I approached, and there may have been something in their looks that prompted me to ask out loud, "Yidn?" ("Jews?")

And they answered, astounded, "Ya, geviss Yidn. Un ver bist du, yingele?" ("Yes, certainly Jews. And who are you, child?")

Our steps slowed. I struggled to say in a few words who I was, where I had been, and where I was bound. At first hesitant, stuttering like a man who has long sat without speaking in solitary confinement, thickly saying a few words, choosing a few sentences to utter for the first time out loud in the light of day, I found myself talking to the first two Jews I had met in many months, in my own language, my native tongue, Yiddish. My surprise was so great, my excitement so strong, that I burst out crying, shedding a river of tears as deep and wide as the rivers below me, tears that had been dammed up and held within me for months, for years.

And this young couple, who had just now emerged from the forest, together with the soldier who had stopped them and was taking them to the police station, all looked abashed at the big boy crying in the middle of the street.

Intermediate Epilogue

I never saw my Daugela again.

I wrote him a letter some time later, then a second and a third. I opened them with "Brangus Mano Gelbetoyas"—"My Dear Rescuer." After she had arrived in Israel, my friend Clara told me that Daugela had once gone to our city looking for me, and met her. But I was already an ocean away.

Thirty-four years later, while writing these pages, I suddenly woke up, as from a deep sleep, and realized that during all these years I had never tried to contact the people who saved me.

Once awakened, I began a search for my Lithuanians. I remembered names and places only dimly. I wrote to the secretaries of labor councils and the editors of newspapers in Lithuania, but received no response. Friends referred me to a person of central importance, the vice president of the Lithuanian Council (Lithuanian Soviet) who was known for his affection for Jews, the poet Miežolaitis. It is he who found Ona Pečkyte for me, and he who told me her name. I also heard back from the village of Liepynų—I received a letter from Ona.

From her letter fell a photograph of an elderly couple standing in front of a house. In her letter—written for her by a young girl—Ona told me that the master had passed away four years earlier. "He always remembered you and thought that perhaps you were drowned in the flood," she wrote.

Later, I learned that a huge flood had indeed inundated our city during those years, a flood of the kind I had been afraid of as a child, and many children from an orphanage had lost their lives in it.

"I am sending you a picture of us by the pear tree, which you probably remember. I myself am now old and alone, with many pains in my legs. I can hardly walk. Some good people here bring me food."

I was so excited, so happy to hear from her. I wrote her back once more, and then again; I sent her packages of food. In my next letter I planned to ask her, among other things, what had happened to her son. Did she see him after the war? She had said she was lonely. If he had died during the war, I may have been the last one to see him that Sunday, the evening of the German retreat from the area.

And then I received one other letter from Lithuania, from Pečkyte, it is for me perhaps the most precious of all. It enabled me to fill in several pieces in the puzzle of my story. She finished the letter in this way: "I don't think what I did was heroic. I'm a woman of faith, and I was happy to be of some help to a person in distress."

I stayed in the city for a year and a half and never once tried to find her, to identify her. Now I wrote to her, thanking her. During the next few years I sent her packages of food, as well as rosary beads made of olive wood from Bethlehem, which pleased her, devout Catholic that she was. Faithfully, in so far as I could, I stayed with her to the last.

12

A New Year

The First Days

In the blink of an eye, at dawn, the Germans were gone. In an instant the death sentence that had been hanging constantly over my head was repealed and was no more. And right away, as a direct result of my great excitement, I felt the need for action, for movement. Staying in one place had been part of the hiding. Now I had to move, to leave, to go on, ever onward, anywhere I wanted, to explore urgently the dream made real.

It was like emerging from a hole after an earthquake, like leaving the ark after the flood. Who was left? What had happened to the rest? The whole point of liberation was to discover that your loved ones had been spared. How else did I imagine what liberation would be like when it came, if not that every member of our family should be reunited, and that we should return to our old home? Failing that, the miracle would be flawed. We must meet, sit down together, and talk and talk and talk. It was a necessary part of the anticipated reunion at the end of it all that we exchange accounts of our experiences. Listen to my story, hear what happened to me.

This last pleasure of liberation was in many respects denied me. Perhaps this is why these pages were born now, so many years later.

One hundred and fifty days had passed between my departure from Mother and the day of liberation. One hundred and fifty days of hiding, leading to my rebirth. But after liberation, why shouldn't she come, why shouldn't I meet her immediately?

Mother never appeared, and something lay shriveled inside me for many years, refusing to give up waiting for her to come and reclaim me.

Shortly after I met the young Jewish couple, I found myself in an office, sitting across from a man who first listened intently to my story, then immediately rattled off to me—and although I was only a child of eleven years and two months, I could sense his smug, businesslike self-satisfaction—the deeds and achievements of the newly founded Jewish committee that was helping refugees return to the city: a soup kitchen serving free food, a clothes warehouse for basic gear, a list of abandoned apartments for a place to stay. Before long they intended to open a dormitory, and perhaps even a school, if they found enough surviving children. Volunteers were at hand throughout the city and region, and such children were already being discovered. He recited these accomplishments with sparkling eyes, but all I wanted was something to eat and a place to sleep and sleep some more.

I went to sleep in a flat that had belonged to the families of German officers, together with other people to whom I had been assigned. The former dwellers had obviously abandoned the flat in haste, leaving much behind.

The next morning I went straight to old Julija, hoping for some kind of continuity to bind together the drastic changes I had undergone. I found her at home, embroidering, happy to see me. She told me of the hard times the city had gone through, days of bombings and battles. Now, thank God, it was all over. She had been an eyewitness to the ghetto's destruction, and told me how it had been wrapped for days in flames, occasionally emitting loud explosions. It was said that not a single house was whole anymore, and not a single Jew remained. Pečkyte had visited her a few days before it happened and had taken some clothes for me. Julija had hidden the rest of my possessions—my books and stamps—just as I had left them. She suggested that I stay with her until my situation cleared up. I didn't feel I had the strength to stay there. She said nothing about her son. She knew nothing about my sister, not having seen the family of Martha for several weeks. Perhaps the blond woman would know more about her, and about my mother as well, but they had moved to a new flat in the center of the town after the liberation. I got their address and went there immediately.

I found them in a nice flat on the slope of Green Hill, which faces the city center. They had evidently received their place from the authorities, perhaps because they had adopted a Russian girl. They met me with great kindness, happy to see that I was alive and had returned, and asked me questions about my adventures. They invited me to dinner, apologizing for the shortage of food in their house. The woman told me a little about her last meeting with my mother, who had shared her worries about how I was doing in the far-off village. They had also discussed my sister, but neither of them had any news about her. Martha had stopped coming to the factory recently; apparently she had followed her mother and my sister to her relatives in the village, and now it was only a matter of waiting for their return.

A heavy, debilitating weariness came over me; my head grew feverish and seemed full of lead. I couldn't refuse her offer to lie down for a short nap. I was put to bed under white sheets and fell into a deep sleep. I woke up near noon the next day, my body burning. It was clear that I was not in the best of health. This was not the time I would have chosen to appear weak. I was uncomfortable now, of all times appearing weak and in need of compassion from people. Before the war I was constantly ill with a sore throat; my parents had considered having my tonsils removed. During the war, amazingly enough, my illnesses had disappeared. This time, too, I would have preferred to ignore my fever, but a swelling in my groin indicated an infection—the cuts in the soles of my feet, received from the barbed wire in the battlefields a couple of weeks before, had swollen and become infected.

My hosts expressed concern for the neglected state of my wounds and began treating them with what means they had in the house. Pharmacies were not available yet in their region. And so my short visit with these Lithuanians turned into a stay lasting several days. Hallucinating with fever, I lay on their sofa in the guestroom, trying hard to make polite conversation or to leaf through old German journals, constantly falling asleep. I hated to trouble these good people, and I was aware of the diminishing store of food in their house.

On the third day of lying abed sick, my condition improved and my fever subsided. Like a wounded wild animal that slips into the forest upon healing, I hastened to take leave of my generous hosts. Tottering and weak, I left their house and never saw them again, although I continued to send and receive greetings through old Julija. I looked for them for years but did not succeed in tracking them down, since I don't know their names.

I returned to the "Jewish courtyard"—the public kitchen where the survivors congregated. The place drew people like a magnet and swarmed like a train station platform, with newcomers always arriving. As in a dream, incredulously, people would find one another—neighbors, friends, and sometimes, if much more rarely, even family members. There was no end to the excitement, embraces, and tears. Some incessantly told their stories and the miracles that saved them; for others, their downcast faces, impassive and closed, spoke for them.

Everyone who came here saw himself, at first, as the only survivor, the last remaining Jew. Now, upon meeting other survivors, they wanted first of all to hear from loved ones and unburden their hearts.

The more I heard about things that happened, about deaths occurring even at the last minute, the more my wonder at my own survival grew. Only now did I begin to grasp the miracle that had kept me alive.

The days were warm and long, the last days of August. New faces appeared and old ones vanished. Some continued to wander, some joined the army. I was one of those who stayed where he was—after all, I had nowhere to go and I was comfortable where I was, and with the adults I felt I was an equal. Among those gathered there I had a special status, the recipient of restrained and painful craving—a child, one of the few who were saved. The camaraderie of survivors enfolded me, and I let myself sink into its embrace with longing and eagerness. Every day I returned to the kitchen.

One of these days, I thought to myself, I will go to the ghetto.

Each night I slept in different quarters, tagging along with people who invited me to join them. Most of them were young people coming in from the forests or rare hiding spots. Friendly and hospitable, they heaped unlimited affection and attention on me. Some said they would like to adopt me, a kind of substitute for the little brother or son they had lost. The dwellings were full of all manner of good things. Preserved food, sausages, and cheeses made every evening meal an extended feast.

Gradually, Jewish partisans who had fought in the forests began trickling into the city. Most of them were young, with noncommittal expressions, older than their years. They went around in groups, smoking heavily and holding tight to their weapons, most of which had flat cartridge magazines that looked like plates attached to the gun barrel—weapons they had used to kill Germans. Again and again I asked about my mother—perhaps she had escaped to them at the last moment? Many knew her from the days of the ghetto underground, but they had not seen her in the forest.

I was entranced by these weapon-bearing fighters. They seemed to me proud and strong. I amused myself with the thought of joining their paramilitary troops, serving like the young boy soldiers I had seen on the front. Every once in a while one of the partisans would be alerted to rescue a Jewish child from a monastery or from a Lithuanian family that refused to return its ward. There were also whispers about vendettas and acts of revenge that they didn't hesitate to perform against Lithuanians.

How long did I wander about on my own? I suppose it was for two or three weeks, perhaps even less. But I recall the period as a long and special one.

One day after my foot had completely healed, I went to the ghetto.

On the way there I must have stopped at old Julija's house, descending from there by the same path I had climbed a few months before. The path I had taken was now a wide paved road, along which there now stood, over the route my boat had taken across the river, a gigantic wooden pontoon bridge bedecked with flags and slogans.

High dirt ramps connected the bridge with Varnių Street on the far bank and the path in the valley. At the entrance to the bridge stood a plaque stating the number of the engineering unit that "erected this bridge in record time to allow the brave troops of the Red Army to pursue the Nazi animal to Berlin." Below it was hung the placard of the battalion, with pictures of two soldier-builders, Stakhanovites, in a special frame, so honored for their outstanding personal efforts during the construction of the bridge.

I was reminded of a river festival to which I was not allowed to go; Father had punished me for not having returned home on time on another occasion. The next day in school they told me how festive riverboats had made wide dizzy circles in the water, accompanied by orchestras and cheering crowds, sending colorful fireworks high into the sky, joyfully tooting their horns. All my friends had gone, and I remembered my disappointment for years.

I walked over the bridge, approaching the other side. The bridge rose high, joining with wonderful simplicity the two banks of the river, taking me directly to the beginning of Varnių Street, where the gate had stood through which I had left a few months before. A strange sight met my eyes—the wide expanse of the ghetto, which I had once thought was infinite, had narrowed. The space that was once packed with scores of streets whose names I knew by heart, the hundreds of houses whose images were etched in my memory, had been turned, incredibly, into a lot a few hundred meters across; you could see from one side of it to the other.

And what was on the other side of the empty lot? Lithuanian houses. Finished, painted, lace curtains stretched across the windows, perky flowerpots perched on the windowsills. They now surrounded and closed off the ghetto in a tight, dense row, like people standing around an open grave. The storm of fire that had raged here stopped beside them and left them intact.

I got closer to the rectangular lot of the former ghetto. I was already familiar with scenes of partial ruins. But here, within the ghetto, the destruction was complete. Almost nothing remained standing, neither wall nor roof. Only chimneys. These, miraculously, stayed upright and intact, lined up in rows like tombstones. Made of brick, they were all that survived of the combustible wooden houses. Their bases began with smashed kitchen stoves; their tops were high in the sky. Stripped of everything that enveloped them in the houses of living people, they stood upright in the ruins like sentries frozen at their posts. Surrounding each chimney was a heap of rubble. Pieces of walls and doorjambs, twisted tin roofing, skeletons of steel beds and oven ranges crumpled by the heat. Further away lay everything that had been thrown in the air by explosions, left where it had fallen—shoes, quilt feathers, torn letters, scraps of clothes. The ruins of human habitation, with all its signs and marks, lay strewn about—once the soul of the house had expired—like spilled guts.

Since most of the houses in the ghetto had been houses of only one or two stories, their ruins didn't amount to too much. This was not the case, however, with the glory of the ghetto—the large apartment complexes. The ruins of these buildings formed veritable hills. I stood and looked. The last time I stood there I had seen Zelda crossing the street. This time I found a scrap of the Torah vellum lying in the dust; I picked it up and took it with me.

Human body parts were visible through the ruins here and there, the remains of those who tried to escape from their houses—they may even have reached the fence—but were caught, their bodies thrown back into the flames and not completely consumed. There were also whole bodies, bloated like big round drums, crammed into the opening of a cellar where the staircase had collapsed, as if they were still striving to break out of the fatal trap that had closed over them. Many other corpses remained hidden deep in the rubble, where only the smell of their slow decay rising from the ground, a heavy, unbearable stench that hovered for a long time over the dead, revealed their existence in the days to come.

Could my mother's body have been among them? The possibility never even entered my mind.

But there were also those who remained alive, thanks to the *malinas*. My friend Alik and his mother, and Bashele and her mother were saved this way. Fortunately, the tunnels of their *malinas* led to empty lots or to a ruined glass hothouse, where the tongues of fire didn't reach. For about two weeks they were confined without movement in their hiding places before they were able to crawl out, feeble and dehydrated, into the arms of their liberators.

It was not hard to find our house at Vigrių 44, since the house was on a corner lot. I found the remains of our closet in the corner. My treasury, my private kingdom, everything I had collected during the ghetto years. The metal objects in the drawer—keys, recognizable locks—were now bent and blackened, and my alarm clocks were melted.

Later, I found a stack of family pictures at the foot of the staircase, about a dozen photographs that stuck together and miraculously survived on the ground near the cellar entrance—the same cellar that had saved my life a few months before and that had somehow survived the waves of destruction unscathed. I cannot explain how these photographs—pictures of our family, no less—reached this spot and escaped the all-consuming fire that raged all about, as if my mother herself had placed them there six weeks before, just as she used to leave lunch for me. Perhaps an explosion or a burst of flames had propelled the bundle of photographs out of the burning wooden closet toward the steps and out of the range of the fire. With trembling hands I took the pictures, hoping to keep them with me for a long time to come.

The ghetto had been emptied of houses and of people, and I found this hard to believe. Where were they all, all my people?

I went down to the graveyard on the riverbank. There were the old graves with improvised tombstones that I had known from before. Among them I seem to recall one carrying a single short name, "Mek." On the edge of the field there were now long, fresh piles of dirt, evidently gathered there during recent days. Lacking tombstones, the mounds were mute, keeping their secret.

And unlike Jeremiah or Job, I could not throw myself on the ruins, wear sackcloth and ashes, and lament my destroyed world. Only a long sobbing cry came over me where my house at Vigrių 44 once stood. I wept without restraint for a long time.

To this day my great lament pulses in my breast, accompanied by a strong sense of belonging. I am still from there.

I crossed the river several times to return to the ghetto territory. After the first visit, I remembered the washtub that Mother had buried. On my next trip I began scrabbling where I thought our corner of the shed in the yard had been; a bad odor still hung over the place. And indeed, after a little digging, I was excited to encounter a tin object. I wasn't strong enough to remove the entire tub, and only dislodged the lid. Most of the contents had been reduced to charcoal by the terrific heat that raged above it. The small wooden board was in place as Mother had left it. And although it was baked at the top of the treasure, the writing could still be read thanks to the glistening lead of the chemist's pencil. I was excited by the discovery, and at first I was inclined to cover it back up and postpone removal of its contents to another day. But there were many signs of snooping and digging in the area by Lithuanians—it was said they had found not a little plunder there. I feared that if I covered the tub back up, others would discover its traces and scatter its burned contents on all sides.

Another Jewish boy happened to be there, and together we hoisted the tub from the dirt and ashes. I loaded it onto a big board and, like a persistent ant, dragged it and its contents—I believe someone helped me part of the way—into the city, to the home of Julija across the river. There I left it as it was for a long time before returning and taking it with me.

In another trip to the ghetto—the visits were never easy, not even in terms of reaching the ghetto by way of a long, tiring walk through Green Hill and over the bridge—I came back and wandered through the ruins surrounding my house, unwilling to let go. Perhaps I would find something where my friends' destroyed houses had stood—Johann of Innsbruck's microscope, chess pieces, or the board for our button soccer game.

At the Dieners' Home

Where was my sister? In August of liberation year she would have been seven years old. Mother was clearly not in the area; perhaps she was in the camps. But my little sister was supposed to be in the vicinity, and she should have been the first person I met within the gates of the city. Yet she wasn't there. Julija and the blond woman believed that, like many others, Martha's family had removed to the country until the storm passed. So I waited.

One day, near the soup kitchen, a couple stopped me and started up a conversation. I had met the man, Nahum, the day before. Who are you, boy? How were you saved? What do you know of your family? These were questions I was used to answering. The couple exchanged glances during our talk. They also asked questions about my family abroad. I named uncles in the United States and Jerusalem, whose address had stuck in my memory from a New Year's greeting they had sent.

We then said good-bye and separated. A few hours later I met them again in the same place. This time, after a few polite words, Nahum's face took on a ceremonious expression and he said, hesitatingly, "There's something we wanted to ask you this morning, but we decided to think carefully about it again. Would you join us and come live with us?"

He went on to say that the thought had not left his mind ever since the day before, when he had first met me. He had gone home and told his wife, Magda, and they had come here together this morning to have a look at me. After they had gone back to talk the matter over, they had made up their minds about making the offer.

Seeing my discomfiture, they told me a little more about themselves. They were a young, childless couple from the ghetto who had been saved by hiding in a Lithuanian friend's flat during the past year. Nahum was a lawyer and was about to win a very respectable position—chief notary of our city, a post with status and many privileges. He would receive a good salary, a handsome and spacious apartment downtown, and superior food rations, so they would have no trouble taking care of my needs. They realized that I was waiting for the possible return of my family, which they wished with all their heart to happen. But meanwhile, or if, God forbid, my wishes didn't come true, I would be as welcome to them as a son, their own child for all intents and purposes.

They spoke more, particularly Nahum. They were obviously moved by the bold step they were taking. They dwelt in detail on the apartment they would be receiving, how I would have a room of my own and would lack nothing. At summer's end I could start school again and start making up for the considerable gap in my education created by the last three years. And they added, to my great discomfort, that I would be their only child, as they had no thought of bringing children into the world anytime soon.

I didn't know how to answer them. I had received similar offers before theirs. One man had said to me, "Boy, what would you say about teaming up with me? As soon as I decide whether I'm staying in town, I'll come and get you." War was still raging not far away; everything was in flux; illusions and hopes bubbled over and filled the air; and, after months of being on my own, I was comfortable with my current fluid state, free of commitments. Like everyone else around me, I was suspended in an indefinite state of waiting, and I made no long-term plans. I had a roof over my head and plenty of food, and I was accountable to no one. I was a young and independent clochard, and I liked it.

The look on the Dieners' faces was grave. I replied politely: I told them that their offer made me uneasy, and that I would let them know in a few days what I had decided. I had no wish to offend them. They did not press me; in any case, the new apartment would not be theirs until the following week.

One day soon afterward I met Nahum again, entirely by chance, and he reminded me that they were still waiting for my answer. I hesitated, conferred a little with the young people with whom I was staying, and I believe I went to see Julija as well. In the end, my decision to accept the offer came about largely by chance, since the people that I was with were about to leave their flat anyway, and I would have had to find another place to sleep. So I told the Dieners that I would try staying with them for a month, and that I would join them in their place the next afternoon.

That same morning I returned to Julija. I probably did so at Magda's request to collect underwear and other clothes for myself, and I probably went to get her blessing as well. At the time, and in those circumstances, my latent feelings of belonging were transferred onto the elderly Julija and onto Daugela in the country—Mother had handed me over, however indirectly, into their hands.

Nahum and Magda's flat was on the fourth floor of a modern downtown building on the river. A family of senior German officers had lived there previously, as could be seen by the nice furniture, the many clothes in the closets, and the cupboards overflowing with food left behind. This neighborhood had seen its share of the war, too: in the courtyard, just across from the interior windows, there was a building similar in size to ours, burned and half in ruins as a result of a direct hit. For this reason, the yard was full of broken bricks and glass, and was unsafe to walk in.

With the Dieners came Sophia, in whose house they had hidden. They insisted that she move into their modern apartment with them as a kind of symbolic reward for her noble deed.

Magda was from Budapest and had a decidedly western European education. With Nahum she spoke German mixed with a little Yiddish. She had landed in our area entirely by chance and very dramatically, arriving from Hungary with a young husband for a vacation on the Baltic coast.

There, one summer not long before the war, she had met Nahum, who was many years her senior, a brilliant lawyer just then returning from his studies at the Sorbonne. Their passionate affair led to divorce, marriage, and settling in our city, all just before the war broke out.

She did her best to be proper and generous with me, casting our relationship in a familial mode. At a certain point she suggested that I call them Father and Mother, even trying to persuade me that doing so might do me good. I declined—I was unwilling to betray the memory of my parents in return for material gain. My conscience gave me enough trouble just for agreeing to move into the house of a strange family as a son.

It was odd for me to return, after four and a half months of being on the move and in hiding, into the peace of house and home. I was like an alley cat being tamed. I went out a lot, back to the soup kitchen and other places, meet-

ing and mixing with people. I returned to my room only at night. To the credit
of my hosts, I must say they did nothing to stop me, and they tried to cultivate
their idea of good manners—Magda's ideas primarily—only gradually and with
a great deal of patience.

She had the manner of a refined aristocrat; next to her, I was rough, messy,
stubborn, and scruffy. During childish fits of rage, I enjoyed the idea of secretly
escaping: I would run away to Julija or to Daugela, and no one would ever know
where I was.

I would lie awake in bed, anxiously following the buzz of airplanes that still
filled the night skies. Watchful, I waited for the sirens to sound. Most of them
were Soviet planes moving west to discharge their cargo far from the front. From
time to time came the familiar sound of anti-aircraft guns opening fire.

The nights. Little by little, a fatiguing pattern of leafing through past pages
began. Even as the days in this new reality grew more peaceful, the nights re-
verted to bygone times, their nightmares and fears. I suppose that as long as I was
on my own, I was also on guard, and the shadows were pushed aside. Now, with
the warmth and comfort of a home came a bit of a thaw, and the price of relaxing was steep. I would wake up drenched in sweat, choking, groaning, shaking.
A weary round of escapes and flights ensued, in all of which I was a hair's breadth
away from the clear, unquestionable doom that lay in ambush around the corner.
Aktion followed Aktion, each aimed at me and at me only. I was like a victim of
recurring fever that must run its full course before I could get over it and become
strong. The Germans filled my dreams until there was no more room; they would
not leave me alone.

Sometimes I would wake and Magda would be beside my bed, trying to calm
me, shaking me out of my world of heavy sighs. This lasted weeks, months, and
only gradually subsided. Reality grew stronger, and the demons moved aside and
seemed to be banished from my life.

Then Lazer joined us, a relative of the Dieners and our neighbor in the ghetto,
and now the nights were filled with his groans. Alone and defeated, he was unable to bear—at least, not at night—his burden of sorrow and the pain of losing
his baby during the Kinder Aktion. Through his cries I relived my own troubles;
the suffering of this bereft father filled my own heart with secret sympathy.

The nights. How I suffered, yet they were perhaps the most important thing
that happened to me that year. It was the realization of the new reality of being
alone.

The days, by contrast, continued to be full of excitement and happenings.

People came back to fill the half-destroyed houses; additional survivors were seen in the city. The radio would sometimes play congratulatory government announcements by the illustrious Jewish broadcaster Yuri Levitan, informing us of a great military feat, a huge advance at the front, the destruction of a large pocket of encircled Germans. At the same time we continued to hear news of new mass graves being discovered and of concentration and death camps being liberated. We continued holding fast in stubborn expectation.

The city slowly regained its strength. The supply of electricity became more stable, and movie houses began opening up, although only for one showing an evening. Streets were cleared of debris, and more and more of them were opened to traffic, much of it the work of German prisoners of war. Every morning they could be seen marching through the streets under heavy guard, like our own brigades had done some months earlier. The Germans were miserable, worn out, wearing crumpled caps, and dressed in rags and heavy, buttonless military overcoats. Their pathetic appearance, their servile expression, filled me with acute embarrassment mixed with loathing. Were these weaklings the same people who only yesterday had lorded over us, the source of last night's dread?

Every celebration in the city found an enthusiastic sympathizer in me. I was excited about the entrance ceremony of the Lithuanian Division, which had fought in the Soviet ranks. With this festive procession the authorities hoped to emphasize the positive role Lithuanians had played in the war. Many of the soldiers were Jews, some of whom were escapees from ghettos who had fled to the forests and joined this division. The battalions paraded through the main street of the city, the boulevard whose length I had once traversed with my mother. Crowds stood on both sides, cheering and throwing flowers. I gathered flowers that were strewn on the street, fashioned them into a wreath, and offered them, with feeling, to an officer riding his horse at the head of his company, saying, "Thanks." He leaned down from his horse, took the wreath from my hand, kissed the top of my head, and said a few words. For an instant our eyes met and I knew that he, too, was Jewish.

But even with all this celebration, deep down, lay the hidden fear of a counterattack and the return of the Germans.

I quickly discovered the city library, which had renewed its services, and became a loyal patron. A hunger, unsatisfied for years, craved fulfillment. I sometimes went there more than once a day, and often finished reading whatever book I had borrowed on my way home. The librarians came to know me and showed a warm interest in me. I was proud to see how rapidly I filled the lines of my borrowing card, and my Jewish name got inscribed in an ever-growing number of books.

It was a strange year, a year of awakening and recovery; it was full of pain and mixed with faint hopes. Perhaps our loved ones were somewhere in the west and might someday return. How and when did I come to know something? When did the knowledge that I was probably the sole survivor in my family take hold? I received information in trickles, but never anything definite.

FRIENDS

That fall a Jewish school opened. This was a welcome initiative of a number of community leaders, aided by the Jewish colonel Rabelsky, a regional psychiatrist for the Red Army who devoted himself to rehabilitating the community. It was he who obtained permission to found the Jewish school and orphanage under the auspices of the municipal educational authorities. He also obtained a suitable budget and a site—a house with a large inner yard at the intersection of two principal streets downtown.

There were only a few dozen pupils in the school, but it seemed amazing to me that only three or four months after the city's liberation so many Jewish children had been gathered. Some of them were survivors from the ghetto and the surroundings; others belonged to families just returning from deep in the Soviet Union. Still others had belonged to the original Jewish orphanage; during the war, they had been dispersed to Tashkent and other distant places and had now been returned by the Soviet government.

The teachers who gradually arrived were mostly survivors who returned to the city. Raphael Levin was named school principal; we knew him from the ghetto. Studies were conducted in Yiddish and since there were no textbooks, the job of preparing class material was left to the initiative of individual teachers. In my class, the upper fourth grade, the main teacher was Berl Kahn. He would read to us the history of Lithuania and Russia from a notebook in his own handwriting and I was amazed that he could recall so many historical details from memory. We were also taught mathematics, English, and Russian.

The classrooms were on the second floor. The first floor housed the children's home, a euphemism for the orphanage; most of those who came to our classes from there were girls.

It was a decidedly odd school. Every child in it bore his or her own special burden. Possessed of minimal self-discipline, unaccustomed to listening, we were unable to concentrate for even an hour at a time. Ancient children. Younger ones had never had any schooling of any kind before. Some knew no Yiddish at all, having learned their first language from Gentiles—Lithuanian, Polish, or Russian.

I immediately became a good, industrious student. And although we sat crowded, four to a bench, sharing the few books in shifts, I have no memory of discomfort.

The best part of school for me, besides the academics, was being with other children. To be once again among peers, to exchange things with them, to compare, cautiously, the load of memories. To this day I find myself faithfully preserving ties created with the children of those days. A similar tribal feeling of belonging comes over me whenever I meet another survivor.

Alik was one of the first children I met after liberation. He and his mother had survived in a ghetto *malina* and now lived in an attic on the main boulevard. When I went to their place I was met warmly by his short, bespectacled mother who, in addition to all that had happened in the meantime, also remembered me from the days before the war. I returned again and again to their house—something about the presence of mother and son drew me. During one of my last visits to their flat, Alik told me, with dry directness, that his mother was very ill, that she had breast cancer. From then on she lay in bed and Alik took care of her. One day he met me in the hall and said, simply, "Zi chorchlt" ("In agony"). Sounds of muted, drawn-out rattling reached my ears, and I didn't dare get close. A few days later Alik's mother died and Alik began, very practically, with a serious expression on his face—I can see his face to this day—to move out of the apartment. At least he has his mother's grave, I thought to myself.

Michael had not only a set of parents but another special person as well—a little sister, Estherke, who was the same age my sister would have been. During the Kinder Aktion they were saved by a double wall in the workshops. I went to their house a lot, too, for no reason in particular. Michael had a sharp memory, and it was he who helped me collect and reconstruct the words of our ghetto songs.

The person I was closest to during those days was Ettele. Her mother, Dr. Gurvitch, was the school doctor. She recognized me, reminding Ettele and me that before the war we had vacationed together at a summer resort. Now we studied in the same class and I gradually began going to their house until in time it became a second home. There were three daughters—Bella, the eldest; Eta, a year older than I; and Noimele, the youngest, a niece and sole survivor of her family whom her aunt had adopted as a daughter. Because Dr. Gurvitch was very busy, the house was run by the girls most of the day, and very pleasantly so. It was a Zionist household, and it was clear that they would one day move to Palestine. In the meantime, we sang Hebrew songs and lit Sabbath candles.

I grew accustomed to life with the Diener family. I stopped rebelling. Magda and Nahum had a good idea: they introduced me to Bussi Yellin, a piano teacher, and she began teaching me to play. I practiced my first lessons diligently and already saw myself, in my mind's eye, continuing my studies in the conservatory, just as I had dreamed.

Sister

May 8 came and the news spread that Berlin was ours and the Germans had surrendered. People filled the streets, flags waved, loudspeakers blared, Yuri Levitan read the day's orders from Generalissimo Stalin, and showers of fireworks and glowing balls filled the night sky. May 9 was declared the official day of victory, and during the days that followed we couldn't see enough of the daily newsreels showing the battles of the conquest of Berlin and the formal ceremony of signing the terms of surrender in Potsdam.

The reign of evil had ended. Now the detention camps would open and all the imprisoned could return to their homes. Father was indeed set free during these days. He was a walking skeleton: forty-three years old and weighing only thirty-two kilograms (seventy pounds). He stayed in a German hospital for months before recovering. Did he hear anything about us during all this time? Having met some of our people in Dachau, he knew in a general way about what had happened in our ghetto.

And meanwhile, in my own city, what about my sister? Where was she? Did I really not begin looking for her immediately?

I asked about her but didn't find her. I was still unsettled and confused by the upheavals of liberation, and I was only eleven and a quarter years old, with the war still raging all around. What was I to do?

Little by little, information began filtering through to me; I found it hard to believe it. Who first brought it to me? It may have been the blond woman, who continued to follow things closely, or my old Julija who told me about it. However that may be, one day I was told that the gossip on Darbininku Street was that Martha had handed over a Jewish girl to the Germans and had left town for a while.

When this rumor reached me, I reacted in an odd way. Instead of going immediately to Martha's house to inquire and investigate, I held back. I avoided doing this on the childish pretext that I had better not expose myself—if they found out someone from our family remained alive, they might disappear and make it impossible to place a hand on them.

I lived, however, for seventeen more months in the city, nine of them in the house of the chief municipal notary. Why did I never go to that family with him, or ask him to send someone from the authorities?

I raise questions and find it hard to answer them, to understand the logic of a child's reactions. Was I not simply weak in the knees and faint of heart, which kept me from confronting Martha and her family, looking them straight in the eye and asking bluntly: Where is Abel, my brother? You were entrusted with her safety by my mother. What did you do with her? Where is my sister?

Certainly I talked the matter over with Magda and Nahum. But they apparently understood better than I that what had happened here could not be put right, and there was no point in bringing it up.

And thus I stayed on in the city, living my life and waiting. Perhaps the matter hinged for me on Mother's return—when she came back she would investigate, she would certainly make inquiries. But during the nights in the years to come, it was my sister who asked me questions.

I did not try to find Pečkyte during these months either, nor did I write to Daugela.

One day while I was sitting on a public bench, a pleasant-faced, elderly Lithuanian man sat down, taking an interest in the book I was reading. I believe he was on his way home from work on the trains. He seemed to be a simple man, a manual laborer. Proudly he told me that he had many books to read at home, and offered to let me borrow them. I accepted his offer and visited him several times. Thanks to him I read Henryk Sienkiewicz's trilogy, the first part of which is the well-known *With Fire and Sword*. He had several grown sons who all treated me well even though they knew I was Jewish. During the course of our first conversation, he indicated that before the Russians arrived they had lived in Green Hill on Darbininku Street, in Martha's neighborhood. They also knew my Julija. Upon hearing my story, the man recalled that on one clear summer day, a black

Gestapo vehicle came to their street and picked up a Jewish girl who had been hiding, so it was said, in Martha's home. They had also seen the girl before, and since Martha was known to be childless, they assumed that she was a village relative who had moved in with them because of the war. All this I learned from a Lithuanian whom I met by chance.

On another day, a housemaid came to the Dieners' residence; she was also an office cleaner at Nahum's place of work. I struck up a conversation with her, and after she heard my history she told me the following story: during the previous June or July, the Gestapo had placed her under arrest for several days. While a prisoner she saw a number of young Jewish children the Germans had trapped in various places. One little girl stood out among them, slightly older than the rest, who gathered the others around her, keeping up their spirits, and leading them about from one place to another. The children were kept there for a few days before they were taken to the Ninth Fort.

And although she was unable to describe any distinguishing features of the little girl, and even though the time of the Lithuanian woman's arrest did not necessarily coincide with what I knew about the time Mother was told that Martha and my sister left for her village, I am unable to shake off the feeling that the woman had seen my little sister in the Gestapo corridors, and that it was she who had protected the other children around like a mother hen, leading and comforting them.

And my friends named Martha have no idea how hard it is for me to be in the presence of their name, to even pronounce it.

Almost a year and a half passed before I gathered the courage to enter the police station up in Green Hill. Reluctantly, I told the duty sergeant my story, a complaint against Martha's family. He promised to make inquiries and told me to return. Several weeks later I did, but the sergeant wasn't there. The next time I found him, he told me he had been in Martha's house. He said they claimed that someone had turned them in and the Germans had come and taken the girl. "Do you have witnesses or evidence that can be presented in court?" the policeman asked me. What proof did I have except the fact that I know my sister was delivered to them and that now she was no more? Another question stuck in my throat: how was it that they escaped from the incident, without having been harmed in any way by the Germans? I left the station, assuaging my great shame with a childish rationalization: now Martha's family knew that their deed had not been forgotten, that someone was watching them. At the time I was only twelve.

On special occasions, on the Sabbath and holidays, I seek my sister. I have habituated myself to do without Mother, but I find it hard to bear the absence of so prosaic a possibility, possessed by others, of saying to my wife, come, let's drop in on my sister's family this evening, let's have supper Sabbath evening with them, let's call and find out how the boy's doing in the army and how their daughter is. The spectrum of subtle daily bonds that tie families of siblings gives them the wonderful feeling that they are not alone.

Like a captain checking the damage to his ship after a storm, I survey my soul, trying to gauge the extent of the stinging wounds from those days, still within me, and I find that those involving my little sister are the ones that cause me the most grief to this day.

Once and once only, I managed to see her during her stay with the Lithuanians. One warm day in May, in the afternoon, through the holes in the attic hiding place, I saw her from a distance, walking down the street as it curved down the slope. How did I know it was my sister? From the way the little girl was holding the hand of the grandmother she was with, pressing close and not letting go for an instant; from the way she occasionally leaned her head this way and that, anxiously, keeping constantly on guard. An ordinary girl does not behave so.

And I could not send her a single sign of love, a small hidden signal that she was not alone. I could only look mutely on from afar, as if through a clear closed bubble, seeing her before me just as I continue to yearn for her even today.

Perhaps it is her tender age that crushes my heart—this little girl only six-and-a-half years old, and the heavy weight imposed upon her soft shoulders, cast alone into darkness among strangers. My only sister, my flesh and blood.

We both hid in the same street, ten or so houses away from each other, so why me, why me, of the two of us? Her life might have been more structured, more beautiful. Was it because I had clamored louder to urge my mother to move me elsewhere? Why only me?

CHILDREN'S HOME

The victory celebrations were not yet over and a special atmosphere prevailed at the Dieners' house. Things were packed, furniture and clothes were sold, emotional visits with friends took place, all leading ostensibly toward a vacation in Vilnius. But the preparations were so extensive, and the secrecy so extreme, that it was clear to me that the outing signified something more. Since I was told nothing, I pretended not to know.

My twelfth birthday was approaching. To my pleasant surprise, the Dieners gave me an early gift—a considerable sum of money. They explained the gift by saying they would be on vacation on my birthday, but I knew, deep down, that their action confirmed my feeling that it was essentially a parting gift.

In those days there was an oppressive sense of surveillance, of inexplicable surprise arrests, and of harsh investigations of honest and innocent people. In our house there was sad talk of one of their friends, a good and dedicated man, who had used all his power to locate and rescue Jewish children, take them into his house, and gradually place them in caring families, all the while checking up on them and aiding them; and then he was suddenly arrested. A scandal broke out in the city at the time—a well-known lawyer simply disappeared overnight. It was said he had managed to get around the authorities and cross the border into neighboring Poland, where a democratic regime was in power at the time. It was said furthermore that Poland allowed movement westward into other countries in the world.

One day I left the house and when I returned, Magda and Nahum were gone. They had urged me to go to a movie, then disappeared.

I gauge again the depths of my feeling—I was hurt to be left behind like one of the objects in their flat, but in spite of the surprise abandonment, I find that I bear no real grudge. When they left I regained my independence, and part of me was happy with that. Was I not waiting for my parents to return? A warm feeling toward the Dieners has remained within me all these years.

The Dieners sold their piano, too, so my short career as a pianist came to an end.

And so, after nine months of living with Magda and Nahum, they exited my life. When I met them again, with much emotion, seventeen years later, they couldn't stop explaining and apologizing. Once they had made the decision to leave the country at the first opportunity, they had debated the question of what to do with me. On the one hand, they wanted to take me with them, since on their own initiative they had taken me into their house and I was their child in all respects. But other considerations influenced them against this course.

First, they were setting out on a dangerous adventure, the outcome of which was unknown. Many who tried to cross the borders in those days were caught and thrown into prison. And although they got across the borders safely, they faced, in the end, years of poverty-stricken wanderings, hunger, and grave illness before they settled in France, the land of Nahum's dreams. There they had a son, Alex, and eventually they supported themselves producing handmade teddy bears.

Second, they were constrained to the utmost secrecy so as not to be arrested before they could leave. What is more—and this, in my view, was the strongest justification—it was at a time when survivors were gradually returning from the camps. Did they have the right to uproot me from this spot when there was a chance someone from my family might return in search of me? They themselves had no one to wait for. I understood their reasoning; it was logical.

In practice there was no great change in my daily life. They left their cousin Lazer to look after the house. In the morning I went to school, and in the afternoon I wandered about the city, which I loved doing. Lazer didn't interfere in my life—he was wrapped up in his own affairs and his own pain. He treated me with respect and managed to give me a feeling of stability in spite of the Dieners' abandonment. Before long one of his female cousins, a survivor, returned from the camps and came to live in his flat. We three got along well and didn't speak much of Nahum and Magda.

I believe that after the Dieners' defection, I began eating noon meals in the orphanage. Arrangements were evidently made by the community or Dr. Gurvitch. Since the place was next to the school, it was very convenient for me.

Our flat began to attract visitors. Since it was an official government residence, various people came to see if it would meet their needs. The possibility that strange people might encroach on my safe corner worried me a lot. Lazer had a letter from Nahum officially conferring on him the right to the house, and he displayed this document to anyone who came. At the same time, Lazer never hid his intention to leave the place too. Just how and when he would do this he did not say.

My street wandering brought me one day to the great synagogue. Before the war, on feast days and holidays, I would run about here on the steps playing with the other children while my father sat wrapped up in a tallit inside. A fine choir was stationed high up, near the great cupola; its singers sang with serious countenances, conducted by an energetic man—Gerber himself, the ghetto choir conductor. Now the great sanctuary was locked shut and neglected, and the Jewish community offices were in the back rooms. Their people tried several times to attract us, the remaining children, with sweets, to come and study the Torah and prayers, but it was a lost cause.

On this particular visit to the synagogue, I noticed on the bulletin board, among the many notes dealing with searches for relatives, a list of people in whose name letters were waiting in the community's offices, and there, to my surprise, was my family's name. Excitedly I went inside and was given a letter from America, from my Aunt Cheina—now Helen—in New York. According to her, she had found my mother's name on a list of survivors. She sent the letter to our city, hoping a member of the family might receive it. I was beside myself with joy—here was clear evidence that Mother was alive somewhere, and what was more, I had discovered an aunt, one of Mother's sisters in America. I was no longer alone!

I sat down and sent back a long and detailed letter. Aunt Helen was a superb collector and saved my letter.

One day Lazer and his cousin urged me to attend a matinee at the opera, and supplied me with pocket money for ice cream and cake. When I returned I found that they were no longer there. Even before that I had observed, as I had with Nahum and Magda, that they were busy packing and preparing for departure. And once again I had pretended not to notice anything. I believe the timing of their flight was influenced by the upcoming termination of our right to stay in the flat. This time, unlike the case with the Dieners, I was left without a pre-arranged shelter. In Lazer's defense let it be said that on several occasions he had suggested that I consider moving to the children's home, and I had refused. In any case, when he left he knew it was an option. I feel no bitterness toward him either.

So I was once again alone.

Lazer and his "cousin"—she was indeed a relative of some kind—wandered far and arrived, in the end, in the United States in Laredo, which is situated on the border between Mexico and Texas. There they married and adopted their remaining flesh and blood, Ileda, from our ghetto. Of her and her sad end I have already spoken.

What now? I do not remember being too anxious. A Russian Jewish family, relatives of a senior municipal officer, came to live in the Dieners' apartment. They were evidently well connected, because at night they allowed themselves to listen to radio programs from faraway stations that broadcast in Western languages. Their food in the pantry was also of fine quality. They kept most of the Dieners' furniture, and some of it was put up for sale.

The new family, though they behaved with a certain arrogance, displayed considerable courtesy toward me. They did me no harm, and made no demands that I leave the flat, yet I still felt hostile toward them. All they asked of me was to move into the small room next to the kitchen, into a place that had once un-doubtedly been the servant's room. They understood something that hadn't oc-curred to me—that I couldn't be on my own for long. I ate breakfast in the kitchen and the other two meals outside the house—lunch in the children's home and dinner, as I recall, in the house of friends like Eta or Michael.

I call the next period "the big decadent period." I was a twelve-year-old boy living alone in a flat belonging to strangers. It was summer vacation, without the structure of school or other obligations. I would visit friends, go to the library, or wander about wherever I chose. I was as free as a bird.

This period, which lasted several weeks, came suddenly and unexpectedly to an end—I came down with measles. The disease had been making the rounds in the children's home, and a special room had been designated and darkened for the sick. One day I was running a high fever, I had a terrible headache, and all my limbs were weak. For a day or two I lay alone in my small room, tossing and turning in misery, saying not a word. A caretaker from the children's home came to see me—apparently the new tenants called her, or Dr. Gurvitch found out about me—and she persuaded me to move into the children's ward. There I lay a number of days more, suffering and in pain, until my body got the better of the disease.

From then on I stayed in the children's home and never returned to my little room.

The Children's Home

In the ward another boy lay near me, tall in comparison to me. He had a tiny mother who sat near him all the time, laying moistened towels on his forehead. I had no idea why the boy was in the children's home when he had a mother. Later I accompanied him every morning—we were the only two Jewish boys—to a Lithuanian school, where we became friends.

Thus I ended up in the orphanage against my will.

Children's Home No. 4 repelled me in many ways. Over the course of the previous year, in spite of having studied on the floor above it, I had only set foot in the place once. It looked to me like a shelter for the destitute and a den of misery. Unceasing sounds of bitter sobbing and unyielding quarrels rose up from below, followed by scolding and silences. All the sounds were accompanied by the sour smell of urine-soaked mattresses and overcooked food. Whining tod-dlers with runny noses and droopy diapers crawled about on the sticky floor.

Like stray kittens, most of them had been gathered off the streets, extracted or rescued—sometimes by force—from their shelters. Some of them had been discovered on the steps of the home wrapped in newspapers or a blanket, or had been located by dedicated Jews in distant villages or behind the walls of monasteries. If my little sister had survived instead of me, her first station would have been the children's home.

Older boys and girls lived there as well, natives of our city who grew up during the war in the depths of the Soviet Union—in the Ural or Kazakhstan—and had now been returned to their place of origin. Some were veteran orphans who had grown up in institutions even before the war, while others had been torn from their parents when the war broke out. Alert and crafty little foxes, seasoned and aggressive petty thieves—nothing was sacred or off-limits to them. They were capable of pilfering, lying, cheating, and informing. I was unaccustomed to such a crowd. One day I myself saw how two of them, in the entrance to a house, "shook down" a drunken sailor by whispering friendly words over his befuddled head, gradually relieving him of his coat and shoes, then taking his watch and leaving him cleaned out. I stayed as far away from them as I could, and they for their part had no particular fondness for an "egghead" like me.

Not all of the children were violent. Some were quiet, and nicer. On the whole we had a collection of wholesome types, wizards at survival. The entire community—about forty children—was housed under one roof and was required to behave in a disciplined manner. All of the children were in need of attention, warmth, and some compensation for what they had lost. The counselors and the few educators who worked with us did not have an easy time.

In my sleeping quarters a dozen or so beds were arranged along the wall, as in military barracks, with an aisle between them. Everyone had a small cupboard by his bed for personal items. Although the quantity of food was reasonable, we seemed to be constantly hungry.

Solomina was the head of the children's home. Sturdy and firm and a loyal communist, she had one wooden leg (apparently a war injury), which she dragged around, and constantly pursed her lips. She ran the institution diligently and with a firm hand. It was perhaps the right way to impose a positive educational framework on such a motley and wild bunch. She was there from morning till evening, almost devoid of a private life, and she conducted all her business with a very serious face. We hated her with an animosity usually reserved for strict school principals and, in the manner of the downtrodden, floated rather cynical jokes about her behind her back. In her own way, however, Solomina was very dedicated and responsible, and she left her mark on the institution for a long time to come.

Solomina had her eye on me and made no secret of her expectations for me on various occasions. Once she invited me to attend a party meeting, and I was proud to do so. We heard a lecture about the worldwide political situation, and Solomina sat at the head of the dais.

They began including me in plays for adults. I played the role of a child in the sketches of Shalom Aleichem, performing to the best of my ability. I was proud that they had chosen me, of all people, to appear in serious plays, and beside me Channele Glushak, the leader of the girls. She had a beautiful voice and was pretty. Her long blond hair, gathered with a colored ribbon, fell onto her shoulders. She was the very picture of femininity. The plays were organized and directed by Yerachmiel Berman, who worked with us patiently and respectfully. Later I learned that Berman was one of the four partisans who, during the week I left the ghetto and after courageous fighting, had managed to escape from a truck that had been stopped on its way to the forest.

The day after the first performance, which had been very well received, I was called aside and, to my surprise, given several folded-up banknotes for me and Channele—our token share of the evening's proceeds. Although they had never spoken with us about payment of any kind, it was still my very first salary and it pleased me to receive it.

MOTHER

Although life in the children's home seemed full of youthful liveliness and optimism, it had hours of sadness and longing. At those times we would sit on benches in the empty dining room or on one of the beds and sing. Our repertoire included sorrowful Russian songs as well as our own Jewish ones.

As if by magic, I was drawn back to Green Hill. Every so often I would leave for a visit with old Julija. Once or twice on my return journeys I visited a women's dormitory on the street that rose from the city to the mountain. In an upper story, divided into rooms, lived women survivors who had returned from the camps. Each time I asked the newcomers whether they had seen my mother.

In the summer of 1945 prisoners from Stutthof began returning to our city, even though they had been freed at the end of January. Some of them came to visit the children's home. With dry lips they tried to frame the difficult question, which we guessed before they asked it. Some of the children would likewise report to the women's dormitory whenever we got word of a new group of arrivals. The older girls took the initiative with this, and they often came back crowing with victory—they had found a cousin thrice removed or some other distant relative, and we all envied them. It was not an easy thing to go and ask questions.

Deep inside I did not believe that Mother was likely to be among those who returned from the camp. She had not, after all, ever planned to leave with the evacuees—this much she had told me herself beforehand. And if she had been taken in spite of herself, she would certainly have been among the first to return, having left behind two hidden children. On her return, would she have spent any time, even the smallest moment, in a dormitory for lonely women, waiting for me to come and ask about her? Not one woman among the survivors I met there and who knew Mother was able to say she had seen her since being evacuated from the ghetto.

The women were worn, beaten down, with sad eyes; they were half bald, wearing wrinkled clothes that did not fit their bodies and that suppressed any hint of femininity. They moved like sleepwalkers, and their questions were sometimes strange mixtures of snooping inquisitiveness and aimless wonder. Whose are you, child? How were you saved? Perhaps you met my child: are there other Jewish children like you in the city? And deep within me arose a feeling of discomfort and guilt, as when I listened, after the Kinder Aktion, to the wailing of one woman to another.

And you, have you seen my mother? I, too, was cautious and hesitant with my questions, apprehensive of the answers I might receive. And perhaps I would meet some acquaintance, Arke and Maimke's Ruchamah, or Zipporah Heiman, the wife of Eliezer the author, or someone else with whom a feeling of closeness might blossom at meeting. Some of the women seemed unwilling to disappoint me and would answer according to the secret desire of my heart: "Yes, I believe so, indeed. I do seem to remember meeting someone just like that." "What do you think?"—here she would turn to her friend—"Wouldn't that one person we met be her?" Because I was late returning to the children's home and was in for a scolding, I foolishly seized upon just such a response to justify my delay. As soon as I got back and saw the rest of the children and the caretakers looking at me, I quickly forestalled the rebuke by relating that I had received greetings from Mother in the women's dorm—she was alive. This time the bookkeeper Hannah Brava was on duty. She became excited, hugged me tightly, and shared in my joy. The rumor spread through the rooms and people came to congratulate me. Later,

I understood that I had gone too far in a contemptible sham. I began giving less weight to the news, reinterpreting it as a rumor I had heard, raising the level of doubt. But it left a poor taste in my mouth.

As the days went by, the dull expectation of Mother's return grew dimmer. But a clear and final moment of closure, like the sound of clods of earth falling into an open grave, that might impress upon me a final separation from Mother never came. We had not parted properly when I stepped out of the boat, nor did we when she left Julija's house on April 20. I feel the want of it to this day.

Some months after my arrival in Palestine, I received, in a roundabout fashion, an urgent letter from my father, who had been staying in the DP (displaced persons'/survivors') camps in Germany. He told me to go on the 22nd of Tammuz to the synagogue and say kaddish. Thus I learned, for the first time, that Father had definite knowledge of the date my mother died.

And what do I know now of Mother's end, beyond that during the first days of the evacuation of the ghetto Mother hid in the Golach family's bunker and was not part of the transports? Later, perhaps when the Germans had begun searching and exploding shelters, she had decided to come out and go through the fence, where she was shot.

Many questions emerge from these dry facts, which Father related to me some years later. He had learned them, apparently, from people from our city whom he met at Dachau. But only someone who remained alive after the final stages of the ghetto's destruction could have told such a detailed story about Mother's death at the fence. Was it possible? It happens that there was an additional transport of those who had been caught in bunkers after the bulk of the transports had already left. To this day I do not know who this amazing escapee might be.

I can imagine how, with her characteristic courage and strength, Mother accosted the sentry in front of her. Intently, as one human being to another, in the pure German she had learned in primary school, she pleaded on behalf of her two children, who weren't far away.

I suppose that at the last minute, Mother wanted to escape and reach the Lithuanians in Green Hill. Was she headed toward the blond woman or Julija, or did she hope to find someone in Martha's house who would welcome her? Only sixteen days lay between the final evacuation and the arrival of the Russians in our city.

And during the very same hours I was stationed behind the shed about a hundred kilometers away, unaware that the prayers I was whispering were in vain.

For two more weeks I kept it up without knowing that my loved ones were no longer alive.

INTERMEDIATE EPILOGUE: THE LAST WEEK

This is an attempt to summarize the last week of the ghetto according to the ghetto records.

Friday, July 7, 1944: Goecke informs Dr. Elkes that the ghetto will be evacuated the next day. They will all be marched on foot to Tilzit (250 kilometers away). For the weaker ones, a riverboat will be arranged. There is panic in the ghetto, and suicides.

(The Luria family's attempted suicide fails; only their young son dies from the poison they take. They request and receive special permission to bury him, accompanied by a Lithuanian policeman. On their return from the burial, they implore him to kill them; he pulls out his pistol and shoots them. The end of Luria, the "Heuchermann.")

Sabbath eve between July 7 and 8: Heavy bombing over the city. Widespread rumors that the Germans will leave the city by 11:00 A.M. the next day. A strong hope arises. A panicked rush to the shelters, with violent struggles for a place in them.

Saturday and Sunday, July 8 and 9: Air activity ceases, but there are no acts of evacuation. It is known that the Red Army changed the direction of invasion, turning toward Grodno-Bialystok-Warsaw.

(The weekend of Pečkytė's visit to me in the country?)

Monday, July 10, to Wednesday, July 12: Brutal evacuation of all residents from their houses, concentrating them in the large apartment blocks in preparation for removal—this time apparently using transport vehicles.

Tuesday evening/Wednesday morning, July 11 and 12: Heavy rains pour onto the people, who have already been kept outside under open skies for two days. They are wet to the bone and very dirty; the only question that matters to them is whether they will be moved. Everyone hopes that Goecke will fail to obtain transportation.

Wednesday, July 12: The order to move comes at 9:00 A.M. Goecke has found transportation after all. Five in a row, they are all marched to the main railway station of the city or to a side line in the suburb of Aleksotu. In crowded railcars new captives are added until noon. All are transported in crowded railcars to Stutthof in Prussia. The men are sent, after selection, to the eleven concentration camps associated with the Dachau camp system in Bavaria, near Kaufering and Landsberg, not far from Munich.

Wednesday, July 12 at noon, to Friday, July 14 at noon: Thorough searches for those in hiding; they are four thousand people short. About a thousand people are cruelly flushed out of *malinas,* using guns, grenades, and smoke bombs.

(The period between the night of July 13 and July 14, Thursday night, the 22nd day of Tammuz, 5704, is possibly the time frame of my mother's death.)

Friday, July 14, at noon: The last transport for the one thousand additional captives leaves for Germany. From this point on there is systematic burning and blasting of all the ghetto houses and structures, along with the people who remain hidden in and under them, until nothing is left standing.

(Sixteen days later, Sunday, July 30: the Red Army enters the city.)

In total: 160 weeks × 7 days + 4 more days = 1,124 days. Sixteen days between destruction of the ghetto and the arrival of the Red Army. Total: 1,140 days of Nazi rule in our city.

Among the one thousand captured there were about fifty children. They were immediately segregated, and the Germans threatened to kill them unless their parents revealed the location of additional shelters. In the end, the children were all shot, and their bodies were thrown into the fire before their parents' eyes. The parents were then included in the last transport. This, then, is yet another time that I might have perished. Among these remaining children may have been Mineleh, whom I sought after liberation but in vain.

Mother once told me a fable she had heard from an eye doctor while he was removing a grain of sand from her eye. It was a fable about two kinds of people: those who raise their eyes and count stars, and the others who keep their eyes on the ground and collect gems.

Which of the two was Mother? She had something of both kinds in her at once. She was born, like the Messiah, on the Ninth of Av, little good that it did her. There remained for her only a few days at the end of the month of Tammuz before reaching another birthday, her forty-first, which might also have been close to the day of our city's liberation.

Did they clean away my mother with the bodies they found in cellars and under the ruins, or had they already thrown her bullet-ridden corpse into the building burning nearby? Two graves belong to me in our city—that of my mother at the edge of the ghetto (perhaps), and that of my sister in the Ninth Fort (perhaps). And for a full year and a half I lived only a kilometer or two away, and this never entered my mind.

I never once visited the Ninth Fort. Yet my cousin Rachel, Mottel's family, and the little French girl with blond curls are buried there. Nor did I try to locate the Pilz-Fabrik where my mother worked or try to reconstruct the route of her secret visits to our hiding places.

And during all these years I have avoided the thought that somewhere, still loose in the world, there is a German soldier who on a July night in 1944 aimed his rifle at a silhouette trying to get through the fence, or a Gestapo agent who drew a pistol on the curly head of a seven-year-old girl. One feverish night I almost identified them among the ticket collectors on a German train crossing the Rhine Valley on my way from Switzerland to Holland, and I never traveled there again. And perhaps one of them passed me today in a bus of tourists, who came with their wives to the Holy Land, marveling and taking pictures. Might the long-haired students roaming here with their backpacks be their children?

SCHOOL

At one end of the wing of the children's home was a small room that served as a library. Here were a few Yiddish books, a ridiculous remnant of the city's treasury of Jewish culture that by some miracle had made its way to this place. After I began living at the children's home I was made responsible for the library. I diligently wrote the names of the few books in a notebook, pasted labels on them, and made up borrowing cards like those I had seen in the municipal library. Suddenly I had a place of my own where I could be alone and do something I liked so much to do. It was here that I dragged, like an ant, the uncharred remnants of the washtub from the ghetto. I declined Meir Yellin's offer to consign its contents—or at least the charred plywood—to the museum for perished Jewish authors that he intended to establish.

The new school year approached and I was to enter the fifth grade, one grade higher than the four grades taught in the Jewish elementary school. Something had to be done with me. I was admitted to a Lithuanian school, and that is where we went, the long-limbed boy and I, while the rest of the children attended the Russian school.

The Lithuanian school, which housed all twelve grades together under one roof, was situated in one of the seminary buildings for Catholic priests near our house and Rotushe. Could I ever have imagined one day studying in one of these gloomy buildings? Among the Lithuanians there was a coldness emanating from the thick walls and from the high-ceilinged classroom halls. Order, discipline, and restrained behavior were the rule. The teachers were stern-faced and serious. They acted very properly toward us, the two Jewish pupils, since they were obliged to accept us. But we could sense a suppressed animosity.

It was an all-boys class. The day began with a prayer from which we were exempted, thus marking us as different. At recess we were met with overtures of friendliness and curiosity, as well as some signs of reserve. I could always rely on my strong friend, whose large stature kept any possible attacker away.

I would watch the children running about the yard, unable to suppress the thought that they had played just so during the last year and each year before it.

In spite of all the unpleasantness, this school was the best solution for me, and I was even proud that my knowledge of Lithuanian made me an equal among the boys in the school. I avoided thinking about the fact that at the school day's end they all went back to the bosom of their families, and I to the orphanage. I made every effort, as was my usual habit, "to be OK." The years of heavy reading in Lithuanian came to my aid, both in the ghetto and in my hiding places.

I attended the Lithuanian school for about two months at the most. The Christmas vacation was approaching, with all that it held in store for me. Every teacher, as usual, gave us homework to do during the break, and I was especially worried about the tasks our art teacher had imposed on us—perhaps because she had asked us to portray a happy event that had recently happened to us.

13

Second Year/Seven Journeys

First Journey/ Two Messengers/ To Vilno/January

My daughter (age twelve): Dad, I don't get it. How many places did you live in?

First Messenger

Things had begun to happen during that summer. One after another people were disappearing. Aided by the repatriation act that allowed former Polish citizens to return to their country, thousands of people in the Soviet Union began moving westward, whether with authentic passports or forged ones. My good friend Michael's family went away, too, and I was left standing on the steps of their house with tears in my eyes. I do not like partings, as I have said before.

One day the Gurvitches bade me visit them in the evening, saying a man was looking for me. When I arrived they informed me, cautiously, that the man apparently had greetings for me from my father. I do not remember being particularly excited, perhaps because I expected something like that to happen to me one day.

I went into the backyard and there, under the shadowy arch of the gate, a man I didn't know was waiting for me. He may have had another person with him. He questioned me at length about my identity, and only after I answered satisfactorily did he extend to me a small note with Father's familiar writing on it. In angular letters betraying his effort to make them clearer, the following message was written, in words to this effect: "Dear child, this is your father, who by miracles was saved from hellish tortures and who is now in a survivors' camp in Munich writing to you. Do not forget your people's heritage and your family's memory. Come join me for a new life in another country. I will love you to my last breath, your father, Israel."

The man hinted that on some unspecified day he could help me reach Father.

Was I dumbfounded, shocked? I do not believe so. I had always thought my parents would come back one day. I was seized with an inner joy. From the moment I read my father's note, a new era began. I was no longer forsaken and forgotten. I had an anchor; I belonged. A year and a half after Mother had cast my basket on the Nile, I was nearing my father's shore.

My life had a new purpose.

As for my mother, no such message from her came from anywhere. Was she, perhaps, somewhere in the camps to the west after all?

But I still had things to do. What would become of the charred remains of my father's journals and the other contents of the tub from the ghetto? How could I bring Martha and her husband to justice? From that day onward I was filled with taut expectation. I waited for the airship that would land beside me, lift me up high, and take me into the distance.

I began preparing for an escape, whenever it might present itself. I asked one of the children who worked in the wood shop to make me a small suitcase out of light wooden panels; in return I gave him some of my things. In this suitcase I placed, in advance, the things I would take with me. There was the album of ghetto seals and a few documents from the washtub. I chose documents that were likely, in my opinion, to be of help to my parents should I meet them—Father's diploma from the Lithuanian university, and Mother's matriculation certificates from the gymnasium and nursing school. I left the rest of the ghetto treasures on the shelves of the children's home library. For years I was sorry I had not accepted Meir Yellin's offer to take these things into his care. I wavered greatly over the wooden panel that had covered the tub, on which Mother had written her words—three times I put it in the little case, until at last, with practical sobriety, I left it out.

Winter came gradually, and its ever-shortening days were filled with anxious expectation. At the time, the Gurvitches were feverishly and secretly preparing for the flight of their eldest, Bella, to a Zionist training group in Poland. Together we lit Hanukkah candles, ate latkes, and sang holiday songs.

And meanwhile, in the children's home, I was given a leading role in the play for the end of the civil year celebration. We had a professional stage director, an old Jew from the Soviet Union. He took his job very seriously—he saw the play as a personal challenge that, if successfully met, would advance his professional career in our city. I took part in the play only because I had to. What would happen, I thought, if just when the play was ready for presentation I had a chance to get away from there? The enthusiasm of the director did not cheer me at all.

One day in mid-December I was informed that the messenger from Poland was returning. This time he could take me with him. Was I ready? He intended to leave Vilno for Poland at the beginning of January. He suggested that when the time was near, I would leave the children's home without a cover story. Because I would be leaving shortly before the time of our departure to Poland, they would not have time to look for me.

I talked to Dr. Gurvitch. The man seemed credible, open, and direct; he spoke of a definite time frame for the journey, two or three weeks hence, left us his address in Vilno, and seemed trustworthy. The journey was timed to happen during Christmas vacation, which would facilitate my escape; the children's home staff would be especially busy.

Although the fear of Solomina was upon me, as it was upon all the other children, I did not feel as if doom were hanging over my head should I fail—I could say I was going to visit my uncle in Vilno. But abandoning our director bothered me. How would he react if he knew one of his lead actors was about to run away at the last moment? I decided to go on with the rehearsals and to look for a good opportunity to hint that he should prepare an understudy. When he realized I would be leaving, he gave me a minor role.

December. The days grew very short. By three in the afternoon it was dark, filling me with a peculiar tension, like that of a similar darkness two years earlier when my little sister left the ghetto during December days just like these. The messenger from Poland came back. We agreed on a detailed plan: I would accompany him to Vilno one day the following week. We would meet at the station and take the evening train. The twilight would also help me steal away from the children's home undetected, and we would sit apart from one another in the cars. He drilled me on the address in Vilno where he would be staying—he reminded me over and over—near the time of our departure for Poland on January 3.

During the last week of December 1945, two holiday parties were being planned in the children's home to greet the new year—one in-house, the other for the city's Jewish population. The night before my departure, I finished packing my little suitcase and went to take leave of the Gurvitch family. Bella was already in Poland and had sent back her first message that all was well. They hoped I would meet her there. I went to bed excited.

The next day I said good-bye to no one, and there was no one to accompany me.

I got to the train station and hid at the top of the front stairs, waiting for the man. To get onto the platforms, I needed a ticket. I looked carefully around me—God forbid that Solomina should happen by. It was to this station that Mother and I had returned from the only journey we had ever taken together, a trip to visit Aunt Libe, Father's sister, in the neighboring town. All day I had played there with my cousin Rivkeleh, and in the evening we went back to the train, which picked us up from a small station. I never saw my aunt or cousin again.

The steps in front of the station were wide. I remember sitting on the left-hand side, my eyes darting to all who entered, waiting. Although I did not remember the details of the man's physical appearance—I had met him only two or three times—I expected that we would recognize one another. But the time of departure was near and no one appeared. I waited as long as I could before moving into the crowd, but when the train was about to leave and the gate was less well watched, I slipped inside and ran up and down the length of the cars—to no avail. The man wasn't there.

Perhaps his plans had changed at the last minute and something had happened to him; why had he told me nothing? The thought that my exit had failed depressed me but it did not surprise me—some part of me always expected the worst.

Drained and beaten, I trudged back to the children's home. I slipped back into my bed undetected. How glad I was that I had avoided taking leave, since nothing had come of it. Had I been wrong about the time of meeting—the day, the hour, the place? Perhaps I had been taken in by a con man?

The next day I consulted the surprised Gurvitch family. What should I do now? Dr. Gurvitch, in her wise and reasonable manner, did not lose her composure. The man had made a good impression; something must certainly have happened. But since his departure from Vilno was still a week away, something could still be done. She recalled that Liuba, a good friend of Bella's, was going back to Vilno in a few days. She would ask Liuba to take me with her and accompany me to the address the man had given me. If in the end my journey didn't take place, I could return saying I had gone to visit my uncle.

Liuba agreed to take me. She planned to leave in two or three days, and I was able to participate in the play after all under the suspicious gaze of the play's director.

Second Messenger

Early in the morning on one of the last days of December, or perhaps the first of January, I left again. This time, to avoid unnecessary mishaps, I met Liuba in the Gurvitches' home, and from there we walked to the train station. Once more

I followed the familiar technique of walking several steps behind her. We even passed not far from the children's home. Liuba bought our tickets, but we entered the cars separately.

The train left on time. Liuba sat not far from me, and occasionally we exchanged glances. She was a young, pretty girl, tall with short black hair. The journey was a fatiguing one, full of stops and delays. I was tense the whole way, sitting ready by the aisle. It was only a hundred kilometers in all, but the journey took an entire day.

We arrived in Vilno late in the evening, too late to go looking for an unfamiliar address. Liuba suggested that I sleep in her flat and look for the man the next morning. I had no reason to object, so we went to her place.

SECOND JOURNEY/TO PONAR/JANUARY

In the Convoy

Liuba lived in an apartment building that housed several Jewish families. And even though people were already asleep—some in improvised beds scattered in various corners—and we spoke in whispers, the news about me spread, and people came from different rooms to see the child who planned to go to Poland. Among the people surrounding me I met, to my surprise, Yaffa Braun, my black-haired kindergarten teacher, whom I had not, I believe, seen since she had been my teacher. She lived in the building with her elderly mother. Among the other residents was one whose name drew my attention because it was a Hebrew one—Geffen (which means "vine"). He was man from our city, a ghetto survivor, who was doing research in chemistry at the University of Vilno and lived in the adjoining flat with his family. He listened silently to my story. Afterward he called me into another room, swore me to secrecy, and with few other preliminaries told me that tomorrow or the next day an organized convoy was setting out for the border. "Why should you depend on a certain man who failed to meet you and whom you don't know at all? I can get you a place in this group," he said authoritatively.

I was a child—why should I go looking in a strange city for someone I didn't know whether I could rely on or who I couldn't be sure was waiting for me, when I had been offered an alternative by a man who seemed credible, who had a name, and who knew my father?

I went to sleep content. Had my absence been discovered yet? Were they already looking for me?

In the evening I took leave of my pleasant hosts. I swore that I would tell no one where I had come from and that I would not reveal the address. I went to the meeting place with one of the women. On the way, she stopped somewhere to say good-bye to someone and pick up something. There I learned by chance an important lesson in conspiracy. The woman received a secret address in Poland that she wrote on the bottom of a box full of matches. She also wrote a few other things on the back of the tin foil from a pack of cigarettes, carefully smoothing it afterward to make it look new. When I marveled at these methods of conceal-ment, she recommended that I hide my important documents. Then and there she opened the seams in the shoulder pads and lining of the large coat I was wear-ing, inserted the most important documents, which I chose, and stitched the seams together again.

The next lesson in secrecy did not succeed. To reach the meeting point in a suburb east of the city, we hired a sleigh. We refrained from going directly to the place and instead got off nearby and continued on foot. But others passed us in other sleighs, stopped right outside the designated house, unloaded their bundles with much noise, and ascended the creaky wooden stairs.

From time to time, whenever someone thought they heard the hum of a motor approaching, the whispering would cease. But the hours ticked by and no signal to move came. Toward morning, it was already clear that we would not be leav-ing that night. We were asked to wait until dawn and then gradually to go back where we had come from.

That day I could have gone looking for the messenger from Poland. But, as I have said, I was only a child. Why should I bother to look for a man at an unfamiliar address when I already belonged to a group? I knew the people now, I was comfortable with them, and their preparations to leave were already underway. Instead I toured Vilno, the capital of Lithuania.

On Saturday night, the fifth of the month, we were called again to the same flat. I repacked my things first. With money that Geffen gave me, I bought a few articles of clothing that I lacked at the market, including a warm cap to replace the one that had mysteriously disappeared. In my little suitcase I rearranged my most important possessions: the photographs of my family, the stamp and seal albums, the collection of ghetto songs, a few certificates, and a large piece of sausage—a shot of iron rations in case I needed it.

At the second meeting, people seemed less anxious and calmer. For the first time I heard names of various Jewish organizations that I had never encoun-tered in the ghetto. Each of these bodies worked to help their supporters flee. I now know that they were only capillaries in the flight organization that operated throughout Europe to help bring Jews to Palestine. This time, several vehicles were ready to set out, some of them belonging to the "Zionists" and some to the "Orthodox." That evening travel passes in our names were distributed right away, a sign that we would indeed get underway that night.

I was introduced to a couple on whose pass I was added as their son. They were pleasant people, and joked about how easily they had obtained a grown son. The man was an ex-officer, tall and broad-shouldered, cheerful and self-assured; his wife was also large and friendly.

Near midnight we were told we were leaving. Group by group, trying to make as little noise as possible, we left the apartment and stepped into the creaking snow. Around the corner waited two high, army Studebaker trucks, equipped with benches along the sides and down the middle. I was seated at the front on the left, as was the couple I was registered with. We put our bundles at our feet under the bench, and I hung a basket of clothes on a bracket above my head.

This attempt to leave was on a larger scale than before—four trucks were leaving at once. The objective was to reach the town of Grodno near the Polish border, about one hundred and fifty kilometers away. Apparently conditions were expected to be right that night for crossing the border. Someone with experience had reckoned that in five or six hours we would reach the border, and if all went well, we might even make it there in time for the morning train to Bialystok on the Polish side.

Only a few minutes passed before the truck slowed down. We heard voices outside. Someone stuck out his head and informed the rest of us that military guards were stopping us. While in the process of slowing down, our truck suddenly spurted forward and swerved sharply from one side to another, as if it was going around an obstacle placed in its path. We heard loud shouts in Russian, followed immediately by a volley of fire. The shots came from the right and behind, and sounded to me like the pounding of hail or gravel on the metal side walls. The truck did not stop, however, but continued to barrel along with a sharp turn to the left, descending to a gravel road. Several seconds of silence followed before we broke into commotion. Everyone burst out with questions. What happened? Were those shots? Were they aiming at us?

Among them was the voice of a woman saying, with impressive self-control, "Well, I'm wounded. They hit my hand. Does someone have dressing or a handkerchief?" They were still trying to help her when the woman beside me cried hysterically, "They've caught us! We're doomed! What will become of us?" We tried to calm her, to shut her up, but she continued wailing.

All at once one of the two girls opposite me cried out, "Oh no, I feel blood on my arm! What is it, what happened? Light a match!" She was crying bitterly, "Dvoireleh, Dvoireleh, my dear friend Dvoireleh."

For most of the trip I had shut my eyes as tightly as I could. As in previous days, the old regimen of prayers came once more to my lips. I prayed that on this night, too, I would be saved from danger. I held my breath and covered my ears.

Oy vey, they were saying, they've killed Dvorah Bod, a blond, cheerful, twenty-year-old from Shavli, who sat in the row opposite me with her friends; it was apparently she who lay there with blood streaming from her temple.

Now there was great commotion and panic. The truck continued to speed along the bumpy dirt road. Through the flapping tarpaulin we began to discern small headlights far behind us. The sky was dark, snow gleamed all around, and the lights grew closer and closer, like pairs of predatory eyes. Once more the truck made a sharp turn, entering a forest. For a moment this was a relief—we could no longer see the pursuing lights and I felt better, as though I had covered my head with my blanket after a bad dream. After going a short distance, the vehicle stopped, and out of it jumped a man who broke into shouts in Polish that I couldn't understand but someone translated: "Spread out! Hide!" Immediately we jumped out and dropped down as if bitten by snakes. Groups formed, and panicked consultations started up: Where are we? What do we do now? They'll be after us soon! I found myself near the couple I had been assigned to. I gauged from their reactions and behavior that they were reasonable people who could be relied on in an emergency.

After everyone had jumped out of the truck, no one dared to venture far from the place where we were. The man whispered to his wife that he knew this area; he had once worked there. He said that there should be some structures that we could hide in nearby. I asked if I could come and they agreed.

While confusion reigned and people were still arguing, each one throwing out his own suggestion, I made a bold decision to climb back up in the truck and retrieve my suitcase. I was supremely conscious of the fact that this was my only chance to try to regain my few most precious belongings before it was too late.

There was no sense in my action—the Russians, though still out of sight, were getting closer, and our people were likely to scatter to the four winds at any instant. It was an instantaneous decision, the kind my mother would have been proud of.

While I was climbing up—the tailgate was down and this helped me boost

myself up—I heard strange noises. From the depths of the truck came a series of low sounds that stopped and started. At first I didn't know what they
meant—was someone still sleeping in the vehicle? I felt a chill on my skin—these
were the sounds of a death rattle, the likes of which I had first heard a year before, during Alik's mother's last hours. For a few seconds I was glued to the spot.
Instinctively I wanted to retreat quickly, to get completely away. In spite of this I
decided to advance as far as I could. The noises were on the right, while I had to
look for my suitcase on the left. Cautiously groping forward, with my eyes tightly
shut and my jaws clenched, I reached my suitcase. I did not bother with the basket of clothes hanging somewhere above me and turned around fast to crawl back
out, trying as quickly as I could to cut myself off from the continuous wave of
sounds that came without stopping from the dying Dvorah Bod.

By the time I jumped back down people had begun to disperse. I managed to
rejoin the couple, who were already leaving the spot. The vehicle remained on
the road, with the girl who had been shot inside it. Among all those people not
a single soul stayed near her. And even though, under those circumstances, it
was every man for himself, among the bundle of traumas from that night there
remains within me perplexity, shame, and a feeling of inadequacy because I
climbed into an abandoned truck where a dying girl lay, just to rescue a little suitcase, a suitcase whose fate—in the end—was already sealed.

In the meantime, the three of us walked northeast, trudging through deep
snow up a slope in a thin forest interspersed with many bare outcrops. The others went westward. The man insisted that he was familiar with the area; he had
been here as a surveyor or engineer under the Germans. As we walked, we came
across an abandoned brick building. While we hid in a storeroom or perhaps it
was later, I became aware of another macabre fact of this delirious night: the forest we hid in was no other than the Ponar Forest, the infamous vale of death, the
equivalent of the Ninth Fort for the Jews of Vilno and its surroundings.

I later wondered what exactly the man surveyed for the Germans. But at
the time, huddled and shaking with cold, buried in the depths of a storeroom,
we only prayed that the rest of the night would pass without mishap and that,
with the first light, we could return safely to the city. In shock, I tried to digest the quick change, how in a few minutes the tables had been turned and a
quiet journey that was to end by catching the morning train to Bialystok had
returned me all at once to a weary escape in snow-covered fields and forests, to
burrowing—yet again—among boards and broken bricks.

And what is more, it was not that the Germans were pursuing us, nor were we in danger of being led to a death pit when we were found. Why was it, then, that I should be seized by so great a panic?

What was the point of hiding, of freezing for several precious hours? Others, luckier or possessed of more sense than we, got away, taking a different direction. They reached a hamlet, knocked on a door or two, offered a considerable price for a horse and sleigh, and already in the last watch of that very night were back in their old houses in the not-too-distant city. I even wondered if it would have been possible to hang onto the cars of the train whose whistles we heard once or twice in the area, using this means to get quickly away.

But the reality was different. Several hours of waiting in hiding began, hours of hearing our pursuers accompanied by barking dogs. It was only a matter of time before they would reach us. So the man decided there was no point in hiding any longer; we were better off going out and heading for the forest.

As it turned out, the convoy leader had been in our vehicle, and it was he who had made the decision to break through the barrier so we wouldn't get caught. In all likelihood his gamble paid off, at least for him personally, although he endangered the lives of the passengers in all of the trucks. After the fact, rumor had it that someone had informed on us or had arranged to turn us in. Some even pointed fingers at a certain Jewish driver who, although he was arrested, was released after a day of investigation.

It was nearly dawn when we started walking. Our path was a tentative one, although the man stated repeatedly that he knew the place, a few steps more and he would start to get his bearings. The route we chose seemed to go further south, but later it curved around and brought us in the direction of the transport vehicle that we had abandoned, which was not where we had intended to go. Far off we discerned headlights circling the area, and we froze in our tracks. The lights approached the place where our truck was—we recognized it—stopped for a moment or two, turned in the direction it had come, and drove away. The man deduced that the pursuers had finished their searches and had left the area. We could now take advantage of the open path, which was the shortest route, and return to the city.

And there, near the truck, where two small gulches came together with a junction of roads and pathways, soldiers stood waiting for us. Stop, hands up, a search for weapons (they didn't touch me), a demand for identifying documents—there was no point trying to get away.

Earlier, in the shelter, the man had destroyed our false papers. He had stuffed the little pieces into cracks and between blocks of wood. I had also hidden the few zloty bills that Geffen had given me. During this act, the couple had whispered back and forth, exchanging worries and fears about what lay before them. It was probably their last conversation for many years.

The guard unit that caught us consisted of four or five quiet, businesslike soldiers. The couple tried protesting the arrest, claiming that we were in a hurry to catch the morning train to the city, but we were simply ordered to stand aside and that was that. It was clear we had erred by returning to the intersection.

The search party came to an end—a truck arrived and collected all the military people and us, and took us away. They spoke animatedly and with soldierly gaiety, grumbling about the Jews who had got them out of their beds on a Saturday night. A blond *katyusha,* the focus of mirthful attention, spoke proudly of how she had fired a machine gun.

In the city, a fresh white morning had already begun. People dressed in their best were walking the streets, going to church. Horns honked, and we were being led here beside them, hunted, bound for an entirely different destination.

I am surprised that I remember the soldiers' talk, the appearance of the city, and the stops because the moment I sat down, on an overturned bucket, I became exceedingly tired. I fell into a troubled sleep, broken here and there by loud noises and sharp turns. When I woke up, we were already entering, through a side door, a large building in the city center. They took us inside and directed us, I seem to remember, into a kitchen or dining room to give us something to drink.

Long hallways, high ceilings, benches for waiting, and doors with high frames—the place had the look of an ordinary office building. No guards or soldiers were to be seen, but I understood that we were in a command post of the NKGB; we were seated in the hall to wait for the registration going on behind closed doors. It was somewhat reassuring that a large number of our people were present. We met the people of our other trucks, mostly women and babies, whose interrogations were just ending. Sometimes they were moved from one room to another; their faces were gloomy and their children were crying. There were no men—they had apparently been taken elsewhere.

The hours passed with much tedium and prolonged waiting. Now and then doors opened and our people came out, were taken away, brought back to wait; it was impossible to get a clear idea of what was happening within. Here and there someone let slip a word to his neighbor—they take everything away, they ask endless questions. I occupied myself with the question of what I would say to them and how I would save my suitcase.

It occurred to me that the album of seals might possibly be the thing that would cause problems, since none of my other possessions was controversial. I considered leaving it in the hall under the bench until I returned from the interrogation. But its colorful cover stood out too much and I had nothing to put over it that wouldn't draw attention. From this point I held the case in my hands without knowing how I would save it.

My turn came; I was one of the last. I was brought into a room with three U-shaped tables and was made to sit opposite the tables. On one of the tables stood a stack of filled-out forms, along with a collection of earrings, gold chains, diamond rings, dollars, sterling pounds, and even gold Napoleons. When I was made to sit down there were two investigators in the room—one asked questions and took notes while the other checked possessions and clothes. I set the album down casually at my side, where it lay unnoticed throughout the interrogation. With a certain courtesy they asked me the details of my identity, where I came from, and where I was headed. I answered and they wrote down what I said.

Up to that point things had happened with a breezy directness. They were obviously not paying too much attention to me, a mere child. But in the meantime the other man had finished rummaging through my case and had moved on to my outer clothing. With little trouble he undid the seams in my coat—even though they had been reinforced since my first attempt to leave—and began pulling from the depths, one after another, the various documents. "What are these?" they asked, their faces growing sober. I demonstrated the innocent nature of the documents, told them I had found out that Father had survived and was in Poland. Some good people had agreed to take me to him and these were his papers from before the war that had been saved with me. But their expression remained severe. I wondered whether this was a professional expression put on to undermine a subject's self-confidence, or whether I was up against people with limited understanding whose brains, since we were dealing with old documents, simply did not register my explanation.

I became much more suspect to them when they found, deep inside the coat, right next to the tear in my pocket, my winter cap, which I had been looking for in vain for two days. They were completely unimpressed by my surprise and joy, nor did they rest until they had mercilessly cut the cap into bits and pieces.

In an effort to satisfy them, I appealed to one of our people, a boy who knew Russian (someone went to fetch him to translate). I told them again about my father, a teacher and researcher who had completed his thesis about the Spanish Inquisition with honors, of my mother the nurse, poet, communist, and partisan, who had graduated from a rural gymnasium in the 1920s; I even told them about the washtub, how the documents had been miraculously preserved and how much it meant to me that I take them with me. They looked at me with glassy eyes, kept silent, and took notes.

The interrogation ended. I got up to go and put my hand out to pick up my cap and the album beside it. "Just a minute, what do you have there?" For years afterward I imagined a different ending to the affair, one in which the investigators never noticed me leave the room with the stamp album in my hand. But it happened otherwise. The interrogation resumed.

At first there were two of them, one Russian, the other Lithuanian. Later, it seems to me, a Yiddish speaker joined them and they all descended upon me at once. What are these strange marks pasted into a bound notebook? Who gave them to you and to whom are you supposed to take them? In a conciliatory tone, with the voice of an indulgent teacher, I tried to unfold the story of my stamps, repeating again in my halting Russian the meaning of the collection and its historical importance, how I had collected them one by one. And with cynical contempt, they asked me again and yet again, and in spite of my answers, not only did I fail to satisfy them but their voices rose, and they hinted, with hidden menace, "We will get to the bottom of this!" And indeed I was trapped in a country where a document stamp was among the most sacred of things, demanding the fullest consideration. I began to see not only that the album had no chance of being left in my hands but that I was in much greater trouble than I thought. Tears of anger and frustration welled up in my eyes. I was doing my best, trying to tell them the whole truth, and they were not listening at all. If only they would pass me up to a senior and wiser investigator who would certainly understand my explanations.

At one point one of the investigators suddenly took a new tack—he accused me of wanting to go to Palestine. "Of course not," I said innocently, I was headed for Father in Katovitz—the name of the place I had heard mentioned during the last few days. When he repeated his accusation, I went so far as to wisecrack, "Why Palestine? They're always shooting at you there."

Whether I managed to anger them with my impudent reply or with my knowledge of international events, there is no doubt that the man across from me grew angry, so angry that he laid hands on me, as I came to tell it later. Some weeks before I had read in the paper—or it may have been on the news marquee hanging at the head of the city's main boulevard, where I had once seen the photographs of world leaders meeting at the Potsdam and Yalta summits—"TASS Tel Aviv. Exchanges of fire were heard all night between the British army and members of the Jewish underground." This is how I knew about the shootings in Palestine.

They finally let up on me for a while and sent me into the kitchen to get something to eat and drink. Then I was taken to a different floor, to a senior investigator, an officer. Once more came the volley of questions and answers that didn't register, with new questions added: Who sent you? Where did you leave from? Who organized the trip? I was relieved to realize that they weren't asking a thing about the children's home. As for the organizer, I made a character up, a man with a black beard who led us into a dark street and into the truck. This time, too, I made use of the boy who spoke Russian, which was convenient for me, since, in the course of translation, I could embellish and correct inconsistent answers. Gravely, the man wrote everything according to protocol and ordered me to sign. The interrogation was over. The album, of course, stayed with them.

My little suitcase, a leading player in this episode of my story—all my efforts to save it were in vain. Even crawling into the deserted truck had ultimately been fruitless. And that is how, in the end, when I finally left that country, I was stripped of every material souvenir of my home and family—the family photographs that I so miraculously discovered in the burned ghetto, the documents in the washtub that Mother had gone to the trouble of burying, and the album of ghetto stamps that had survived so many pitfalls with me. What the Germans had not burned the Russians confiscated; nothing remained.

And the day was not yet over. All the children in the convoy were brought into the workers' club and were given something to eat and drink. Dozens of children of different ages, some alone, others brothers and sisters, all of them younger than I. There was much weeping—they were the real victims of the affair, having been separated from their parents, who were likely to be sent to prison for a long time.

Evening fell and we were told we would be moved temporarily to the local Jewish children's home until the investigations were over. I did hear that we would very likely be sent to a "juvenile delinquent camp" near Minsk. Sad and downcast, we were taken in a closed jeep, in several trips, to the children's home for supper.

I was tired and depleted. The orphanage had several children who had been transferred from ours and I was ashamed to have them see me in my disgrace. I was also fearful of Solomina's long arm, lest she come immediately and take me—and then what would I do?

The wait for dinner grew long—they were not prepared to take in dozens of children so suddenly—and we were famished. The Lithuanian director of the children's home moved among us, trying to reassure us, saying a comforting word, promising we would all have a place to sleep. I decided to take advantage of the chaos. I discovered a back door that could be opened, escaped through it to a neglected backyard and from there into the street. And although I had never been in the northern region of the city, I got my bearings and made it to the center, from which I could find my way. Where to? Straight to the flat of Liuba, Yaffa Braun, and Geffen.

When I entered the apartment, they looked at me as though seeing a ghost. Liuba lay in her bed with a cold, and Yaffa Braun's mother was applying cupping glasses to her back. When Liuba saw me she jumped up as if stung, and the cups started dropping from her like beads from a broken chain. Knowledge of the previous night's failure had of course spread all over the city. She began interrogating me forcibly: Did you give anything away? Did you tell them the address of your starting place? Crushed, I swore that I had kept my promise and was careful not to say anything. But I felt as if a cloud of anxiety was still hovering around me: perhaps they had freed me on purpose so they could dog my footsteps or—even worse—had persuaded me to become their accomplice. If not, how could a child who had never before been in the area find his way back? And it was indeed a grave error on my part to return to the flat I had left, especially with Geffen living there, the chief organizer of the escape. But where else could I have gone? To a certain extent I was aware of the problem—I had made my way back slowly, partly out of fatigue and dullness of senses, but also so as to give the impression of an innocent passerby, all the while throwing an occasional backward glance, as in a spy movie, to be sure no one was following me.

Yaffa Braun put an end to the many questions and took me under her care. She prepared a large and tasty meal for me that I finished as though my stomach were a bottomless pit, and in a reassuring tone she offered me a bed in some out-of-the-way corner, perhaps in another apartment or the adjoining, half-destroyed building. Tomorrow they would decide what to do with me. And I considered whether to return the next day to the children's home, since they had promised us that they would return our possessions.

Late the next morning, after a troubled sleep, I found Geffen beside my bed. Cautiously he repeated his questions about my story and the interrogation. He recommended that I not return—I had no chance of being given back my possessions. Until the storm passed I would have to hide somewhere, and he would see what he could do about that. Geffen himself went to live at a new address.

At the Goldbergs' Home

It was clear I could not stay in the apartment. Once more I took a clandestine journey across the entire city, a child following an adult, trailing along some distance from him, looking about for possible dangers, to the home of the Goldbergs: Hasia and Yasha, their little girl, Oka, and a grandmother—a warm Jewish family. Later they told me how I came to be with them. Yasha had been a Zionist for a long time and had been active in the Beitar Youth movement. During the war they had escaped to the Soviet Union, where he had served in the Red Army. After the victory, the family was reunited and returned here, hoping to continue their escape westward. One day Geffen called Yasha and asked urgently for his help in hiding a boy.

A chimney stove was lit in the center of the flat and the family crowded around it. Although Yasha had a senior position in a government general store, food was scarce, and I was embarrassed to be another mouth to feed from their limited store.

During the first days there I was still in shock. Yet to a certain extent I wasn't too surprised—some part of me was always ready for every catastrophe that might occur. Rumor had it that Solomina was looking for me. So I returned to my old habits from the days when I had lived with Julija a year and a half before—moving about the flat without shoes, and hiding in a closet and staying there until guests left. Five-year-old Oka was sworn not to mention my existence to anyone, adult or child. Because these were cold winter days when no one played in the yard anyway, it wasn't difficult for her to remain silent about my presence.

I was trapped once more, at the mercy of strangers, suspended next to the full lives of others, as if I was observing them from the darkness and the frost outside, through the lit windows of a warm house.

The house was on Rudininkų Street, in the area of the former Jewish ghetto of Vilna of two or three years ago, an area that had evidently been evacuated without fire and smoke. It was odd seeing a ghetto left standing. On the walls of the houses, in halls and passages, the graffiti of the former inhabitants could still be seen: "We do not wish to die," "We are dying of hunger," "Revenge, Jews."

What does one do all day in captivity? I read the few books that were in the house, flipped through the newspaper from front to back, and kept myself busy with small worries. What happened to the second play at the children's home without me? The thought of having to go back to my city and the Lithuanian school bothered me, for I had not finished the homework we had been given over

Christmas break. Much later I was told that when I left, a fight broke out among the children over who would sleep on the large pillow I had left behind.

In the evening by the stove, Hasia would sing in her soft, velvety voice. She loved folk songs and knew many.

Third Journey/To Poland/February

With the Ciocia

The three weeks I spent in hiding at the Goldbergs were depressing. I returned with full force to old habits (being tense, alert, and cautious) and was gloomy with despair. What chance did I have of getting out of this dead-end situation?

But one day Yasha came home from work with news—a woman had arrived from Poland who was willing to take me back with her. At this stage of my life I had become skeptical about such offers; I was careful not to get carried away with enthusiasm. At the same time I was so desperate that any change seemed better to me than prolonged, futile hiding. Let them take me wherever they would, I thought, as long as I got out of there.

A day or two later I went to meet her, clandestinely, in the market booths in the old city of Vilno. The Goldbergs made me swear not to tell her my story lest she be put off and withdraw her offer. She was an elderly woman with dyed blond hair, and a round, pleasant, if worried face that had clearly once been well cared for and beautiful. We talked a little, and I understood that she had papers that would enable her to have me join her. Moreover, I felt she had a special interest in taking me, because she checked and verified my identity. When we parted, she said that after she finished her business, which could be within a few days, I must be ready for the journey.

Several days of anxious waiting passed, and then came the hoped-for signal. The Goldberg family parted from me with warmth. They wrapped me in a big scarf and warned me not to talk with anyone on the way, lest they recognize my features or voice. Once more I began a cautious journey on foot through the city, once more the suspension of breath at the train station. Inspections, inspections. Buying the tickets, entering the cars, moving from car to car. How was I to get through it all? I felt as I did before crossing the river. But, in spite of the somewhat weak appearance that made her appear as though she didn't quite know what to do, the woman completed all the arrangements without a mishap, and after making our way through the maze we found ourselves in a sleeping car on the train.

To this day it is not entirely clear to me how the connection with this woman was formed, or who directed her toward me and how. She had come to Vilno with the express purpose of retrieving her grandson and bringing him to Poland, but in her papers two grandsons were already registered. I later learned that this all had been prearranged. When she had gone to Warsaw to put her travel documents in order, she had been given to understand it would be worth her while to bring back with her a certain other child as well.

In the last moments before the train started, I was overwhelmed with anxiety. Move already, move. As in Rotushe Square, waiting for the truck, as in the futile wait at the train station in Kovno—the minutes turned into hundreds of separate split seconds.

The first part of our journey was eastward to Minsk—only half a day's journey. From there we would continue to the border town of Brest-Litovsk, and finally take another train on the Moscow-Berlin line, which would bring us to Warsaw, our final destination on this journey. There were three legs to the journey, each one evidently no more than a few hours in all.

In the train compartment I got to know my travel companions for the first time, Ciocia ("aunt" in Polish) Frieda Gorfinkel and Yolik, her eight-year-old grandson. For about a week we three were like a tightly knit and intimate family unit.

At first Ciocia seemed to be a delicate and fragile person. But she accomplished her mission with determination and courage, carrying it off under the guise of a helpless figure when necessary. She had valid passports and money, and she drew upon an inner source of strength. To me, she was a rescuing angel who perhaps was not at all aware of the importance of her mission. I felt guilty for exploiting her innocence and endangering her without her knowledge.

We arrived in Minsk late at night to the freezing cold of late January. Minsk was a ghost town weighed down by its ruins. We had to wait there for several hours for the early morning train from Moscow. We gathered in a partly heated room designated for mothers with little children, but we nearly froze anyway. That night of waiting may have been what produced in each of us, about a day later, a nasty cold, high temperature, and sore throat.

Brest-Litovsk was the hometown of many of my father's family, not one of whom survived. Although signs of destruction were not lacking, there was a large and spacious train station serving those who were leaving the Soviet Union. Dozens of people sat on their baggage in different corners of the station, waiting their turn. Even if one had all the required documents for crossing the border, getting tickets to Warsaw was as hard as parting the Red Sea. We sat down in a corner somewhere and Ciocia began running back and forth between offices and ticket windows. At first she returned totally disappointed—no one could promise her tickets within the next week. As her cold grew worse, so did her despair. But a few bank notes passing from hand to hand had their effect and, in the end, she returned content from one of her forays—she was promised tickets within a day or two.

Finally, at midnight one night, we got on the renowned Moscow-Berlin train, which moved quickly out of its berth. One more inspection of Soviet passports, and another immediately after by officers wearing unfamiliar uniforms, sporting ridiculous four-cornered hats—and we were in Poland! I wanted to cheer, to break out shouting hooray! But I didn't. It was always better to be careful, for the train was full of Russians. The engine picked up speed, dark evergreen forests hugged the shuddering rails, my riverboat chugged forward, and I was in a stupor with a high fever and a sore throat. Flush against the cold windowpane I tried to measure with my gaze the forests speeding toward me. Here, although I was burning with fever, the Erl König would not overtake me.

With Weisstein

The train sped forward, without stopping at the smaller stations, and after a continuous journey by night and day, we approached the outskirts of Warsaw. Ruin was everywhere, the result of prolonged battles at the gates of the city, similar to the sights we saw in Minsk several days earlier. So it would be in the coming days throughout all of Poland, and Germany as well—a long journey through ruins.

Only here, during our unsettling wait at the end of the journey, did I dare reveal to Ciocia some of my adventures of the last month. I felt the need to share this information with her as a measure of the gratitude I felt toward her.

In the dark we stepped down, drained and weary, on the Warsaw platform, and I was like a dreamer, like a drunk, unable to believe I had really crossed this river as well. Perhaps my mother would be waiting here, and I would run toward her and be gathered into her arms. Here, too, my story was supposed to end.

The train station was noisy. Among the arrivals milled poorly dressed people insistently offering "notz i kolatzia" (bed and breakfast). I was amazed that Ciocia didn't lose her bearings in the busy station; she found her way, carried baggage, and, finally, after haggling, showed the sleigh driver how to find a certain address in a street with a familiar ring to it, Yeruzalimska.

In the morning I saw a window overlooking an inner courtyard. There, beside a yellow wall, rested a laurel wreath entwined in black ribbon; above it, fastened to the wall, was a copper plate engraved with a name and date. "Shot by the Germans." I had not yet gotten very far after all.

After a wonderful breakfast (rolls, butter, a soft-boiled egg), we went to meet a man named Weisstein. My journey with Ciocia was over. It had lasted a total of five days—from Monday to Friday. The significance of the journey for me was out of all proportion to its actual length. I parted quickly from Ciocia and came under Weisstein's wing.

Weisstein was short, somewhat dwarfish, and in his forties. He had a full face, a high forehead, a deeply receding hairline, and a wise Jewish countenance. He had a reserved smile that seemed to guard a secret, a pleasant expression in which was mixed a measure of courtesy, tolerance, and kind-hearted generosity. I never saw him get angry or frown. He remains in my memory as Dr. Weisstein, although my father says he was not a doctor. He struck me as a well-educated man, albeit a very practical one. In the ensuing years I tried to contact him but had no success. He took me with him wherever he went, received me with cordiality and respect, without being patronizing or lording over me, and bore my expressions of independence and silence with patience and self-restraint.

I never learned who gave him the job of transferring me and who paid him for it. I marveled also at how he came to know so quickly that I had been stuck in Vilno after the truck incident, which caused him to send Ciocia for me. I also have no clear answer concerning the identity of the first messenger, the one I was to leave Vilno with, nor whether Weisstein or someone else had sent him.

Weisstein, in any case, was decent, a good uncle. I was much in need of such an uncle. He accorded me friendly protection along with a good deal of personal freedom. I went out every chance I got. For me, wandering freely was the best expression of my happy, intoxicated feeling. The gloom and tension of the past few months were gone, and my long process of liberation, begun a year and a half earlier, was over. I was free!

A couple of special events occurred while we stayed in Lodz. The Anglo-American Commission had come to the city to study the problem of Jewish refugees in Europe and their connection to Palestine. Posters were distributed and the entire populace was urged by the city's Zionist institutions to demonstrate outside the hotel windows where the commission was staying. Many were there, including Weisstein and me. Not since Democrats' Square had I seen such a massive Jewish gathering. There were speeches, they sang Hatikvah, and I was excited and moved. Once more I had a people, and I was flesh of its flesh.

That evening an assembly was called in the theater building. After the speeches came the artistic program, in which a world-famous ballet dancer appeared, doing De Falla's Fire Dance. The dancer moved with the stormy rhythms against a backdrop of flaming, trembling screens made of strands of shining glass threads. It was the first artistic performance I had seen for many months, and my first encounter with ballet and modern Spanish music. It made a deep impression on me.

We went back once or twice to Warsaw. We were seeking suitable opportunities to continue on our way to Germany. Weisstein also had to decide which escape route to take—whether to go south through Czechoslovakia, Austria, and into Bavaria, now under American rule, or to go west toward the conquered regions of Germany, which were in Russian and English hands.

Fourth Journey/To Berlin/March

On the Road

Some weeks after I arrived in Poland, Weisstein finished making his arrangements. He had found a convoy suitable for crossing into Germany and we set out for Szczecin, a port city near the Baltic coast in the northwest part of the country.

We went to Szczecin through Poznan, a two-day train journey. I could tell which passengers were going to continue with us from their bundles and faces. Like us, they too were moving toward the collection point. When we reached the city, we all found ourselves in the same hotel-like structure, perhaps the only one operating in the half-abandoned city, and the tumult was great. We were ordered to keep our presence and our destinations secret, but these instructions were unrealistic. It was impossible to explain away the presence of so many Jewish families, all carrying bundles, on a certain day in the middle of winter, in an outlying, half-deserted city. I, who had been burned once before by a similar assembly, found myself shaking in trepidation at the sloppy disregard for secrecy.

For two or three days we waited for trucks in the temporary hotel. These were supposed to take us by way of the Polish border and German territory to Berlin. It was said that the drivers were Russian soldiers returning to their bases in empty trucks, and that this was an everyday occurrence with no special risk. But stories were also told about acts of looting or extortion committed by drivers, who would stop their trucks on the way. The fact that our route would take us through German territory under Russian rule also worried me. I did not hide my fears from Weisstein. I was disturbed—might not any coincidence bring upon me the many-tentacled octopus of Solomina and the NKGB? He dismissed the possibility with a wave of his hand: "Such a young child. Where does he get so many worries?" said the amused Weisstein.

As our wait dragged on, we were instructed to move from the hotel to an outlying suburb on the edge of the city. The morning found us stretched out on the dirty floor of a deserted house, full of abandoned objects and broken pieces of furniture. The scattered books were all in German, testifying that these were the family quarters of German officers. Once more I was snooping through the abandoned spoils of war. In a half-flooded basement I found some treasures—German stamps and envelopes from the days of the war.

I also found a 1938 pocket calendar from a German coal supply company, and in this I began, on that same day—for the first time—to write, with a dull pencil, dates, names, and places. I even reconstructed the words of ghetto songs. It was my first attempt to look back. This booklet, in which I continued to inscribe important events during the coming months (in Berlin they were written with a different pencil, a sharper one), is with me even today, and it is my earliest written evidence that my memories are true, and not the figments of a wild imagination.

The trucks came during one of the following nights, two trucks, I believe. We clambered aboard and settled ourselves among our bundles on the floor. Someone tried fastening the edge of the back canvas flap, but without success.

We drew close to the border and I became very tense. The course of events was so similar to the scenario I had already been through that it was hard to shake off the comparison.

On the face of it, what was there to be afraid of? There was not a clear border with the Soviet Union, and yet we held our breath at every stop or delay. The voices of guards and investigators would be heard, after which the journey would continue. Which of these halts was at the former border and which were merely checkpoints I could not tell. In any case, my eyes were shut. Once the guard even came around to the back of the truck and shone his flashlight on the swaying canvas. We lay flat and held our breath. But even this check passed without incident. Who knows—it may even have been a staged inspection, conducted to increase the payments that found their way into the driver's hands toward the end of the journey.

The further we proceeded, the fewer stops we made, the motor humming solidly and surely. A certain calm joined my great weariness, and in the end, my senses dulled, I settled into a troubled sleep. And suddenly there was bright light—the morning of a new day, in one of Berlin's suburbs within Soviet-occupied territory. The truck stopped in a small village square, and we were told to scatter quickly. From here we could proceed, using municipal transportation lines, to other parts of the city, those held by Western powers. There lay the camps for displaced persons to which we went our weary way.

It was still early on a Saturday morning and Berlin's subway train, which operated on a skeleton schedule only, had not started running. We were advised not to use bus and trolley lines because of the many inspections. But it was no more advisable to stay in the area, loitering in the streets that were subject to Soviet rule. Weisstein and another family or two did something that surprised me—they knocked at the door of one of the houses. It was opened by an elderly German couple. They took us in and offered us chairs and sofas to rest on. They helped one of the women warm a container of milk for her children and served us a hot drink and slices of bread and jam.

This was a German family home with windows jutting out of thick walls, facing the street. Through the heavy curtains we saw a small stone-paved square, gleaming with cleanliness, surrounded by colorful, toy-like houses, with slanted roofs like those on Swiss postcards. The wooden floor was covered in rugs. A massive wooden table stood in the room, a cloth with lace embroidery draped over it. Mute, filtered light penetrated inside, silhouetting the cups and plates arranged around the walls. On the walls hung embroidered works with sayings and proverbs in Gothic letters, on the order of "He who works the land has bread aplenty," and "Bless us, O Lord." There was order and sobriety in everything. Deep in the house was a polished kitchen range with wave upon wave of burnished brass utensils on one side and rows of spice and herb jars on the other.

I was in the house of a German family who had probably owned it for hundreds of years. Portraits of their ancestors hung on the walls in a certain order that none of them had ever disturbed; layer upon layer, generation after generation, with never a break. From here their descendants rose to kill and destroy.

Our hosts spoke little but treated us with courtesy. With decided generosity they showed consideration for our confused, weary, and wild appearance, our many bundles. The division of roles between us was clear with no need for talk. They had been defeated, and we were Jewish refugees belonging to the victorious side.

They lamented the trying times, the destruction all around—pointing out the bombed houses in their midst—and the shortages of food and coal. They told, with lowered voices, tales of family members who had not returned from the war, their fate unknown.

No mention was made of certain subjects that both sides in the conversation were fully aware of. Already I had an inkling of the frustration one feels in the face of the tragic symbiosis between victims and executioners. A few years ago I saw in our newspapers an astonishing advertisement: "Travel in Germany's trains to the finest health spas in the world."

Weak and exhausted, I sensed that important things were happening around me even though I was unable to follow them. Even afterward, during our voyage on the subway—the first in my life—from one end of Berlin to the other, I could not shake off the heavy fog and the shock.

We emerged somewhere from the dark tunnel and approached the camp gate. With shaky steps we passed a guard's booth and here we were, shipwrecked survivors coming into port, among our own people, Jews.

In the Camp

Jews, a crowd of Jews all around: the Schlachtensee Camp for Displaced Persons. Delegates and caretakers greeted us warmly, offering clothing, packages of food, even pocket money. In the dining room food was abundant, tasty, and unlimited. In every way we were given to feel that we were there by right and not on sufferance; we were to be pleased, pacified, compensated.

We were given a room and blankets. I underwent a meticulous registration process to receive an "index" certificate—identification papers from the occupying powers. I now had the honorable status of a DP—a displaced person, one without a home. With these papers I could wander the length and breadth of Europe, like thousands of other refugees, and receive support services in various camps.

I walked, awestruck, through the camp. On the one hand, it was a kind of huge ghetto. It was a former German military camp, surrounded by fences and gates, and in its barracks the inhabitants: broken families, individuals, Jews, and non-Jews—everyone who had been rescued from concentration camps and had ended up here. There were people from different countries, speaking different languages and various dialects; there were quarrels, animosity, and conspiracies; and there were black market businesses.

On the other hand it was a protective shelter, an unlimited stay free of material worries. Some were lingering here, hoping to find relatives, and some were hurrying east or west to their next waiting place. Some remained in order to recover, both materially and emotionally, and some got their bearings quickly, using the place as a base for wide-ranging deals, smuggling, and other black market enterprises.

Weisstein tried by various means to continue our journey in the direction of Munich, but it was not a simple matter. The way from Berlin southward appeared to be blocked. To get there we needed special travel papers from the Soviet authorities, since upon leaving Berlin we would once more be traversing Soviet-occupied territory. He appealed to several agencies and made urgent calls to Munich, but had no success. He berated himself for not taking the route through Czechoslovakia and Austria. But every smuggling route had its own dangers, disadvantages, and uncertainties.

Our outings brought us to the much-praised Unter den Linden Boulevard, formerly the heart of the city. On either side slumped the ruins of hundreds of houses, and beside them the burned Reichstag and the charred Brandenburg Gate. Later, I imagined, when I grew up and became an adolescent, a soldier perhaps, I would fly a huge B-47 bomber straight over this Berlin and release an atomic bomb on it. My desire to do this was firm, though I wavered sometimes. Was Berlin target enough for my cargo? Would its destruction satisfy me? Accordingly, I extended my plans to take more bombs and drop them, methodically and single-mindedly, on every city in Germany, not sparing a single one. I never worked out the details of this thought. At some point in the planning a fog of distraction would always settle over me, like the fog that keeps airplanes from taking off on their missions.

Once Weisstein tried to attach us to an American military convoy, and another time he tried joining a group of refugees that received permission to take a train west—but in vain. Was I very frustrated by these delays? I think not. I was used to obstacles in my path. In all, our stay in Schlachtensee lasted about two weeks. One day I was told there was a way out.

Fifth Journey/To Nuremberg/March

These were the days when the Nuremberg trials were just starting. To the Schlachtensee camp came Bernstein, one of the American journalists who covered these major international trials. He came in his private car for a tour of the displaced persons' camps in Berlin. Weisstein struck up a conversation with him and asked him to help us get to Munich. He introduced me as well. He talked to us a little and later that evening gave his consent—he could take us to Nuremberg, where he was staying. If all went well we would reach our destination in two days. It was only a few hours more from there to Munich. Weisstein hurried to pass this message on to Father, and we got ready for the last part of our journey.

On a springlike morning in March we got underway. I was in the clouds—a ride in a private car for hundreds of kilometers.

Weisstein sat next to Bernstein, I in back, and with much curiosity I began following our crossing of the great city of Berlin. Improvised road signs in English, put up by the military police, meticulously directed us to a specific point in the western part of the city, all the while repeatedly warning that we were nearing the end of the area under the Western armies' jurisdiction. From here we had a journey of several hours through the Soviet zone before arriving in the territory occupied by the other forces. Because Bernstein was a reporter equipped with all the required passes, we expected no particular difficulty in crossing the Soviet sector.

The British guard at the last Western barrier refused to let us proceed. Without the appropriate documents, he claimed, the Soviets would not let us through. Bernstein tried arguing with him, but to no avail—Bernstein could continue his journey, but without us. We, he ruled with polite insistence, would have to get out of the car and return to Berlin. What desolation. With heavy hearts we began removing our baggage from the vehicle, then got ready to take leave of Bernstein, but at the last minute he tried a different tack. The boy, he asked. Will you let me take him with me? And he told a little of my story.

The British agreed to let me go on, but Weisstein had to turn back. After quickly conferring, the two decided on the following plan: Bernstein would take me and Weisstein would look for another way to come after us. I was asked whether I agreed with the plan or whether I preferred to return with Weisstein to Berlin. Weisstein urged me to continue my journey. The practical considerations prevailed—my first goal was to reach my father and he was no longer far away. I had to let go and take the risk.

And so we parted hurriedly, with a certain restraint on my part; I felt I was betraying Weisstein. I got back in the car, and Bernstein and I took off. I looked back and saw Weisstein standing at the guard booth, waiting to hitch a ride back to the city.

So once again I changed companions and protectors.

Our path wound westward at first, toward Hanover, I believe. The ground was flat and the traffic—military, most of it—was heavy. This was the main access corridor of the Allied forces to and from Berlin. After a few hours of travel, we passed Magdeburg and reached the furthest boundary of the Soviet-occupied territory. I was tense at the thought of going through the last barrier, and it was a great relief to cross into the British zone. I felt the tension inside me melt away. No additional borders loomed for the rest of my journey. I took pleasure in the speed of the car.

Bernstein was very nice to me. Our conversation was in fractured Yiddish and halting German. He regaled me with offers of military rations that he had in his bag, whose contents fascinated me, representing in my eyes all the power and wealth of America—packages of Wrigley's chewing gum, Hershey's chocolate bars, Kraft cheese, rubbery tubes of sweetened condensed milk, canned meat and sardines, and even some wonderful cocoa powder, with an aroma reminiscent of home. He chain-smoked much sought-after Camel cigarettes, and he had unlimited gas vouchers. I enjoyed being in the company of such all-powerful abundance. I never met him again after our ride. When I began to make inquiries about him years later, I found out he had died a few years after our shared journey.

And as for Weisstein, as it turned out, he did not go back to Berlin that day. At the checkpoint, perhaps not entirely by chance, was a man from the Jewish Brigade of the British Army. After a brief wait, when no car going back toward Berlin came by, the man approached the Soviet barrier—it was still possible in those days—and cordially pleaded with the Russian to let Weisstein through. "Poor refugee, we just split him and his kid up. Come on, let him go on." The guard agreed. Weisstein caught a ride to a nearby city, where he caught a train that took him southwest without any further incident.

That evening we reached Frankfurt am Main, and the next morning we continued southward. I didn't know whether Father was already in Nuremberg waiting for me or whether he would reach me later. I did know, however, that at the end of that day I would reach the end of my journey. Few are the days—although I have had my share—when, within the space of a day, life can change completely.

What was I feeling that day and in the following days, heading for my meeting with Father? I wanted a protective father who would take me in his arms and say, from now on, son, your troubles are mine, I will take care of you. What would I say to him? What would the first words be when we met? How would we tell one another everything that happened to us during the fifteen hundred days since we parted? What would I remember of all I had to tell him from Mother? How would I describe my sister, whom he had hardly known? We would need entire days and nights to sit and do nothing but talk, talk, and talk. And where would we live? How would we try being together again, two instead of four? How would we be a family again without Mother? What if he already had a new woman in his life?

At twilight we reached Nuremberg. Bernstein expertly navigated his vehicle to a villa in one of the suburbs. It had belonged to a senior Nazi official and was now occupied by American officers dealing with and for the Jews—people of the "Joint" or another army aid unit. It was a handsome two-storied building with many rooms surrounded by a garden. Although the house had not been confiscated by the army, some of the former servants had remained, including the original estate manager, who kept an eye on his master's possessions.

We were greeted cordially by a number of people, some of them in American military uniform, most of them Jewish. It was apparent that they had already heard about me and they were openly curious to see me. I thanked Bernstein to the best of my ability, we said good-bye, and he went on his way. I was invited to supper with the entire staff. Later I was brought to a lovely room, where one of the servants had made up a nice soft bed. I sank into it as in a dream.

A series of telephone calls the next day resulted in the news that within a day or two Father would apparently come to get me himself. Until then I could stay there.

Most of the people staying in the villa went out to work, and I began poking around the place. Almost immediately I discovered that the guest room walls were lined with books from floor to ceiling. I had never before seen such a large private library. Row upon row of colorful book covers, sets of finely bound volumes, books of many sizes, were neatly arranged. Most of the day went by while I browsed the length of the shelves. That all the books were in German, most of them in Gothic print, did not disturb me. And yet I could not forget who had owned the collection. When the Americans saw how much interest I had in books, they told me I could take all I wanted, though they added, with a wink, that I needed to be sure the house manager did not see me.

Huge windows stretched the full height of the wall with bookshelves in between. There were also wide doors that opened into a large garden. I had never before seen such a villa and such windows.

Among the staff one young woman paid special attention to me and treated me kindly. That evening she asked me to join her for a special night at the opera. I was not sure about saying yes—in my boyish way, I saw this night as a potential arena for flirtation and romance by young people that I would only spoil. She overrode my protests—everything would be fine; I was no bother at all. She would enjoy taking me, especially after hearing me say that I liked opera. And so I raised, with much embarrassment, yet another objection: how could I go with her in the shabby, ill-fitting clothes I had been traveling in, which I had received from the Berlin Joint? She looked me over kindly and declared that there was nothing wrong with my somewhat too roomy clothes and, she added, the coat I had on looked quite suitable.

And so, in spite of my deep reservations, we went to the opera after dinner. We were late; the entire staff of the house had gone before us and we almost didn't find a car to take us. Our late arrival did not bother my companion at all. She commanded the cowed ushers to take us inside to the best available seats. With a mixture of embarrassment and disapproval, they opened one of the doors and we found ourselves in a private box, one of the plushest ones in the central balcony.

The Nuremberg opera house! Heavy crystal chandeliers, velvet curtains, tier upon tier of balconies decorated with gold and purple flowers, a festive crowd in its best clothes, an inspiring sight the likes of which I had never seen in Kovno. On the stage was Mascagni's *Cavalleria Rusticana* in one act, performed by the best singers. After the intermission there was another short opera, by Donizetti, I believe.

It was a special gala performance in honor of the international court. In the central gallery just across from us sat the venerable judges and delegates from the victorious nations and their entourages, and my searching gaze wandered alternately from the stage to them and back. Only a year or two before, these theater seats had been occupied by those now sitting on the defendants' bench.

During the intermission, the elegant audience promenaded slowly in an elliptical course through the spacious corridors to a lavish reception in the glittering vestibule, and among the crowd—as in a surrealistic play—was a boy of twelve and a half with an oversized coat. Only last night I had landed here from another world, after an interplanetary journey of hundreds of light years, and here I found myself treading in my big coat in a shining palace in the enemy city of Nuremberg. I wanted to be swallowed up by one of the walls. Without the slightest hesitation my hostess took me along wherever she went, totally ignoring my ridiculous appearance. Only when she tried entering the hard-liquor bar with me did an insistent usher prevent her in spite of her entreaties. Children are not allowed, he declared.

I felt tired and out of place. The next morning we were sitting down to a late breakfast when messengers came in with the news: your father is here.

I did not have enough time to go out to meet him. I just got up, moved a short

space away from the table, and already a boat on the river made a short grace-
ful turn and hove ashore. Several people disembarked, all smiling, looking at me
with faces that I didn't recognize. But the eyes of one sparkled more than the rest.
Everyone was looking at me and I understood that I had a definite part to play.
So I turned to the man with the most welcoming look and fell into his arms, murmuring broken words, something like "at last," or "after all these years," perhaps
both phrases together.

We hugged, and probably kissed. Father immediately straightened up, took a
step back so that he could reach into his pocket, and pulled out a wrapped present, a watch. With a kindly expression he put it on me. He may have fumbled a
little with the strap or the buckle.

At that point, as in an opera, we were joined by the others on the stage: the
journalist Klugman, Father's friend, his redheaded son who had brought Father
to the villa from Munich, and others from the local staff surrounded us. They
all talked and smiled, looked on, perhaps were excited. My eyes may have shed a
tear or two, but I did not cry. Neither did Father.

Then we were invited back to the table. It may have been lunchtime already;
I do not remember the details. We all sat down to eat. Throughout the meal, Father talked incessantly with the people around him, occasionally throwing me a
warm glance, then continuing his conversation.

After dinner we had time to look at the Nazi's large library. Father looked at
various shelves, browsing and wondering. When he heard that I had been invited
to take a few books, he helped me choose them, and I took away three volumes
(in Gothic typeface) of Mark Twain's writings.

Sixth Journey/To Munich/March

By the time the car brought us to the outskirts of Munich, Father had managed to tell me where he lived. Unlike most of the survivors, who lived in displaced persons' camps, Father, because of his work in the city and perhaps also
because of the medical treatment he was receiving, lived inside Munich itself.
He spent the first half year or so in the hospital, at first because of ill health and
later merely to get stronger and have a temporary place to live. In the meantime
he began working for the survivors' institutions. Later he was able to get a room
with a family inside the city, where he was now living. As we got closer to the
place where he lived, he described to me the special character of the quarter,
named after its builder, Borstei—it had been built to house employees of the

nearby power plant. His landlords were Germans but—he hastened to add—they were reasonable, anti-Nazi, and in fact communists at heart, and their attitude toward him was very good. They, too, for their part, had suffered terribly during the war: their only daughter had committed suicide when she heard that her husband had been killed on the Eastern Front. Father whispered to me quickly before we entered the apartment that the Knabenschuh family put a high value on neatness and order; it was one of the things they were very strict about and would not be willing to forgo. I would have to be very careful.

The owners of the house opened the door. My first impression was that they were quite old. Frau Knabenschuh was tall and thin, with a long thin face, black hair drawn carefully back in a tidy braid. Through the rectangular frames of her glasses she gave me a warm and friendly look. Her husband was older than she, white-haired, also bespectacled, a little withdrawn and shy. He worked as a technician or engineer at the power plant. The apartment sparkled and shone: the floor was waxed, dishes gleamed, and the beds were high and fluffy, piled with blankets and topped with a cover folded in straight angles without a wrinkle, as in that house in Berlin. They put me into Father's room, where another bed, large and deep, had already been made up for me.

They offered me a hot bath with a large, sweetly scented towel. Mrs. Knabenschuh treated me—the *bub* (boy), she called me—to good, homemade food, perhaps hot cocoa and chocolate. In the coming days she discovered that my favorite dish was corn flour pudding with cocoa, and she made it for me every morning thereafter.

Through the thick curtains I saw the silhouette of the huge gas tanks that fed the factory, which stood next to the main road. At the time, I did not know that this road also led to Dachau.

Did we talk any more that night? I dove into warm featherbed quilts with shiny satin. Once more, the first night in a new place. Beside the bed was a rug bearing the image of a springing tiger; far down the hall shone a tiny bulb. Did this one also shine on a crucified savior?

The next day, through the window, I saw a row of six-storied apartment houses, presenting a uniform facade of windows, balconies, and side doors. I had never before seen such a large block of buildings. For the first part of the new morning Father spent a good long while showing me how to negotiate the labyrinth of buildings with their identical entrances, each marked by a large letter of the Latin alphabet. The unique design by Borstei, said Father, was that the building included a laundry, a common supply of gas, service corridors to take

out garbage, and even an electric tram that wound through the buildings. Father explained to me where to find the nearest station of this train and which
city station I could reach to change lines, in case I wanted to visit him at work.
He indicated that certain times of the day were better than others to make such
a journey, since during rush hours the ticket price was higher. He drilled me on
our new address—Lampadius 28b, fourth floor, and on and on. Once again he
reminded me how important it was that I keep order in the house. Every object
had to be put back exactly where it belonged, every crease had to be smoothed,
and every speck of dirt required immediate and unconditional removal.

I remember the next few days only in a general way. As is the case for several
other periods of my life, certain segments of time escape me; they are swallowed
up and gone.

In the first few days Father took me to his workplace at the Central Committee for Liberated Jews. He introduced me to his supervisors and coworkers.
All of them had heard about me and my adventurous journey. Father worked
on the historical committee and for the survivors' newspaper, *Unzer Veg* (Our
Path). Once more I spent time with him in settings familiar to me from before—
manuscripts, proof sheets, lead casts, wise old typesetters and editors. I was an
attraction and the object of everyone's attention.

On several occasions my father told me a little about what had happened to
and around him during those years. He had nearly been hanged because the Germans found writing materials among his belongings; once during a short rest the
man next to him suddenly died of heartbreak over having missed some job that
morning that guaranteed a large piece of bread. And although these were strong
snippets of stories, I felt that Father was choosing them carefully, holding back
from me the full story of how he lived from day to day. He never told me any details, not then and not later. He had, however, deduced moral precepts from the
course of his adventures: walk humbly. Be not envious, be not greedy; have no
strong ambition; be ordinary and do not stand out. Thus he would explain the
miracle of his survival.

Two or three days later Father turned to me in the street and said, "Do you
see that sign down the street?" "I see it," I said. "Can you see what it says?" "Yes,"
I replied. "Now I'll do it," he said, closing one eye and reading the sign's contents. Then he closed his other eye and read it again. "What is so remarkable in
that?" I asked him. At the end of the war, only a month before the surrender,
they had been taken on a death march on the roads of Bavaria; even at that late

hour the Germans never loosened their hold on their prey, driving them without mercy, and people were dropping like flies. Father's knee was injured from a previous incident when a German soldier had pushed him into sharp, rusty barbed wire. An infected abscess had developed, causing him to lie several weeks in the Krankenbude—a hut for the sick (this is also the title of a story Father wrote). He got what treatment they gave, the abscess was opened and cut, and by good fortune he slowly recovered without being selected for elimination. Now, during this cruel march in southern Germany, his swollen knee got the better of him and he fainted with pain, dropping on the side of the road. The collection squad that came after them threw him into the cellar of an abandoned building, where bodies lay, waiting for disposal. Had one of the body buriers—who arrived later—not been one of his acquaintances, he would have met his end that day. Seeing signs of life in Father's face, the man woke him and took him to a kind of first aid station, and so he remained alive. When Father, unconscious, had been thrown down, he received a blow—his head had evidently hit the floor—and he lost his sight in his right eye. A day or two later the Americans arrived and liberated them all. Father, a walking corpse weighing only thirty-two kilograms (a "Mussulman," as the Germans would have called him), was taken to a hospital where he received medical attention for a long time.

The Gordian knot, the symbiotic bond between the victim and his murderers. It was a German hospital, and Father received many weeks of dedicated treatment from respectable professors who, only a few days before, had been helping high-level Nazis. Thanks to their efforts, Father slowly regained his strength. When they checked his eyes, only one of his many afflictions, they found no damage to the ophthalmic nerve or in the eye itself. There was a good chance, they said, that he would one day see again out of his right eye. And here—Father concluded his story—the day after our meeting in Nuremberg he discovered that his eye was functioning. At first he didn't believe it. He checked himself, again and again, every few hours. Now he was absolutely sure of it, both eyes were really working. So it seems that Father was very moved by our meeting, even if I couldn't tell.

But of Mother and my sister, he never said a word, never mentioned them. He never spoke with me of his pain, his longing for the wife and daughter he lost. Fifty years went by before Father admitted to his eldest granddaughter that he was unable even to say the names of his dear ones, his daughter and first wife, my mother, in the Yizkor prayer on Yom Kippur. And I know the thought bothers him that I, his son, might certainly believe he has forgotten, but even talking to me about it is beyond his power.

Years later, I found myself returning to the memories, feverishly and stubbornly, slowly and repeatedly rolling back the film of the twenty-some days I spent with Father in Munich, repeatedly poring over the first hours of the journey from Nuremberg, like a man who has lost something on his way home and tries to retrace his steps, to understand how and why it happened, how it began in the first place.

We met on Sabbath in Nuremberg. In the first moments he gave me a watch. In the taxi on the way to Munich, I sat on his left in the back seat. Perhaps he and Klugman asked me about the latest stages of my journey: when did I leave Lithuania, when Poland, how it was in Berlin. We might have talked about the affair of the four trucks, the news of it having reached Munich. Father spoke incessantly. The trip to Munich went quickly.

And this was also the model for my next three weeks with Father—he spoke to me, spoke with the people to whom I was introduced, he never stopped talking. And isn't that just how he behaved at Democrats' Square, and during the selection for Riga? He talked and talked, but never once turned to me with the question: What did you go through, my child, what happened to you?

Certainly he was bruised and battered, weak and enfeebled. He was a wreck of a man, a Mussulman. He did not ask because it hurt too much. I was for him the only living reminder of a world that had been destroyed, of his father's house, of his wife and small daughter who died. That is the logical explanation.

He never asked. Why should he ask? After all, he worked for the history committee. Already during the first days of his recovery he would slip out of his sickbed and go to Flakkaserne, formerly a German air force camp in Munich. There they began concentrating the first survivors, and there he took their valuable fresh testimonies—later it served as the fundamental collection of the Yad Vashem Archives—including no doubt from people from our ghetto. What need had he for me to tell him the history of the ghetto?

What happened to me, to me and no one else, what I had lived through and was hurt by, what frightened me and grieved me, how I worried and feared—he never discovered that, because he never asked.

Once we went for a long night walk to visit friends on the other side of the city, perhaps on a Friday evening. Once more, as long ago, we strode side by side a long way and were free to talk about any subject that came up. Father spent that extended walk discussing Hebrew grammar. Another time, during a long trip by train, he drilled me on the five rules for the definite article in the Hebrew language.

> And I think to myself if, God forbid, I was in his place, meeting my own son in the same circumstances, I would rush upon him like a lion with a roar, hug him and kiss and cry and press him to my breast, never stopping, never ceasing to murmur and speak and chuckle, and with eyes closed and endless tears squeeze his hand and not let go even for a single instant, not even for a fraction of an instant, and all the while asking and answering without hearing what was said, just both of us talking and talking, both at once both interrupting the other, never stopping, never ceasing, day and night without end to the last of our strength until half fainting, wrung out, and emptied we would fall into a brief sleep and then we would wake, and go on and on until slowly like the Sambatyon river that gathers its strength anew and rests from its rage, we would grow calm and be still and a little sated until in the next outbreak we tried to fill what was taken away, never to return, during the four years one month and two weeks, in all, one thousand four hundred and ninety-eight days and nights of the separation forced upon us.

When I had the chance, years later, to raise this sensitive topic with my elderly father, he answered me with dry directness. Yes, he said, he remembered that Mrs. Knabenschuh told him even then that I had complained to her about a father who does not hug me at all.

Father continued to do his regular work and left me in the house in the company and under the care of Frau Knabenschuh.

The matter of my studies preoccupied Father. I had lost the regular lessons of at least the last half year, not to mention the years before. Until arrangements were made, he asked that I begin to study alone, at least by reading the Bible. I agreed. He suggested that I start with the book of Amos. During the day I was to learn certain passages by heart, and at night I would recite them to him.

And so in the mornings I stayed behind, alone in the neat, gleaming flat with Mrs. Knabenschuh, studying chapters of the Bible. A dream and its solution. On the one hand, I wanted to please Father, but on the other I felt inside a fierce resistance to the tiresome rote learning of heavy texts. I conceived another arrangement that seemed logical to me: instead of memorizing incomprehensible passages from Amos, I would memorize some of the Jewish Brigade songs that I found on Father's shelves. That way I could impress him with my ability; he could not say I was lazy. The songs I chose inspired and appealed to me, gave me a feeling of pride and belonging.

I felt the need to tell Mrs. Knabenschuh about this curriculum of mine; perhaps I thought I could enlist her support for the change I was making. The good-hearted lady weighed my alternative proposal in a unique way—she took thread and measured the length of the two passages, the prophecy of the visionary Amos on the one hand, and the "Regiment Song" that I recited to her on the other, and came to the sober conclusion that my idea was a reasonable one; the deal seemed honest and there was no deceit in it. On Father's return that evening, I showed him my progress for the day, accompanied by the helpful opinion of Mrs. Knabenschuh. Father answered what he answered and I had no idea that from this matter a literary anecdote would grow. I discovered a year later what he had felt in the face of my businesslike exchange when I came across a feuilleton that he wrote in response to the incident. He published it in *Nitzotz* (The spark), the journal of the Zionist Youth Movement and continuation of the underground newsletter of our ghetto and the camps. His sketch portrays the ironic situation in which a German woman approves of the daily scope of studies for a Jewish child and Holocaust survivor—a secular song in place of that prophet of wrath, Amos—by measuring the two in centimeters.

Now it became clearer to me who had been the source of the messengers that had reached me during the previous half year. In the course of his work taking evidence from survivors, Father had heard from people from our city that a bright little boy was taking part in plays, reciting and singing. His heart told him it was his son. He sent a messenger. Upon receiving my positive answer, he enlisted the aid of a central figure among the survivors, Rabbi Abraham Klausner, the principal chaplain for the American occupation forces in Germany. This good man occupied himself, among other matters, with operating a network of emissaries who brought child survivors from the east to their relatives in the west. Thus he reached me.

Father added that at one point he thought of going on his own, but he felt he could not depend on having the strength and ability to bring me.

He paid a price for this help. In the time to come, after I had already continued my journey to Palestine, Father's employers in the Central Committee persisted, with no small amount of cynicism, in reminding him that they had taken the trouble to bring me to Father; he was required to continue his vital work and could not leave. So my grateful father postponed his own aliyah. It was two and a half more years before he made it, by then to the state of Israel.

Natives of Kovno stood out in those days as leaders of the survivors. The chief rabbi was Snyeg, whose wife had given me the precious school stamp. Dr. Zalman Greenberg was the head of the survivors' organization; he had been the head of the Pilz-Fabrik brigade, Mother's brigade. I met them both. It occurs to me now that I might have talked to Greenberg and others about Mother. At the time there were many who knew her from the ghetto, who saw her in the last days, perhaps even during her last hours. But my hands were heavy.

Father told me that my friends Michael Kaplan and his family had arrived, and that they were in the Fernwald refugee camp. I went with Father to see them. The meeting with Michael was a joyous one—the first friend from the ghetto that I found in my new home. Right away I raised the question: what had happened to the collection of ghetto songs? I had diligently gathered them while we were in the ghetto but later lost them. My good fortune was that Michael had also been one of the collectors. I sat down immediately to copy them. I gave the songs to Father, who published them little by little under their collectors' names, Michael's and mine, in the historical periodical *Fun Letztn Churbn* (From the last extermination), which he edited.

Father wanted me at his side. But what could he do with me, practically speaking? How, in a German city, could he take care of my studies, my social life? If he were staying in one of the DP camps, with educational facilities and boarding schools, the situation would have been simpler. In his current circumstances, a physical and emotional wreck—ten months after liberation—he was able to keep me with him.

After I joined him, his old hope of emigrating to Palestine was renewed. There he was likely to solve the problem of educating me. But certificates to emigrate were hard to come by: only 1,500 were rationed out each month by the British. Now that I had arrived, Father hoped his chances to obtain a certificate were better. In his letter to his sister Rachel in Palestine he told her of my arrival and asked her to obtain certificates for us, despite the fact that she, an elementary school teacher, did not really have access to the people who made such decisions.

A few weeks after I had arrived in Munich, Father learned that a group of children within the Youth Aliya framework was being sent to Palestine with certificates. There was a chance I could join them, but we had to decide fast. He resolved to take advantage of the opportunity and send me to his sister, even though he had not yet received her consent.

I was fitted with more clothes from the Central Committee's stores, and Father's friends charged me with greetings for their relatives in Tel Aviv. One morning we left—once again—to a large open lot, next to the train station.

SEVENTH JOURNEY/TO THE LAND OF ISRAEL/APRIL

The train set out early in the afternoon, stopping in Frankfurt, where we picked up other passengers. Its final destination was Marseilles, on the Mediterranean coast.

It took a great deal of effort to transport hundreds of children, all survivors of the Holocaust, for whom certificates had been obtained. So unique was this event that years afterward I ran across articles about it, even in the *New York Times*. By and large the children were orphans, having lost one or both parents. We consisted of groups that had formed in refugee camps, on farms, and in training camps under the auspices of various political groups in Eretz Israel (Palestine). Every passenger on our train, and later every one onboard the ship, carried within himself his own wounds, which he hoped to heal.

And still, why to Eretz Israel of all places? One of the few privileges of refugees, who are homeless and have nothing, is the ease with which they can adopt a new dream, a new goal. In my immediate surroundings, the question of where to go was never even raised: we took it for granted that our sights were set on one place only, Eretz Israel.

We spent four days and nights on the train. Worries crept in, especially at night: perhaps the way would no longer be clear; perhaps there would be a horrendous crash; perhaps at one of the stations, when cars were detached and rejoined, a number of cars might be left behind. It was better to stay on guard here, too, as everywhere else; it was always better to be alert and prepared for the worst.

In my car I met a boy named Gabriel who, like me, had been in a ghetto (Tchenstochov) and had hidden with the Polish. Like me, he did not belong socially to the group we were in, and he was also a "good boy"—quiet, reserved, and different from the others. We found ourselves sitting at the entrance to the car, where we slept out in the open, leaning against each other back to back.

At daylight on the last day of the journey we approached a large city. At one point we plunged into a long tunnel and then emerged into the heart of Marseilles, in the middle of a slope on which houses and streets sprawled to the Mediterranean Sea.

At one tip of a bay a camp waited for us ("Les Arenas"), nestled up against distinctive sharp cliffs. Here we had to wait for our ship. Before us lay the sea whose other side lapped the shores of Eretz Israel.

The next day we set out to climb the cliffs. All of our pent-up energy, the anticipation we could barely conceal, we poured into clambering over boulders, scaling the slopes to the summit above us.

Gabriel and I climbed together. We stayed apart from the others, trying to outdo them by getting farther ahead and mounting higher. Every hilltop we reached we gave a different name—Zion, Herzl, Jerusalem—which we shouted from atop the cliffs in a loud voice. It is perhaps not by chance that some years later Gabriel and I, each following his own path, became experts in the geography of Israel, working also as tour guides.

Passover evening. Neatly arranged tables were put out on the asphalt pavement between the camp buildings. The entire assembly, nearly a thousand people, feasted together with songs and readings, sheltered by the white cliffs gleaming in the full moonlight. Delegates said blessings, and rabbis spoke: "Today you are as bondsmen, next year freemen: today you are slaves of your memories here, tomorrow or the next day you will sail to Eretz-Israel and be free."

On the third day of Passover we left for the ship. It was huge and white, a gigantic wall looming above the pier, studded with little round windows like precious stones. Like grasshoppers we encircled the ship, gazing up in amazement: throngs of children filled her decks, waving banners and cheering. Where had so many Jewish children come from?

Cautiously, we walked up the long and trembling gangway to the head of the gently swaying giant, this large white ship, and were guided into one of the holds below. As on riverboats, here, too, we had round portholes shut with large screws.

We lay down our bundles and immediately burst onto the decks to watch the preparations all about us. In a few days this very ship with its decks and passengers would anchor off the shores of Eretz Israel. It was hard to believe. Her sailors exuded a confidence that roused envy. On the ship's deck, I outlined a letter that I planned to send to Father. My notes are still with me, undeciphered, to this day.

The *Champollion* was 18,000 tons. We were told it was the biggest passenger ship to ply the waters of the Mediterranean Sea, a fact that filled us with pride.

Our worries about the danger of sailing the sea subsided somewhat. Newspaper accounts of the time tell us that on this voyage, organized by UNRRA (United Nations Relief and Rehabilitation Administration), there were about 650 children who were onboard by virtue of possessing certificates, unlike those who were involved in illegal immigration, whose path to Palestine was strewn with severe obstacles. In addition to the children, there were more than 200 public officials, group leaders, and relatives of officials, 880 people in all. Among these were the wife and young child of Dr. Greenberg of Mother's Pilz-Fabrik brigade.

Twilight fell. The throb of the engines could be felt through the metal floors. Muffled whistles announced our departure. Unhurriedly the *Champollion* raised anchor and turned with aristocratic grace to leave the harbor. Lights were lit in her honor on the surrounding slopes. The tall lighthouse gave her a rhythmic flickering salute. We sailed into the open sea.

The first night was the stormiest. The next day we saw a quieter sea, calm and awash with sunlight. The ship sliced steadily through the waves, leaving behind us a long wake of water that scarcely succeeded in regaining its calm.

I look back, unbelieving, over the more than twenty years behind me of trying to write my story. Hundreds of pages. The first page dealt with Belka, the Jewish dog; I pecked it out with one fumbling finger on an old manual typewriter. It seems to me now that I am more at peace with myself, more able to carry the load of memories as they are, aided perhaps by the very act of writing them down. I sometimes feel that as my notes proceed to completion, the memories trapped inside me melt away, dissolving after fulfilling their function.

And what will I do when the writing is finished? An abundance of energy will free itself. Perhaps I shall learn to play the piano. Perhaps I will start a home for homeless children.

I have had two great surprises in my life, in addition to rescue and liberation: one, that my memories of those years have not grown dim; and two, that my family should bear, against its will and with no choice in the matter, the shadow of my story, which happened so many years ago.

One could look at what happened in terms of energy: a mighty evil invested tremendous energy in a system that resulted in death, conflagration, and slaughter, and left behind survivors with crippled souls and distress for them and their children, unto the third and even the fourth generations. So great was the destructive energy concentrated here.

I once thought my story was meant for Mother, who never returned to meet me; or perhaps for Father, who never asked. Later, I supposed it was meant for my children. Now, I understand that I cannot necessarily expect them to read it. I am approaching the end of my journey. Who am I, essentially? I am number 132 in the convoy of children to Auschwitz; I am from Children's Home No. 4; from Vigriu 44; from Vilnius 18; from the group of Beitarists onboard the *Champollion;* from Tel Aviv and Tel Yosef; from Ein Gedi and Yotvatah; from Rehovoth and from Jerusalem.

I am a child of the Jewish people.

We stayed two full days in Alexandria. We were not allowed ashore, but the oriental panorama, full of color and sound, filled our senses. Merchants, peddlers, porters, longshoremen, and fishermen boarded and debarked with no small commotion while we looked on in wonder and curiosity. These would be our neighbors in years to come. Quantities of large juicy oranges were passed out to us, bringing home to us our proximity to Eretz Israel. I could not know then that the color of their skin would one day become the subject of my own scientific research.

We left Alexandria in the evening, knowing that the next day we would reach Haifa. I was swept up in a flurry of packing. I was exhilarated. With the first light of morning I began peering into the distance through the round porthole. Then slowly, through the brightening dawn, the white wisps began shrinking, and off the prow of the ship we could see a thin line of mountains holding the edge of the rising sun.

The mountains grew larger, spreading out to the left and right like wings, and we began to discern in the heart of Mount Carmel the silhouettes of trees, houses, streets, and towers. One street rose straight as a ruler through a golden dome in the center of the mountain, glittering in the light of the rising sun. Near the coastline a large square building stood out: it was one of the largest hospitals in the country, someone explained to me. The remaining strip of sea grew narrower, becoming a kind of silver river in which my riverboat slipped silently and slowly to the shore.

Now, in view of Haifa, I burst onto the decks, running their length like a pup gone wild. How and with whom could I share the huge tide of emotion that came over me? Toward me came our journey's leader, one of Father's acquaintances, and without hesitation I threw myself into his arms. We embraced and kissed; I needed to share the tremendous wave of emotion with someone.

A similar emotion seized me seventeen years later, once more in the springtime. It was Sabbath morning, and I was hurrying to return to my wife, who the night before had brought our firstborn daughter into the world. As on the wings of an eagle I sped along on a bicycle through the Aravah plain, for the forty-two kilometers between Yotvatah and the hospital in Eilat, where we were going to decide on her name. I intended to suggest—with many reservations—that she be named after my little sister.

I pushed the pedals with all the strength my thirty years had given me. I wept and sang the entire way. A friendly northern wind pushed from behind as I forged ahead, singing. It was a splendid Sabbath, a festive Saturday, and I was alone in the Aravah, holding it in my arms from the east to the west. The mountains of Edom across from me skipped like rams; gazelles sprang up behind bushes, antelopes sprang forward to congratulate me. A unicorn galloped in front of me, and after him Puss in Boots sprang out to announce that I was approaching the city. From all the piers colorful pennants were waving, and riverboats blew congratulatory whistles. And my boat, sails drunk with joy, cut swiftly through the gladdened river. More than ever before in my life I felt that I had finally passed through the eye of the needle, that I had finally come to the other side of the river. I was no longer alone. How lucky I am, how enormously lucky. And had Mother not promised me all of it?

The shore came closer, taking definite form. Land embraced us from both sides. All of us stood on the decks, cheering. The first boat reached us, putting aboard the ship a navigator and two policemen. We stared at them like native tribesmen on a desert island. The rumor spread instantly: the navigator was Jewish!

On the shore people were waiting; they seemed very friendly. Even the row of British soldiers along the waterline, all sporting red berets, looked anything but threatening. All day long we made arrangements, filled out forms, passed inspections, and endured roll calls, until at last they let us disembark by the swaying plank to the shore, where we got on buses immediately. Under the close guard of British soldiers with Jewish drivers, we were taken to our transit camp in Atlit.

The first night in the Land of Israel. Once again, barbed-wire fences, shacks with three-story bunk beds, formations, and inspections. Powerful searchlights raked the area.

Five days went by before they began to let us out. The organized groups were the first to leave and be sent to their destinations. Those joining relatives, myself included, were released last and put aboard a special bus.

With wondrous ease we passed through the gate. The Jewish driver was a friendly older man. I sat alone behind him, carrying on a conversation in my be-labored Hebrew. On the way south we passed Binyaminah and Pardes Hannah—he told me their names—and let passengers off there. In Hadera he stopped in the main street, went into a grocer's, and brought me two oranges; they cost five Palestine mils.

Our final station was the Sha'ar Ha'aliya (Gate of Immigration) in south Tel Aviv. We begin to disperse, and there was Aunt Rachel. She had smooth hair and a round face, resembling her sister Libe, whom Mother and I once visited. The good-hearted driver offered to take us to Rachel's neighborhood.

From Aliyah Street, we turned to Allenby Street, then to Rothschild Avenue, which was lined with handsome buildings. From there we went on to the sparse Chen Avenue, which struggled against the surrounding sand. The avenue was flooded with strong and joyful sunlight; the bus chugged leisurely along, leaving behind white foam. Around us, mothers speaking Hebrew with their children waved handkerchiefs. On all the platforms people were singing, "There in the Glorious Land, in Our Brethren's Dwellings," in four-part harmony. Trees, similar to those I had once met after crossing the river, raised their tall green crowns around us, shouting and cheering.

Ya'akov and Rachel welcomed me warmly into their apartment. Their porch, closed off with concrete blocks, would be my room. We ate lunch together in the kitchen and talked a little. Mrs. Pnini and her daughter from the opposite apartment, Katzman from the labor union and his son Dvir, who lived upstairs, all came to greet the new immigrant and marvel at the Hebrew he spoke. Although I was somewhat distracted, we spoke of my entering school, as a seventh grader, which I would do in the near future, and about a date for my bar mitzvah, as I was approaching the age of thirteen.

I went to bed early. Only two years before, a mere two years, I had begun my subterranean peregrinations. How many light years that was from me now.

Epilogue

I went to bed early. Much had happened to me that day, and much would happen the next.

One of Mother's poems reads:

Un gut azoy iz trachtn izt vun blumen
Vos veln sich zevaksn mit dein trot.

(How good to think of flowers now
that will bloom with your step.)

In the morning Ya'akov cautiously opened the door, raised the shutter, and said, "Good morning, Sholik, how did you sleep? Care to come with me to the May Day parade?"

A new morning had begun.

Epilogue

Back to the River

But Lot's wife looked back,
and she became a pillar of salt.
—*Genesis 19:26*

AND IN THE END, DID I EVER RETURN?

Like so many of my friends, I had deep-seated reasons for rejecting the idea out of hand: the abhorrence, amounting to hatred, of this land of blood, where so many of its citizens had served as enthusiastic hangmen. And whom will you visit there, with all your dear ones absent; your rescuers no longer alive; the ghetto long since destroyed and its land built over again? Will you go to find out who the Lithuanians are who now live in the house you lived in before the war, who might even have kept for themselves some of your family's furniture?

What point can there be in enduring the pain once again?

And what would be the point of confronting again those silent witnesses—the tranquil landscapes, the forests and lakes, which like a pastoral blanket cover up the murders and atrocities that took place in their midst?

And, on the other hand, to try once again to confront the difficult memories, to bring them up to the surface, and attempt to diminish their strength. To return and test your own strength, to see if you are able to look back.

But Lot's wife looked back. My heartstrings cry out at the interpretation that says Lot's wife had compassion for her married sons' wives, who remained in Sodom. She looked back to see whether perhaps they, too, were following in her footsteps. And when she saw what was happening to her birthplace, her heart broke.

After I had safely crossed the river, my mother had commanded me not to look back. I obeyed her, got out of the boat, and headed straight for the gully that led to the opposite hills. That was the first step I took on the journey to my salvation.

Thirty years passed before I began to look back and to write. The writing itself lasted twenty years. It was hard to remove old bandages that had long since
merged with the living flesh. But once the book was completed, my body could
breathe again.

And that's when the desire awoke to go back for a visit. Twice even. The first
time after fifty-five years, and a second time, four years later.

A great curiosity took hold of me as well—how do those places where I passed
the first years of my life look? How wide, in truth, is the river I crossed? How high
is the green hill from whose hideout I looked down on the ghetto on the other
side? What was the size, in truth, of the field in that distant village across which
I suddenly saw the sugar factory rise in the air in one piece and crumble into bits,
with me there in a field of fire and exploding shells?

And my home—my last stable, thick-walled house, with its wide windowsill from which I looked safely out over everything happening in the world, the
adjacent yard where I played with my friend, the enfolding streets—essence of
early childhood—what are they really like? How will they appear from my present point of view?

And so the moment came when the time was ripe to return.

The first time we went as two families, Aliza's and mine. With deep excitement, and not without fears for the safety of our bodies and souls. But we went.

I did not regret it.

I was shocked by the visit. How had the landscapes of my childhood waited
for me here in secret, and I knew nothing of them? A world preserved fifty
years and more, where time had stood still; like a lost city in the depths of a
jungle that had retained, beneath the thick vegetation, the contours of its former
houses and streets as they had been long ago, remembered, familiar. Nothing
seemed to have changed, although the city had grown older and more dilapidated.

It was a wonder how utterly oblivious I was the first dozen years of my life.
After all, these sights were there all that time. Did I merely never think about it?

As though a fog were slowly lifting, specific questions sprang up and spurred
me to find answers. So I went a second time. At the end of the second trip, after
I had seen and visited nearly everywhere I wished, I left behind me sites that my
longing will continue to caress, that will go with me for years to come. But since
I now know just what they are I feel that I may be able to live with them without
turning to a pillar of salt.

In the City, Towns, and Villages

As my car approached the city and signs appeared indicating the decreasing distance to the city limits, the suspense grew.

Just before I reached the city, a billboard appeared with a compelling jingle whose message was suddenly so timely for me: "Tu Nori, Tu Tori, Tu Gali!" (You want, you need, you can!)

A dizzy ride down the main artery of Green Hill, and I was in the lower city. We settled in a fine hotel near the old quarter.

At dawn the first day—during the summer, the nights are very short—my wife, Miriam, and I hurried with suppressed excitement into the adjoining Vilnius Street. Once more I was treading through the streets of my childhood to my house. Here was the president's palace, surrounded by the same fence with round iron posts, topped with spearheads, but without any poker-faced guards around. We proceeded into the heart of the old quarter, to our street, which was paved for pedestrians. All along there had been various stores to which my mother used to take me in search of pieces of cloth from which to sew a dress, summer and winter clothes, shoes. This had been a Jewish area, a bubble lined with shops and workshops, carts and porters, all of them Jewish. Now there are no Jews. Only the street signs of Mapu and Zamenhoff have kept their original Jewish names. The district has become a complete tourist attraction. Most of the shops have been converted to coffeehouses and boutiques.

It was odd, my curiosity about the house and yard of my childhood. I was in the city for a year and a half after liberation and it never once occurred to me, so far as I remember, to go back for a visit. And the building, at that time, was wholly preserved—just as it was when we lived there. Perhaps I felt some discomfort, some anxiety even, about peering into places where we had lived before the storm, and where Lithuanians who had seized our apartment and household goods now lived. And perhaps it was an aversion to peeking down the stairwell of the abyss into which we had been cast.

I had known beforehand that the building that housed our apartment had changed in form. Now, with a single glance from the adjoining corner of "Butcher Street," the mystery of my house became clear: the building was still standing but had been remodeled—our story at the top, which had been roofed with tin, was gone. In its place was a wide, colorful tile roof, bordered in decorative relief. In the first story, facing the street—where the bakery and Meltzer's pastry shop and another small shop had been—ancient red bricks showed through from under the demolished plaster.

I had heard it said that our building had once been a monastery. I had found certain evidence for that when we sought safety in its catacomb-like cellars during the first days of the war. Now a copper plate affixed to the facade testifies that the building has been pronounced an ancient historic landmark and listed for restoration and preservation.

My home. What is a man's home? It was natural during my childhood for us to move from one flat to another every few years, according to my parents' economic situation. My inner home, the one that was destroyed, was not the one we left against our will in the city's old quarter. My last home had been in the ghetto, at Vigrių 44, and it had been burned and destroyed.

During my second trip, I found an old article in an architectural review thanks to which I understood the changes that had rendered my home unrecognizable.

The building originated, it says, in the Middle Ages. Because it was situated where two rivers met, on the main road from the ancient fortress to Vilnius, it served as a hostel for foreign merchants.

At the beginning of the twentieth century another unstable story had been added. The sketches accompanying the article show our flat. Here was my parents' bedroom, which was also the dining room; here was the room that had been rented to the student Sioma; the room where my sister and I slept, in one corner of which stood my father's writing desk. Here is my life's fortress nakedly exposed, a shaky addition wrapped in tin, an eagle's aerie with a wide windowsill from which I could, or so it had seemed, look out in safety over a stable world. From this same window, in so far as I was brave enough, I had also been able to follow the last days of the world when it was safe. When restoration was begun, the added third story had been removed. I have therefore no place to look for our flat's windows, and I was relieved. Without a family, there is no need for a home.

At least the courtyard had kept its former shape, although its size as preserved in my memory was much reduced.

A glance across to the opposite street corner reminded me exactly where the flat of the girl Yehudith was, to whose dolls I had given shots as a "doctor"; where Arke and Maimke, my childhood ghetto playmates, had lived; the flat of my friend Yehoshua, who had disappeared at the start of the war; and the dentist's house. Nearby were the enormous cathedral and the priest's quarters. How did we have the courage to live next to a Jesuit compound?

The Rotushe—the town hall—stood in the central square like always. I could reconstruct exactly where the authorities had erected the demo shelter as the war loomed, opposite the Society for Jewish Ethnography Museum. I stayed only long enough for a photograph on the spot where I waited for the truck that took me to that distant village, a journey that brought me back to the shores of life.

I walked the city with Aliza, who was my age and from my city; we reconstructed sites and places. Everything as it had been. Here was the promenade beside the river ("nabrezhna" in popular Russian slang), the market alleys and the nearby streets in the old quarter. We identified the Hebrew gymnasium and the public school from the days of the Russians.

The wonder is that this period of my life did not leave me with many more memories. I was in the city for sixteen months after liberation and my return from hiding in a village, and I was already more than eleven years old. I was burdened with the struggle against the memories of the previous three years, with waiting for my parents to return, with the fact that my sister had been torn from my life.

We went to the town hall and requested birth certificates. With some suspense, we waited a good while behind a large wooden door. And when the door opened, we were both issued birth certificates. We had indeed been born in the city, and though we had gone as far as we could from this planet, here our names remained, many years after we had been as good as dead. What is more, on my certificate my mother is listed as having two first names—Leah-Margola, a name I had never before heard. As it turns out, the municipal archives registered local rabbinical marriages in the years before the war.

Both of us had lost younger sisters during the war—would it be possible to get their certificates?. The technocratic reply was "only the parents have the right." Go find the parents who can exercise that right.

Then we went to the synagogue. Aliza's youngest daughter decided to say mourner's kaddish in memory of deceased relatives. At the sound of her sobbing voice, my strength left me and I, too, was seized by deep weeping, the first during this visit. Perhaps it was a wail for all my childhood friends, with whom I hung around on prayer days and during Holy Days; or perhaps a lament for the Jewish congregation, wrapped in *talitim,* which would gather here and listen to the sweet voice of the *chazan* and the choir above the *bimah*. I was a witness to the gradual disappearance of all of them.

And perhaps—yes—for my entire childhood world, which was buried here in smoke and fire.

Now we went to the fortress of death, the Ninth Fort. Until that time, all I had known about it was the way up to it, the path that rises diagonally from left to right up the hill, as I saw it from the ghetto full of our people being led during the second day of the Aktion. Now, for the first time, we ascended it ourselves.

There was a persistent drizzle and I gave up on my deep desire to walk the length of the road on foot, perhaps even on our knees like the pilgrims in the Via Dolorosa in Jerusalem. I wanted to try to look back, through the eyes of those who were taken, down and to the right of the ghetto at those of us who were left, who stood there watching, frozen and horror-struck.

And at the top of the hill, past the line of vision from the ghetto, the fortress of death appeared. From here the victims could have clearly seen God in heaven.

Not in the depths of a dense forest; not beyond the ridge, as in the Babi Yar quarry; nor in the treacherous showers of Auschwitz. There, atop gently rolling hills, clear, sharp, and definite, sat the fort and its moats, like a beast of prey, perched securely on its belly, waiting to swallow the rows of victims as they came closer and closer to their end. They saw it and recognized it ahead of them, before they were led, group by group, to the killing pits. It is beyond my power to imagine the process of execution, where they were detained and where they were taken, since the pits were opened two years later and the remains were burned, leaving no trace behind.

Above the plain on the other side of the fort, in the place where the pits were dug, stands a frightening giant statue that seems to stretch out its arms, either in mourning or crouching to fall upon its victims as they came ever closer. They numbered at least 50,000 over the course of three years.

And beyond the sidewalk, which abuts a peaceful and tranquil village, there stretches a green plain. The sight of the western moat restrained me, all of it punctured with bullet holes. This is without a doubt the very execution site, in use daily during the years of occupation, the maw that swallowed the relatively small shipments. Here were sent, according to the memorial slabs and documentation, people not only from our city but also from distant places—the Lord knows why—prisoners from Berlin, Drancy, Marseilles, and Vienna.

I wonder whether my little sister—after she was delivered to the Gestapo by her protectors one or two months before the Germans retreated—was led to this place, together with other Jewish children that they had gathered up here and there.

Choking, I said kaddish aloud in a sobbing voice while we fell into one another's arms. Every one of us in our little band had someone to mourn here.

I had returned home from my first journey with a feeling that I had not completed my mission. On my second trip, my first stop was at the office of Shirdyte, the city archivist. In her hands were bits of information that could make many things happen. Was she aware of that?

Survivors of the fire went to her, knocking at her door, looking for traces that disappeared sixty or more years earlier; the echo remains from the voices of parents who were lost to an abandoned child. She listened, creased her brow; you felt her deep and full attention. I could only imagine the tears and emotion that welled up in her gray room.

She brought to each of us, Aliza and me, unexpected documents about our lost little sisters: the release forms of our mothers from a private midwife clinic! What a coincidence—two mothers, in different years, went to Dr. Levitan's clinic to give birth. On these documents are listed, for the first and doubtless last time, the names of each of our sisters, in black and white. One who died two years later deep in Russia, and the other who lived to be only seven years old.

Immediately Aliza and I rushed to the address listed at the top of the document. To our amazement we discovered there a long, gray two-storied building that carries a sign: "Women's Clinic."

And so the puzzle was solved: now I knew why we had returned with my baby sister from a birthplace so far away, while the Jewish hospital was not far from our home in the old quarter. The document confirmed that—our mothers had preferred to give birth in the private clinic rather than in the public hospital.

And, as in a complex puzzle, I stumble upon an unexpected revival of two early memories as a four-year-old boy. . . . A long hall on the second floor, rooms to the left and the right, and I am running forward with all my might to find Mother. I turn to the right into her room and, to my surprise, a strange baby rests on my mother's breasts, suckling with great intensity. The shock was so great that I burst from the room and stood in the doorway. I would not leave the spot, nor stop crying, despite the attempts by passersby, doctors, and nurses to comfort me.

Yet in spite of that, I went back to visit her in the coming days. My mother stayed there eight days—as shown by the release form—and then we went home in a black taxi with my new sister, down the main avenue of the city. On its way the taxi was blocked for a time—this I remember clearly—by a "Maccabee" demonstration, marching the same day in the city center. When we got home, we ate salami sausage and drank tea, and to this day salami is my favorite among festive foods.

How many of the babies that left that clinic during the 1930s won longer life? Such calculation is pointless.

Years ago, after having woken from my deep, decades-long sleep, I had been able to locate my rescuers—Pečkyte, who had taken me to the country, and Ona, the spouse of the peasant in the country. I owe my life to these three and to two others; in all, five Lithuanians.

Rima, a good-hearted Lithuanian who lived in Kaunas and who was an engineer in early retirement, took it upon herself to investigate for me, persistently and diligently, throughout the city. She discovered, at the edge of the city, the grave of Pečkyte, the woman who found shelter for me in a distant village and led me there. I managed to send Pečkyte a few parcels, and even a sum of money, which reached her just a few days before she died and apparently it helped her have a decent burial.

Now we went together to the grave, where I planted flowering begonias. Rima also looked for the grave of the old woman on Green Hill, Julija, but she was unable to find it.

"We're photographed beside the pear tree that you no doubt remember," wrote Ona, enclosing an old worn photograph. During my brief correspondence with her, I received a letter whose return address was unfamiliar to me. "It is the local postmistress who writes to you," the letter said. "I used to bring your letters to Ona. I am sorry to inform you that she did not see your last letter, having died after a prolonged illness." I wrote back, thanking her, and I kept her address. Now her son Algis was waiting for me in the town's train station, and in his car I began to cross the town toward the village.

Was this the same route I had taken when I first arrived in Vincas Daugela's wagon, and the same by which he brought me back after the liberation? I cannot know. Fifty-five years have passed, and the town has grown, paths have become paved, and a convenient road cuts through the outskirts toward the village I was seeking.

At that time there appeared a certain stretch of fields between the town and the village, and I could recall the sight of the town in the distance like a picture.

A railroad track bordered it in front, and in the left corner of the site had stood the giant sugar refinery.

Now the town's buildings advanced, filling the space to the edge of the village, and town buildings now abut the edge of Daugela's former property. The house no longer stands, and had it not been for Algis, I would not have believed this could be the place. The property is still green, a long rectangle as it was then, but how narrow it is! At one end was a ridge, and in it a spring flowed where I once bathed. Now, at the end of Daugela's land, stands a new house, marking the border between reality and memory.

Of the house nothing remained; because the Soviets identified Daugela as a dissident, they did not allow him to renovate the house, and the structure gradually became dilapidated.

But I could distinguish, rising in a front corner of the property, a mound of dirt covered with vegetation typical of ruins—here the house had once stood. Now, like its owner, it has returned to dust. A vigorous growth of young pear shoots that sprouted from the felled tree mark the traces of the man's yard, and that is all.

I wish I could have wandered about more and tried to reconstruct the path of my escape from the farm on that night of battles, in the wake of which dawn brought my liberation, but it was not to be.

From there, back with Algis. I wanted first of all to find the gravesite of my rescuer. We went through the fields, first to the sugar refinery, to its tall chimney stacks that tower over the expanse—a cornerstone in my memory—that had been rebuilt after it had exploded in that night of battle. I naively thought that I could find Daugela's grave in the Catholic cemetery by myself, but I was wrong. Algis offered to take me to his brother's family, who still lived in town; they would doubtless be able to find the gravesite for me.

"But meanwhile," he said casually, "there's a Jewish memorial stone nearby that you might like to see."

We approached the place, above one of the bends in the beautiful Šešupe River to whose beauty I, too, like all the denizens of that country, have sung nostalgic songs. In that pastoral landscape, adorned with picturesque birch trees, there stands a memorial stating that in this charming spot, one thousand Jews from here and the environs were executed in the summer of 1941. A few steps further was the rectangular mass grave, bordered by a low fence.

That was the first mass grave I saw in Lithuania.

To my surprise, in a quiet street nearby, I met Daugela's sister-in-law, a ninety-one-year-old woman whose existence I had not known of. And not only did she remember me, but she was also able to quote back to me the words I had apparently shouted when I heard the news of liberation: "I'm alive! I'm alive!" demonstrating how I waved my arms. Amazing. She is now the last living witness from the world of my memories, about which I myself sometimes wonder whether those memories are real. These things indeed happened; I did not imagine them.

On my second trip I went back to see her. The now ninety-five-year-old sister-in-law welcomed me once more, this time from her bed. And this time, her daughter-in-law took me to Daugela's grave, which he shares with his mother, and I laid a wreath of flowers on it.

Once more I went to the lot in the village; once more I tried to reconstruct the path of my flight beneath a shower of gunfire, the shelter into which I fell; once more I tried to locate the descendants of the good Lithuanians who took me in for a few days until Daugela's village was liberated—but to no avail. Houses that have grown up and roads that have been built have obscured the dim pictures in my memory beyond recognition.

Since my return from there, I have at last made use of the various pieces of information I have gathered, and I have finally been able to nominate Daugela and Pečkytė for a Righteous Among the Nations certificate from Yad Vashem, something I'd known for years that I should do but which I hadn't the strength to do.

And within me are still buried certain stones of memory, enveloped in a kind of unclear longing. A part of me would like to return and visit these places again, extend my investigations and inquiries, talk with the neighbors, peer at maps, try to understand and assimilate the changes that have taken place there—and perhaps in my soul.

Ostensibly, I went there to visit the Jewish shtetls, the dwelling places and settlements of generations of my family. I knew in advance that there was no point in searching for their houses—there is no one to ask, and no one who wants to answer. The memory of my visit to my grandfather's home would not be enough to find it; the photograph of my mother's home from the 1920s is unlikely to help locate it in her town. I knew only that all my family members were killed in their respective towns.

I went to visit the living places, where they had lived, and I found myself unwilling to deal with their graves. More precisely, the mass graves, called by a more sanitized name: common grave. Since my visit there, I never leave the pits, the groves, the silent road crossings that lead to the depths of the forest. I cannot pull myself away. I return and dive into reconstructing the details of the great killing: How did they imprison them? How and where did they lead them? How did they murder them?

I have always had, embedded deeply within me, pictures of the executions, assembled over the years from photographs and television screens. Images of the last moments of life, captured by the murderers themselves and burned into my flesh. Among them—how can I sort them?—the image of a mother with a child on her lap, leaning toward the barrel of a gun aimed at her head, or the backs of a group of women, standing crowded next to one another, leaning over a cliff.

But where are their mass graves? These graves are now the only evidence of the lives they had. In the regular, traditional cemeteries, the gravestones are mostly shattered and the mounds obscured, and during the last sixty-five years, thick trees and shrubs have grown up there.

During my first trip back, in remote Siad, I was shown the mass grave of my mother's mother. In the records of Vidukle, where my father's father was the town rabbi, there exists a description of how he lagged at the end of a line of people as they were led to a grove beside the train station. But we were unable to locate the site of his mass grave.

Signposts to these places are mostly missing. The locals didn't like the signs and vandalized or removed them.

Before my second trip, I equipped myself with a book of photographs of 220 mass graves in this country. Most of them are local killing sites, each of which swallowed only a few hundreds or several thousand; they are hidden in thick, refreshing, and blossoming forests, approached by an innocent dirt road that winds like a snake to its deadly end. I have visited six of them, in Mazheik and Plungian, Vidukle and Shavli, Nemoksht and Zhezhmer. Six among more than two hundred like them throughout this country. Little workshops of death, operated by the locals, mostly for a short period only—two or three months of the first summer of war.

O land of forests, rivers, and lakes.

I set out to find traces of my family and I found towns with a Jewish presence in its very absence. Even if there is no half-ruined or tightly locked synagogue or empty lot preserving the outlines of the structure that once stood there, the small wooden houses with colored shutters and modest doorways in the center of town are hints of this absence. In these towns, the Jewish shtetl often accounted for more than half the population; most of these houses belonged to the Jews.

The daily round of the local residents' lives goes on as before, like a theater stage with the same setting and props throughout the entire plot, except that a large number of the characters have disappeared and are gone. In a big city, the missing presence is diluted among the population. But in a small shtetl the Jewish absence seemed to cry out to me. As if its former occupants, who filled the space for many generations, were ghosts.

Irena, a Lithuanian woman whose house sits next to the Jewish cemetery of my grandmother's village, where they had led the hundred women and children of the town, tells me of her childhood memories: "When the shooting started, my mother would take me into the shelter, so I wouldn't hear."

How then did it happen? How, with orchestrated steps, did someone send circulars and instructions to all the villages as to how and when to kill their neighbors? Or was it that, with wondrous inner coordination, they set their sights, in every corner of this land, on the Jews in their midst, leading them on a similar path of death?

And I, unwillingly, on the tips of my toes and with great trepidation, I am drawn into a kind of comparison between those who were led to death in the gas chambers and those who were led to the pits in the forest.

The anonymous, industrial scope of sealed transports in train cars to a place unknown. And in contrast to them, the country Jews, being led along the village's main street, their homes of several generations, in the presence of friends and acquaintances, among them their clients, people they had helped in time of need, classmates and playmates, while from the windows all around they are looked down upon with scorn and glee over their downfall.

I recall one of the short and poignant stories of Ida Fink about the elderly people being led through the main street in heavy rain on their last route, and a daughter running after them and calling out to her grandfather: "Farewell, zeide—be well!"

At first—for days or weeks—they were collected at the synagogue, and then they were marched to the edge of the village, to a thick grove where, when things were as they should be, they had wandered and played, on paths that they knew. And there they were ordered to dig long pits, and before they understood what it meant, a shower of shots put an end to their final minutes.

Here I stop. It is impossible for me to imagine what the women and children went through while they waited, imprisoned in the synagogue for as much as a month, before their turn came. And throughout this time—this model was repeated in Vidukle and in many other shtetls—their neighbors—again, their neighbors—did not refrain from describing to the women in detail, through the barred windows, how they had killed their husbands and brothers, and what awaited them on one of these days. And those days did indeed arrive. Sometimes, of all days, on the Fast of the Ninth of Av, or at the New Year and the Day of Atonement.

It happened in at least 220 places in that country. More precisely, 220 signed and catalogued sites, many of them collection points for Jews from the surrounding area, for several villages and towns.

O land of forests, rivers, and lakes.

Who were the people who carried out the systematic killing? I look at the people around me, some with impassive faces. Some whose body language tells of the hard years they lived through, some still young—dressed in jeans with shaved heads—blasting loud rhythmic music from their cars like every other place in the Western world. Who among their parents accompanied people to the pits and pushed them in? Who shot them and buried them alive? Who stripped and robbed them and plundered? On 220 sites? Let us say that at every killing site fifty to one hundred "local abettors," as most memorial plaques delicately put it, participated. This rough calculation yields a sum of at least ten thousand. Ten thousand in the shtetls and villages only. And what about other places in that country?

Is there another Eastern European country where mass participation by the natives, not the Germans only, was as great in sending Jews to death?

And once more, on tiptoe. I approach the subject with the greatest caution, trying to touch and understand—how did they determine where the killing would take place, where the pits would be dug? Why just "there"?

In Kaunas, the ancient fortresses—the underground vaults and catacombs—were chosen as suitable sites for the killings. In Ponar, near Vilnius, it was giant pits that had been dug to store fuel. In Marijampole, they imprisoned the Jews in empty military barracks beside the Šešupe River, and on the banks of that river the victims met their death. In dozens of other places, the margins of the Jewish cemeteries were the natural choices, as it were, for the killers.

But sometimes they led the victims many kilometers into distant forests. That is what I saw near Zhezhmer, Nemoksht, Vidukle. The Jews of Shavli—the third-largest ghetto in Lithuania—were led tens of kilometers to the Kozhi Forest. So it was in Plungian; they went to a hilly thicket west of town, bringing victims from half a dozen other places.

Why there? In Kozhi, there is a row of mass graves. Eleven giant pits, long and rectangular, each at a distance of several meters from one another. In what order did the digging, and the killing inside them, take place? First deeper in the forest, then toward the perimeter, or the other way around? And similarly in Plungian. It is a nagging, pointless question that will not leave me alone.

Friends ask me: What about the people? Did you meet any people there? What are they like?

I reply: They look similar to people in any other country. There are all kinds.

In one townlet, when we stopped and asked where the Jews had lived, where the synagogue and the mass grave were, the man shrugged and went on his way.

And there were places in which people helped us, as in Vidukle, my grandfather's village. One man went so far as to keep asking his neighbors until he got to a more distant neighbor, the oldest of all. And that man knew that his current house stood in the town's Jewish neighborhood.

Here, somewhere, Jewish life had bustled around the synagogue and the house of my grandfather, the rabbi. Once, as a child, I had been taken through narrow, winding passageways to a corner where a lad, who certainly seemed then to be much older than I, and certainly more skilled, had proudly shown me his chef d'oeuvres—a wooden car cab and wheel he had built himself.

Of the synagogue there remains only an empty lot. And the lad most likely suffered the same fate as the rest of the town's youth.

As for the Jewish cemetery, we were referred to the outskirts of Vidukle, near the Catholic one. There, beyond some lonely old gravestones peeping here and there among tall trees, on a back slope, near a small lake, we discovered a fenced, rectangular mass grave.

My slow-moving grandmother, and with her all the children of the town with whom I used to play, who grilled me about the big city that I came from—here all of them met their death.

At least she hadn't had to march a long distance like my grandfather had. Him they led, with the other men of the town, on a march of two or three kilometers to a trench behind the railway station. There now stand a few defeated trees, remnants of the thin grove that perhaps provided the killers with a measure of cover for their abominable act. Among the trees is a concrete stone bearing a plaque that tells the story.

"For years, human bones would rise and stick out of the ground on this lot," a neighbor told us.

I have childhood memories about the open space between the town and the railway station. My father and I used to walk along this road during vacations in the shtetl.

But no one then imagined a scene about a mass of innocent people being led on a hot August day to be shot at the edge of a pit.

Siad, my mother's birthplace. My albums are crammed with photographs that I collected from the belongings of her brothers and sisters overseas, pictures brimming with the romance of youth.

Those were days of enthusiasm, of dreams whose fulfillment they pursued across the sea, far from the small and stifling village. Only their aged parents and a few members of their generation remained behind.

They are the ones I found in mass graves. The women and children, among them my maternal grandmother, on the edge of the local cemetery. The men and boys are twenty kilometers to the north—they dragged them that far.

A village full of wooden buildings strung about a main street, sprawling on the shore of a small lake, with a stream that traverses it. And all around it, a forest.

I would like to stay here for a number of days. To get up at dawn and go out of town, to the edge of the forest; to feel the cool dampness and smell the scent of pine and oak trees, the odors of dairies and goats that had been in the yards of Jewish townspeople.

To wander, toward evening, in the paths that lead to the nearby stream and lake, to try to reconstruct the position captured by the photographs I have in my hand. To walk into the thick forest, where "youth full of life and joy," in the words of the caption written on the back, would be photographed in a certain pose while leaning against a tree trunk, or at a professional photographer's studio, holding a guitar, decked out in holiday clothing, their expressions suffused with indefinable longing.

They whispered words of love and courtship, recited poems by Jewish poets, dreamed of distant lands, quoted words of philosophy and spirituality about the soul's salvation and the pursuit of happiness. "Remember, my sister, friend of my soul, these marvelous, magical days that we shared before I sailed across the seas."

By which of these paths did they go to the forest? Where were their favorite haunts? Could I still find, etched in dry bark, the initials of lovers who finished their signatures with a heart pierced by an arrow?

And as they passed from house to house, did they not have shortcuts by which to steal silently behind the houses, goat barns, and wood houses leaning and about to fall?

And the entire town, bustling with the activity of its Jewish residents, the school, the synagogues, Maccabee soccer leagues, recitals and dances whose proceeds were pledged "to support World War I refugees and their children"—where did all of these take place in this tiny peaceful townlet?

Now there is no one to lead me through the streets and paths of the village, to tell me a bit about the area, the views that attended my mother when she grew up here nearly a hundred years ago.

I wish I could pull at the wooden planks of the houses' walls, like a child tugging at his mother's apron strings, begging and pleading—tell me, tell me what memories are buried in your boards about the days gone by before the new tenants invaded your midst.

And there is no one to ask.

But to my surprise, one living witness remains for me—they took me to Kizulauskas, a Lithuanian man of ninety-five years, and told me, he probably knows where your grandfather's house was.

In a shack that was threatening to fall, in a neglected, untidy room, sat an old toothless man, leaning over his plate. He was hard of hearing, but his gaze was clear. They repeated my question to him several times, and suddenly his eyes lit up: "Greenstein? *Blechar*! [tinker]. I worked for him!" I was agape—my grandfather Shalom Zvi and his son Idel (who had even migrated to Palestine with his family, and because it had been too hot for him there, had returned to his town and to his death) had been the local ironworkers—blacksmiths and locksmiths.

And other evidence stands in the town: its main synagogue. On my first trip I had been surprised to see the wooden, two-story building, still in one piece. I was told that about fifteen such structures remain standing today in Lithuania.

In the intervening years, the building had been used as a workshop, a garage, and a storehouse. It now stands empty and neglected. The stylistic trim on the edge of its roof, the remnants of the latticed partition in the women's section, left no doubt about the structure's past, although I could find no traces of a mezuzah in its doorways.

I went back and circled the building with wonder and excitement. Here my grandfather—according to my aunt—would emerge at times and, in a good-humored way, shush the children playing outside during the hours of prayer.

During my second visit to the place, four years later, the building had already begun to fall down. Its second story and roof had collapsed, and no one is there to repair or preserve it. With no one to gather under its beams, it is no longer needed, and it, too, sinks into oblivion.

In Zhezhmer the archivist produced for me documents and a picture of my aunt and uncle. The photographs are wonderful in their crispness—mounted in glass panes that were discovered only in recent years in the ruins of an abandoned house, apparently that of the regional Jewish photographer. In the pictures are Aunt Libe and her husband, Shmuel Sidrer, both of them teachers, in their classrooms. She is in the girls' classroom, he in the boys'. The children, Moisheles and Shloimeles, are beautiful, tender, and bright-faced, good, beaming souls. With the photographs is an annual report from the district supervisor about the school for 1939. There were four classes in the elementary school, "Yavneh." The staff consisted of the principal, Moshe Sheifer, and two teachers, my uncle and aunt. There were 138 students in all. Lessons were in Hebrew, according to my father's books—*Dawn* and *My ABC Book*. The supervisor's summary: positive.

Two years later, most will be led to the nearby forest. I wish I could cry to them, "Escape while you can!" The men and youths were led to one place, and the women and girls to a different woods (among them Rivkelch and Zionah, my aunt's daughters). And buried half-alive.

O land of forests, rivers, and lakes.

One of the survivors of the village who was identified in the pictures tells me how, on the third day of the war, a relative came from another town with a truck and took them with him to escape to the east. At first the rabbi went too, but immediately decided against it—he must stay with his congregation, he said. So he got down. To his doom.

FAREWELL TO THE SHTETLS

> *It is spring, moonless night in a small town, starless and bible-black*
> *Young girls lie bedded soft or glide in their dreams.*
> —Dylan Thomas, *Under Milk Wood*

Not in Vidukle, Zhezhmer, or Siad had it been possible to hear voices as I heard them in *Under Milk Wood*. You will find in these places neither Captain Cat, the center around whom voices burst from their graves, nor Mrs. Ogmore-Pritchard, who keeps everything clean. When death arrives violently, there is no way to preserve sounds of comfort, of human feeling.

No, this is no comforting village, wrapped in slumber. Here, the young girls—and their mothers—waited for a full month before they were led to the edge of the local cemetery.

Here all is mixed together with screams, protest, and shock. I doubt whether on the Day of Judgment the dead will find their own bones.

Siad, Mazheik, Vidukle, Nemoksht, Zhezhmer, Marijampole, Kozhi, Ponar, and the forts of Kovno—they are now among my possessions, places deeply rooted in my world; I took them home with me.

On Green Hill

> *The gray willows of my longing, . . .*
> *Whose real location on earth I never did find out.*
> —Marina Tsvetaeva, *The Demon*

Until I had finally paid a visit to my city, I didn't know what I was looking for. I knew I wanted to see once more our house, the last one we lived in before the ghetto, as well as my two hiding places, in the city and village.

It became clear to me, with ever sharpening focus, that Green Hill was still a special place of great significance for me. Here was my first path of escape. Here began the one hundred ten days of my rescue. My mother had ascended its green slopes, under cover of darkness, from the Pilz-Fabrik brigade where she worked to visit her two children, each in their own hiding place.

In all, half a square kilometer.

Green Hill is the part of the country that falls from the plain to where the rivers meet; along it extends most of the city. To the inhabitants of the ghetto, that slope rising on the other side of the river did indeed look like a kind of hill. Along the line of its ridge, sharp roof edges peeped through the trees, hinting at a world that we could no longer reach. Some days before my escape, I had already known that in one of those houses my hiding place was waiting, and there I went after I crossed the river.

I was confident that I would be able to identify the house of my old Lithuanian woman, since from its attic I could see in May the ghetto's buildings, when I was allowed to climb up to the attic to catch a little sunshine. In this way I could even see another stretch of the river and follow my mother's boat brigade as it returned at day's end to the ghetto.

I also had in my memory the deep gully that cut through the hill alongside the old woman's house; I had walked up it to reach her house.

During my first trip, I went to the place at the city itself. From the perspective of ghetto dwellers, it was as if I arrived from behind the scenes. In one of these streets my parents had once lived as a young couple, and here—if I were to invest some time in exploration and inquiries, I could reconstruct, using the photographs that I have, exactly where my grandmother could be seen in the window, or where I had been photographed at the age of ten months at my mother's side, on the veranda through which could be seen buildings, most of them still standing, after sixty or seventy years.

But I was in a hurry. Here we were on Workers Street, which later became Little Workers Street, and at its end, standing apart a good distance from the houses in front of it, house number 59a was supposed to be.

Though the street had changed its name, we came easily enough upon house number 59, and my suspense grew. But here an impenetrable mystery began. New houses were interspersed among the old in an unbroken line—the numbering starts anew, in a street with a different name that stretches to the top of the slope. Where is the house that hid me; where is Julija's house?

On this house converge my distress and my desire. Here traces are preserved, perhaps, that I can find in no other place. This is the house where, for several months, my feelings of anxiety and loneliness penetrated its walls, the constant fear, the endless longing for my home and my family, for the ghetto. The walls of this house contain the memory of my mother's last footsteps during the only visit she paid me, a visit that lasted one full day of apparent tranquility, a full day that I could not know would also be our last.

I wandered dizzily about, trying the residents. No one remembered where Little Workers Street was.

I was still looking for a landmark, a point from which I could see the opposite riverbank, now full of new neighborhoods, when suddenly a dark-haired woman darted out of the gully, somewhere beside the river, from Jonavos Street where a number of factories stand. She was returning from work, taking a shortcut.

At once I understood—here was the one end of the path I had ascended after crossing the river. At which point did I leave the path, turn right, and take a steep path to the yard of my old lady?

In that gully there now is a stream of automobiles on a highway that crosses the river at about the place I had crossed it by boat. It even continues across the ground of the former ghetto.

And more. I saw that the same path coming out of the gully ended in a small open place, and I realized—here, in this forgotten corner, nearly hidden from its viewers, in this empty, partly hidden place, the old Lithuanian grandmother had taken my sister on a walk of sorts, instead of taking walks as one would with children in parks and gardens.

The tense body language of that seven-year-old child, who looked restlessly behind her from time to time, was what persuaded me that it was my sister, and not just any girl. Thus I had seen her, from a distance, by leaning far out of the opening in the attic. One and one time only.

On the second day of my search, I found a house that seemed to me to be standing where Julija's house had stood. From its roof one could see the ghetto out front, and, toward the back, looking down, one could make out the opening of the end of the path from the gully. The generous current occupants of the modern duplex could say little about the new house's history except that its owner had been a famous sculptor. And who owned the lot before him? Had the house that held my hiding place stood here? There was no one to ask.

Here, a few houses away from mine, was the house that hid my sister. Her presence there was not so invisible after all. Julija and the blond woman on the other side of the wall who shared our secret had both been able to tell me that they had seen her walking with the grandmother, and both of them knew the house where she lived. After the liberation, they had told me about my sister's disappearance and the rumors in the street. And two or three times I had gone out, under cover of night, stealing under the shadows of trees, approaching what I thought to be my sister's house, to look at it from a distance.

I wish the house's appearance were better fixed in my memory, for I never saw the house itself but rather its presumed direction. In my memory there is no concrete trace of activity, of voices, of lights in windows, that could help me make the connection, then and now, between a certain house and the one where she stayed.

When I returned to that street after the liberation I never dared to approach that house, to knock at its door and to ask direct, pointed questions.

Now I was walking to the place where my sister had presumably been, following my dim memory. Once more I stood across from it, examining the houses across the street, but they were silent. We talked to the oldest neighbors in that row of houses, but they knew nothing. They had passed their youth in Siberia, and they did not know their neighbors in the first years after the war.

And so, here too remained a question, as before.

Then, for the first time, another question occurred to me—hadn't my mother visited us directly after her work in the felt-boot factory? What, then, had been the secret path that she had taken? Where exactly had the factory stood? It should be somewhere nearby. Perhaps with another visit, after I had discovered traces of the factory, I could fully reconstruct my mother's path.

At the end of my visit I descended to the river, slowly. Heavy-footed, I reconstructed my ascent from the shore. And once again, going up the original path, I climbed up the slope as I had done fifty-five years before.

On my second trip, waiting for me on the archivist's desk were a number of documents, each one exciting. One file contained a list of voters from Workers Street in 1940; another, reports of municipal supervisors during the war period; the third, a file on the Pilz-Fabrik Company, the felt-boot factory where my mother worked.

The 1940 Soviet voters list, region of Little Workers Street, a year before the Germans arrived. The Green Hill neighborhood belonged to simple people, and Jews had always lived there. Their names fill these lists; within a year or two most of these names would vanish without so much as a gravestone.

Here my father had lived as a bachelor with the Motl family; here I had passed the first years of my life. I was about five when we moved down to the more modern city. In the voters list I quite easily found Julija's, but then I came across two other occupants of the same house, the Orentas couple—an exciting discovery. Perhaps I had finally found the name of the blond lady, the key to the whole operation of my rescue. She was the one who worked with my mother in the factory and persuaded her elderly neighbor to conceal a Jewish child. During all these years I had tried to discover traces, or to find some indication as to her name, which I didn't remember. Now I had a definite clue.

Or did I? How could I be sure the registered tenants of 1940 were the same as those in 1944? The puzzle remains a puzzle.

This seemed to put an end to my searches, yet I didn't want to be finished with the lists. With hesitation, with some aversion, I decided to go back to the lists and find the full name of the woman, the one who—perhaps it had been her husband—had turned my little sister in.

Were it not better that they sink into shameful oblivion? But I had practical reasons for discovering their full names—I wanted to know exactly where my sister stayed hidden during the last half year of her life, and how close I had come to the house during my clandestine nightly forays. I took a deep breath and once more combed through the list of voters, looking for the woman's first name, the only one I knew. But I found nothing there about Martha.

The municipal records verify that Grincevičiene was registered in Little Workers Street no. 59, as I remembered, so says a form from the municipal tax inspector of September 17, 1942.

The description of her home matches exactly what I recall: "wooden house, property of 80 square meters, one living room of 24 square meters. Heated by stove." The inspector sums up: "to add 10%." At the bottom of the document she testifies by signing that the details she has given are true. Her handwriting is shaky—an old woman who knows only how to sign her name.

A child's imagination. I had remembered her as an old person. On a form from 1941, in the blank for her date of birth, is written "49 years old" (by all appearances, she did not know her exact date of birth). This means that when I met her in 1944 she was only fifty-two.

And the house was gone. How could it be? Our good aid Rima came to interview people, and found an old man who had also worked in the Pilz-Fabrik. At the top of the slope he pointed down in a certain direction and said, "That's the factory's roof." And as for the old woman's house, he said it was demolished because it was in danger of collapsing at the edge of the gully. While I was still urging Rima to return and ask the man more questions, the man died. A narrow opening closed once more; once more there is no one to ask, and no one knows.

A surprising and precise document awaited me in the municipal archives—a professional labor force roster from the felt-boot factory, dated the end of August 1941, that is to say, only seventy days after the Germans had taken over the city. At the top of the form, in German and Lithuanian, was the following:

Ostland—Faser Geselschaft m.b.h.
Aussenstelle Kauen
Valstybinio Veltinis fabriko "Žvaigžde"
Kaunas, Jonavos gtve 74, tel 26806

And with a single stroke, an unknowable mystery became a concrete reality in the form of an address, ownership, and organization.

Under cover of the Pilz-Fabrik brigade, at the end of the Kinder Aktion against children, I left the ghetto one chilly day at dawn. Only by virtue of the special circumstances in this place, where women from the area worked without being separated from ghetto people, one could smuggle and make deals, not only in matters of barter and commerce but also in matters of salvation.

Here my mother arranged hiding places for my sister and me; from here the blond lady brought me Mother's letters; and from here Pečkyte set out to her distant birthplace to find me another hiding place.

So, in this place, between these walls, while their hands were kneading boot felt for the Germans, my mother and two Lithuanian women wove the first fibers in the rope of my rescue, which led me back to life.

Jonavos Street, which runs along the riverbank across from the ghetto, leads to the townlet with the Jewish name Janeve. Here is where my mother's brigade turned every morning. I remember that after they crossed the river in the boat, its people were to turn right in that street, to the west. I hadn't known how close their destination was to my hiding place.

Together with Rima, we hurried to the place.

Jonavos 74. On one side of the street lay the river. On the other side of the street stood a row of industrial and commercial buildings, bordering the slopes of Green Hill. At the end of a row of factories, we saw a compound, enclosed by a low wall, with a gate at the entrance, and a one-story building with several wings. A shack to the left of the gate doubtless housed the guards. How many German soldiers had stood sentry at this place? Had the German firm paid the army for them?

The compound is now divided into a row of offices and small separate workshops. In a nicely restored and painted office we find a secretary and a manager. Neither she nor he knows a thing about the place's past. They look at us in silence and with a certain reserved wonder, a complex look that I encountered in many places in this country. They seem not to understand, these Lithuanians, the meaning of the bold investigations of Jewish tourists in these places.

Cautiously I leave our group, circling slowly once and once again through the surrounding area.

Where did she work here? Where could she move around a bit and pass from one point to another? Somewhere here, other traces of my mother are preserved. Since it was Sunday, the offices are closed, and there is no access to the space inside. There might be an address, some graffiti perhaps, that testifies to the former presence of the Jews.

At the beginning of July 1944, at the end of Mother's last week of work here,

they announced to the last remnants of the ghetto that they would be transported westward during the next few days. The forced evacuation of those who
obeyed the order took four days, and on the fifth, they began to blow up and
burn all those who were in hiding and who hoped to avoid evacuation, my
mother apparently among them.

Perhaps somewhere in the compound I will feel my pulse quicken, like what
my friend Aliza had felt—with reason—across from a certain house in a distant
resort town. Perhaps something that I felt near the fence of the Catholic cemetery next to the ghetto: there my mother may have been shot when she tried to
escape from the fire on the last night of the evacuation.

I was in the city for a year and a half after the war, and it never once occurred
to me to look for this factory. How could I now easily leave the place? I went back
and walked around it, unable to let go.

I turned to the back of the building. I had to find my way among huge piles of
old worn-out tires, which looked like mythological creatures guarding the door
to a great secret.

I clambered past the tires until I got behind the building, to a gap between it
and the hill close behind it. Was there some passage here, a hidden opening of
some kind that would allow captives to steal out to Green Hill? The wall abuts
a slippery incline here, the beginning of the steep slope, leaving only a narrow
space beside the building. Passage is impossible.

If it were possible, I would wander about here constantly, round and round.
How many of my friends have found similarly clear traces of their lost parents' workplaces in the barracks at Auschwitz or in the trenches of Dachau and
Stutthof? Here she spent no less time than with me in the ghetto, in the half
room that had been our home.

I shall sit upon a stone here and wait. Perhaps she will yet return; in the end,
she will surely come back.

Some weeks later, when I had returned to my home in Jerusalem, I mustered courage and turned to the wizards of the Internet. "Ostland—Faser
Geselschaft"—what would land in my net?

Windows and gates emerged, each of them containing clues verifying that
such a firm once existed. To flesh out the information, I went to the archives at
Yad Vashem. An entire vista stretched before my eyes.

I now know that a month after the invasion into Russia began, on the initiative of the German minister of economics, a corporation was formed to manage
light industry (wood, paper, textiles, clothing, and so on) throughout Ostland

(the occupied territories east of Poland—the Baltic countries, Belorussia, and the Ukraine). The corporate headquarters were in Riga, with branches in Reval in Estonia and Kaunas in Lithuania. In one of the tiny cages of this economic whale my mother's brigade thrashed about.

The corporation's annual reports list the number of workers, by nationality. On the last row of this table are listed, separately, the Jews. So many in 1939, but 1943 is marked by a hyphen. That is to say, their number was not important. In 1942 the corporation supplied 190,000 pairs of felt boots to the German army, the Wehrmacht.

How many of them had been shaped by the bare hands of my mother and her colleagues?

After the factory had been identified and located during my second visit, I still wondered how Mother slipped out from the place and ascended the hill. A look at a map of the city revealed only a single alley rising from Jonavos Street to the top of the hill. It nearly adjoined the felt factory from the east.

At the end of the workday, my mother had two choices. The first was to wait until the brigade returned to where the boats were anchored, taking advantage of the commotion of crossing to leave the ranks and go up the path I had climbed to make my flight. The second was to dart to the right into the steep and winding Kapsiu Lane immediately after the brigade left the factory gates. I had to walk it myself.

Kapsiu Lane. Tense, full of hidden anxiety, I turned into the lane with my companion, Ari. His mother, too, had been saved by being concealed in this country.

The steep ascent was partially paved. It would have seemed fitting had I crawled it on my knees—here my mother's feet had trod.

It was Sunday. The few residents at the start of the lane sat on their porches in the garden and sipped drinks, sending suspicious, quizzical glances at the two of us.

Then came the first sharp curve. At the turn, girls were playing with a ball; they cast wondering looks at the two strangers, while the inexplicable tension in me grew. Tall green trees hugged the path on both sides, like those that met me when I climbed the hill on the day I escaped. The dimness they created must have been good for the figure slipping out of the factory, after she had removed the yellow patches and buried her face as deep as possible in her shawl so that her long nose and the sight of her suffering face would not give her away.

The climb was tiring, but in this stretch there are no houses or people, allow-ing one to proceed without fear of prying eyes. Then came the top of the hill, where streets are straight and wide, with sidewalks, landscaped trees, windows that face the street from both sides, people coming and going, dogs barking, children lingering before going home. I found these streets unsettling. It seemed as if we were being watched from all sides, with suspicion.

So how did she pass here? How did she overcome the immense fear of exposure, identification, entrapment? They would point to her and shout, "Šita Žyde!" (It's a Jewess!) "Quick, run her down, stop her!"

How many obstacles must Mother have passed before she reached Martha's house? And after staying there for the night, she had to retrace the long route back. How had she done it? I am somewhat consoled that her visits began in January, during the bitter winter months, when hours of light are few and the faces of pedestrians are buried in their coats. But there were also visits in the warm months of April, May, and perhaps even June, months when darkness falls late. How many such visits did she make after April 20, the date of her visit to me? I cannot know. Martha had asked Mother to limit her visits, leaving behind a restless and capricious little girl.

And this thought comes to me suddenly: if they had invited the Gestapo to take my sister, what would prevent them from doing it on a day my mother visited? But perhaps their resolve weakened only during the last days of the war, when Mother had stopped visiting.

And for us, how long did the entire climb take? About forty-five minutes. Forty-five minutes, and forever.

CLOSING

At the end of my two journeys, after having seen nearly all I wanted to see, I think I have had enough.

I count the possessions that are left to me: a roofless building in the old quarter, a pile of rubble in the back country with shoots of a pear tree sprouting from it, a factory that holds traces of my mother, a stone path that climbs Green Hill and guards her footsteps, a little open place where the image of my sister is etched, and a patchwork of mass graves in groves saturated with blood.

These are my properties in that country; no one will take them from me. I may not have found an actual home where I belong, but at the least I located my longing for it. A person needs an identity, a place to start. I need be envious no more. My longings found a definite spot in the universe.

After my voyages, my possessions increased—they also include my forebears' towns. My grandparents and uncles now sit on both sides of me as in a family portrait, perhaps like a Yossel Bergner painting.

Jack, an American who joined our second journey, dreams of buying the old house in Slobodka, where, according to documents, his parents lived as a young couple, before they had the urgent need to rescue their young baby. In that spirit, I must buy up half of Green Hill.

Perhaps for both of us, our searches are variations on the theme of Faulkner's *As I Lay Dying*—we drag with us our mothers' corpses, refusing to part with them.

Time passed. Aliza and I were sitting in a café in Tel Aviv, talking again about our visits in Lithuania and events of the past.

"Aliza," I ask, "will we ever leave June 22, 1941? Will we ever stop hoping that we'll still wake up again on that summer day and go to camp as planned?"

Even sixty-five years later, the question is still open.

And I also ask myself, still, endlessly, how is it that from that crowded press, from the piles of thousands of corpses, the rows of mass graves and mounds of ashes, how is it that I, a random creature like me, was pushed out to remain alive?

That question, too, remains unanswered.

Another year passed, and I was at the home of friends who live in a small village on one of the southern slopes of the Alps in France. Our host in the tranquil village is Michèle, who, like me, had the good luck to be hidden in a remote village in southern France where the Germans didn't reach. But they caught her father, an underground resistance fighter, a few days before the liberation, and managed to ship him to Auschwitz on the last train that left Drancy; she has been seeking traces of him ever since.

From the veranda one has a breathtaking view all the way to Grenoble, low and far away. Across a deep gully, a lushly forested slope surges toward us, as if setting up a large green screen across from the house.

A few days before our trip, I had received a letter from Abrashke the Tsigayner or, more accurately, from his wife, with a bundle of photographs enclosed. She does not hide her excitement over their visit some months previously to Tel Aviv, attending the birth of their first grandson, and over attending a meeting of the survivors of the 131: the group of Kovno Ghetto children who were sent, after the ghetto's evacuation, to Auschwitz via Dachau. I joined their reunion again.

The photograph of this group, with me among them, showing us in front of the restaurant where we dined, sang, and chatted, would not leave my mind, even while I was staying in France, as if it were propped up, enlarged, on the green mountain range opposite me and across the expanse of time. A surrealistic sight like one of the riveting paintings by Sam Bak, a child survivor from the Vilnius Ghetto, that returns again and again to this day, never ceasing to project upon canvases his childhood anxieties. And I, I gaze at this giant photograph beyond the gully, wondering incessantly about the sixty-two years that have passed between now and that summer in 1944, when I was in hiding and my friends were sent to the furnaces.

Here, now, and alive. Sixty-two years that might not have happened.

Here, now, and alive—and by my side a warm family, three direct descendants, and five much-beloved grandchildren planted around. And a deep inner joy fills me, as if for the first time I have discovered and fully comprehended the privilege I had been granted, the privilege my mother had won for me, in giving me life for at least another sixty-two years. As the years add up since then, so grows the magnitude of her sacrifice.

Later, we went for a trip through the rural landscape, across the Chartreuse Mountains. High-crowned forests hug the winding road, exuding secure, green freshness. The trees here are peaceful and upright. No, they hold no mass graves in their midst. Through the trees we glimpse little green valleys, with springs seeping through them. If the Garden of Eden is anywhere, it occurs to me in passing, it is no doubt built on the model of this magical corner.

And then we come to a small village with a monument standing in its center: "On April 12, 1944, Lieutenant André Mouche, a French soldier fighting in the lines of the French resistance, fell here in a battle against the Germans, dying for France and for freedom. His friend Robert Kahn and family members Jean Pierre and Henrietta Kahn, and their 4-month-old daughter Francoise were arrested and killed by the Nazis: the men in the Kaunas concentration camp, the mother and baby in the gas ovens of Auschwitz."

So here they are, right in the middle of the peaceful French countryside: Kaunas, Auschwitz, and April 12, the day of my escape from the ghetto.

We continue north, to the village of Izieu, where a hidden dormitory for Jewish refugee children was surrounded one morning by the Germans. The forty-four children and their five teachers were deported to Drancy, the transfer point to the east, and most of them were sent to Auschwitz from there. And again—

one or two of them—to Kaunas. Evidently transport no. 73, among the seventy-eight death transports that left Paris, was directed to "our" Ninth Fort.

And when did this Aktion against children take place in Izieu? On April 6, 1944, eight days after the Kinder Aktion in the ghetto. I could no longer repress this thought: if it's true that the children from our ghetto were also sent to Auschwitz (no one has been able to verify this), and if I had been among those ensnared, it is likely that I would have gone up in smoke with the children of Izieu.

But Lot's wife looked back, and she became a pillar of salt.

How hard it is to look behind, and not turn to stone.